Mummies, Myth and Magic
in Ancient Egypt

CHRISTINE EL MAHDY

Mummies, Myth and Magic
in Ancient Egypt

With 155 illustrations, 22 in full color

THAMES AND HUDSON

**This book is dedicated to my
beloved husband Abdel Hamid**

Above: Horus falcon carrying *shen* symbol.
Half-title: The *wadjet* eye, a powerful magical symbol.
Title page: The coffin of Queen Meryetamun, wife of Amenhotep II.

Text © 1989 Christine El Mahdy
Layout © 1989 Thames and Hudson Ltd, London
Editorial and Picture Research: Elizabeth Longley

First published in the USA in 1989 by Thames and Hudson Inc.,
500 Fifth Avenue, New York, New York 10110

Library of Congress Catalog Card Number 89-50542

Printed and bound in Spain

D.L.TO:738-1989

Contents

Chronology 6

Introduction 9
*Features: Heroes of the Middle
Kingdom* 16 · *The Mummy of a
Tanite Queen* 22

PART I: THE ROAD TO ETERNITY

Chapter One 24
Discovering the Mummies
*Features: Resting Place of Kings:
The 1881 Royal Cache* 36 · *Mummies
in the King's Tomb: the 1898
Royal Cache* 38 · *The Mystery
of Tomb 55* 46 · *Revealing
Tutankhamun* 48 · *Mummies in the
Tomb of Iurudef* 50

Chapter Two 52
Making a Mummy
*Features: The Father of a
Queen* 54 · *The Unknown Mummy* 66
*Styles and Uses of Canopic
Equipment* 67

PART II: UNFOLDING THE PAST

Chapter Three 74
Analyzing the Mummies
*Features: The Minneapolis Project:
The Mystery of Lady Teshat* 80

*The Bravest Fighter of Them
All?* 84 · *Family Trees of the
Pharaohs* 88 · *Ramesses the Great*
89 · *The Bristol Project*
98 · *The Manchester Maiden* 102
The Lyons Sailor 104

PART III: MYTH AND MAGIC

Chapter Four 110
Burial in Ancient Egypt
*Feature: Evolution of the
Sarcophagus* 114

Chapter Five 139
Gods, Spells and Amulets
Features: The Heart Scarab 153
The Osiris Legend 155

Chapter Six 158
Animal Cults
*Feature: Cult of the Apis
Bull* 166

Epilogue 170
The Curse and Other Myths
*Feature: The Mummy as Movie
Star* 174

Mummy Factfile 177
Glossary 181
Suggested Reading 184
Acknowledgments 187
Index 188

Chronology

The long span of Egyptian history from unification in 3100 BC is traditionally broken down into major time periods or kingdoms. Rulers are grouped chronologically into dynasties, each dynasty usually consisting of successive members of the same family. Listed here are the principal kings known in each dynasty.

Egyptian kings are often known by two names, one Egyptian and one given to them by the Greeks. Cheops, for instance, is the Greek version of Khufu. Rulers have been listed under the name by which they are most popularly known.

EARLY DYNASTIC PERIOD
3100–2650
(Also called Archaic period)
First Dynasty
Narmer (?)
Menes
Aha *(may be another name for Menes)*
Djer
Djet
Adjib
Semerkhe
Qaa

Second Dynasty
Hotepsekhemwy
Raneb
Ninetjer
Peribsen
Khasekhem

OLD KINGDOM
2650–2150
Third Dynasty
Sanakht
Netcherikhe-Djoser
Sekhemkhe
Khaba
Huni

Fourth Dynasty
Snofru
Cheops
Radjedef
Chephren
Mycerinus
Shepseskaf

Fifth Dynasty
Userkaf
Sahure
Neferirkare
Shepseskare
Raneferef
Niuserre
Menkauhor
Isesi
Unas

Sixth Dynasty
Teti
Pepi I
Merenre
Pepi II

Seventh and Eighth Dynasties
Ephemeral kings for whom very little evidence has been found

FIRST INTERMEDIATE PERIOD: 2134–2040
Ninth and Tenth Dynasties
Composed of kings who ruled from Herakleopolis and partly contemporary with most of the Eleventh Dynasty kings who ruled from Luxor (Thebes)

Eleventh Dynasty
Intef I, II, III
Nebhepetre Mentuhotep *(referred to as both I and II)*

The First Intermediate period ended with Mentuhotep's defeat of the Herakleopolitan kings

MIDDLE KINGDOM
2040–1640
Eleventh Dynasty
Nebhepetre Mentuhotep
Mentuhotep III
Mentuhotep IV

Twelfth Dynasty
Amenemhet I
Sesostris I
Amenemhet II
Sesostris II
Sesostris III
Amenemhet III
Amenemhet IV
Sobeknofru

Thirteenth Dynasty
Wegef I
Amenemhet V
Sobekhotep I
Hor
Amenemhet VI
Sobekhotep II, III, IV, V

This dynasty collapsed after a succession of short-lived and little-known kings

Fourteenth Dynasty
A little-known group of kings contemporary with the end of the Thirteenth Dynasty

SECOND INTERMEDIATE PERIOD: 1640–1550
Fifteenth and Sixteenth Dynasties
Composed of the Hyksos kings, who were not native Egyptians and who ruled from the delta. These two dynasties were contemporary with each other, and included such kings as Salitis, Khyan and Apophis

Seventeenth Dynasty

Composed of a number of native kings who ruled from Luxor. This dynasty was contemporary with the previous two and ended with the expulsion of the Hyksos rulers in the north. Among its kings:

Intef V
Sobekemsaf
Seqenenre
Seqenenre Tao
Kamose

NEW KINGDOM
1550–1070
Eighteenth Dynasty

Amosis
Amenhotep I
Tuthmosis I
Tuthmosis II
Hatshepsut
Tuthmosis III
Amenhotep II
Tuthmosis IV
Amenhotep III
Amenhotep IV (Akhenaten)
Tutankhamun
Ay
Horemheb

Nineteenth Dynasty

Ramesses I
Seti I
Ramesses II
Merenptah
Seti II
Amenmesses
Siptah
Tawosre

Twentieth Dynasty

Setnakht
Ramesses III–XI

THIRD INTERMEDIATE PERIOD: 1070–712
Twenty-first Dynasty

Smendes
Psusennes I
Amenemope
Osorkon I
Siamun
Psusennes II

Twenty-second Dynasty

Sheshonk I
Osorkon II
Takeloth I
Sheshonk II
Osorkon III
Takeloth II
Sheshonk III, IV, V
Osorkon IV, V

Twenty-third and Twenty-fourth Dynasties

Ephemeral kings of whom little is known. The Twenty-fourth Dynasty appears to comprise two kings:

Bakenre (Bocchoris)
Piankhy (Piye)

LATE PERIOD: 712–332
Twenty-fifth Dynasty

Shabaka
Shebitku
Taharka
Tantamani

Twenty-sixth Dynasty

Necho I
Psammetichus I
Necho II
Psammetichus II
Apries
Amasis
Psammetichus III

Twenty-seventh Dynasty

A succession of Persian rulers:

Cambyses
Darius I
Xerxes I
Artaxerxes
Darius II

Twenty-eighth Dynasty

Amyrtaeus

Twenty-ninth Dynasty

Neferites
Psammutis
Neferites II

Thirtieth Dynasty

Nectanebo I, II

A second period of Persian rulers, including:

Artaxerxes III
Arses
Darius III

GRAECO-ROMAN PERIOD
332–AD 395
Thirty-first Dynasty
(*Macedonian*)
Alexander the Great
Philip Arrhidaeus
Alexander IV

Thirty-second Dynasty
(*Ptolemaic*)
Ptolemy I–XV, with Queens Cleopatra I–VII

After the death of the last Cleopatra, in 30 BC, Egypt became a mere province of the Roman empire. When the empire divided in AD 395, Egypt was controlled from Byzantium until the Arab conquest in AD 641

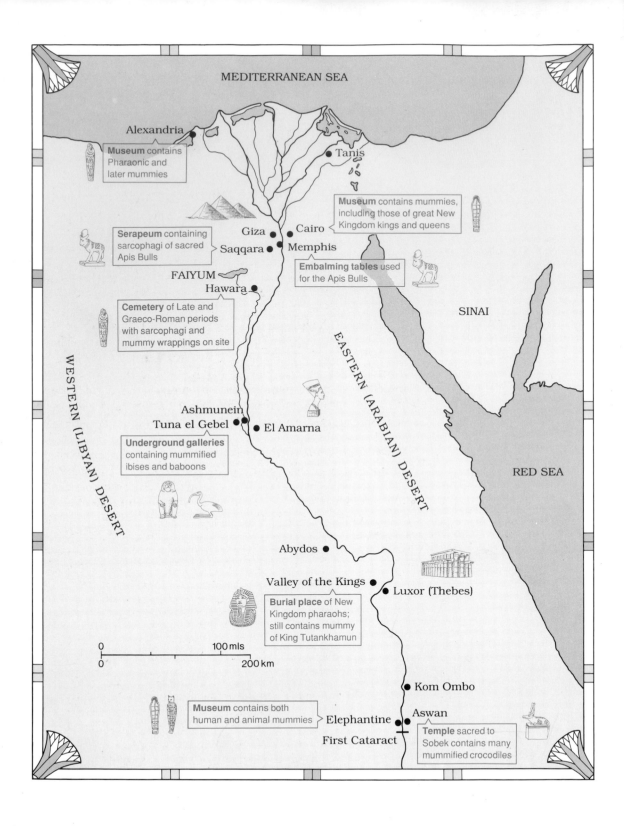

MEDITERRANEAN SEA

Alexandria

Museum contains Pharaonic and later mummies

Tanis

Museum contains mummies, including those of great New Kingdom kings and queens

Giza Cairo

Serapeum containing sarcophagi of sacred Apis Bulls

Saqqara Memphis

FAIYUM

Embalming tables used for the Apis Bulls

Hawara

SINAI

Cemetery of Late and Graeco-Roman periods with sarcophagi and mummy wrappings on site

WESTERN (LIBYAN) DESERT

EASTERN (ARABIAN) DESERT

Ashmunein
Tuna el Gebel El Amarna

Underground galleries containing mummified ibises and baboons

RED SEA

Abydos

Valley of the Kings Luxor (Thebes)

Burial place of New Kingdom pharaohs; still contains mummy of King Tutankhamun

0   100 mls
0   200 km

Kom Ombo

Museum contains both human and animal mummies

Aswan

Elephantine

First Cataract

Temple sacred to Sobek contains many mummified crocodiles

Introduction

A R O U N D 1970 B C, the pharaoh of Egypt, Sesostris I, wrote to a former palace servant who had lived for years in foreign countries as an exile. The unfortunate refugee, Sinuhe, languished and mourned the loss of his homeland, and his sovereign lured him with words sweet to the ears of any Egyptian: 'Think of the day of burial, your passing into a state of perfection. A night will be made for you with ointments and bandages at the hand of Tait [a goddess associated with weaving]. A funeral procession will be made for you on the day of the entombment. The mummy case will be of gold, its head [ornamented] with lapis lazuli. The sky will be above you as you lie upon the bier; oxen will drag you, musicians walking in front of you. The performance of the *muu* dancers will be done at the entrance to your tomb. The list of offerings will be read aloud for you and an offering will be made on the offering table. Your tomb stela, made of white stone, will be in the midst of [those of] royalty. You will not die abroad!'

These words voiced the feelings of every Egyptian, whose great ambition was to achieve immortality and to spend a peaceful eternity in a land identical to their beloved Egypt in every way save the problems. This does not mean that the ancient Egyptians were morbid, thinking their whole life long only of death. On the contrary, they loved life to the full and were reluctant to leave it, but they faced the inevitability of death with equanimity and tried to ensure that they would never be forgotten. To this end they would build a home for their body and soul to last many lifetimes, attempt to preserve their bodies through mummification, and surround their remains with every possible thing they might need eternally.

What is a mummy?

A mummy is the preserved body of a human being or an animal, by any means, either deliberate or accidental. Mummies survive from many ancient cultures, some preserved in a wet state, others dry. The bog bodies of northern Europe, such as the 2,000-year-old Lindow Man, found in Cheshire, England, in 1984, belonged to people who had either fallen, or been thrown, into wet, marshy places. The exclusion of oxygen and acidity in the peat of the bog effectively

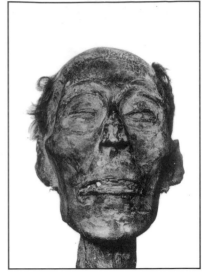

preserved their bodies. Most mummies, though, were preserved by being dried, or desiccated. Many civilizations, including the Egyptian, Chinese and some South American cultures, tried to achieve this artificially. The Incas of Peru kept their mummified kings in the Temple of the Sun at their capital city, Cuzco, bringing them outside for special ceremonies.

The mummies of Egypt
Some of the oldest examples of these bodies come from ancient Egypt and were the result of centuries of experimentation by embalmers. Preserved in every detail, many of the dead look as if they had simply fallen asleep. The body appears to have been soaked in a black, glassy pitch-like substance. Early observers remarked that these bodies appeared to be covered with bitumen. The Persian word for bitumen, *moumia*, has resulted in our term for these remains – mummy.

10

The face of Ramesses II *(left) is of a man serene in old age, probably in his late eighties when he died. Examination of his mummy has shown that he suffered badly from arthritis in the hip, advanced heart disease and bad teeth. The lid of the coffin (far left) in which his body was found at Deir el Bahri would once have been gilded and inlaid with precious stones – these were stolen in antiquity.*

This well-preserved anthropoid coffin *(below) is from the late New Kingdom. The narrow bands began as an imitation of the bandages around the mummy and were used to carry inscriptions. The mummy itself (below left) has been coated with resins which turned black with time. Later, the Persians confused the appearance of such mummies with bitumen – or moumia in Arabic, hence our word for the bodies, mummy.*

The first attempts to preserve the bodies of the Egyptians appear to have taken place during the First Dynasty, around 3000 BC, perhaps within a few decades of written Egyptian history beginning. Early techniques were crude, but gradually became highly sophisticated. During the Fourth Dynasty, the body began to have its internal organs removed. There is evidence that natron, a natural salt, was used to preserve these organs; by the Middle Kingdom, natron was employed to extract moisture from, or desiccate, the bodies themselves, making them stable. When dry, the bodies were elaborately bandaged and gallons of perfumes and resins poured over them. The hope was that the bodies would be saved forever from the natural processes of decay. The process itself became more refined in the New Kingdom, and in the Twenty-first Dynasty it reached its peak.

No one can look dispassionately upon the face of an Egyptian mummy. Even the seasoned Egyptologist cannot remain unmoved. In 1930, H.E. Winlock, then curator of the Egyptian Department at New York's Metropolitan Museum of Art, tried to express his emotions on entering the burial chamber of a queen, dead for more than 3,000 years: 'From the doorway on the other side [of the entrance passage] there was one step down and then inky blackness. I turned on my torch and flashed it around. I was in a chamber just high enough to stand up in, seemingly interminably long in the gloom – and blankly empty. For a moment the bottom seemed to have fallen out of everything, and then my light shone upon a narrow doorway at the far end. I took eight or ten strides across the empty chamber and came to a standstill just within the doorway beside three little empty saucers and a dried and shriveled [sic] bundle of leaves lying at the foot of an enormous recumbent figure. My light flickered along it and came to rest on a great placid face staring fixedly upward in the deathly silence of the dark crypt. Then it flickered down a column of hieroglyphs announcing that "The King gives boon to Osiris, the Great God, Lord of Abydos . . . for the spirit of the King's Daughter and Sister, the God's Wife, joined to the Crown of Upper Egypt, the Mistress of the Two Lands, Meryetamun, true of voice, with Osiris." The silence, the dark and the realization of the ages the coffin had lain there – for it was a coffin – all combined in creating an eerie effect; and whatever one may expect, that does not happen so very often in digging.'

Why mummify the dead?

We think of ourselves as divided into body and soul, but the Egyptians developed a different explanation for the nature of their existence. According to their beliefs, the survival of the body was necessary for the survival of the other aspects of their being: the *ka*, the *ba* and the *akh*.

11

The Egyptian idea of the spirit

The infant, it was believed, was placed in its mother's womb after being created on a potter's wheel by the ram-headed god Khnum. But as Khnum formed the body he also fashioned a spiritual copy, resembling the body in every way, with all its needs, desires and expectations. This was the *ka*, ghostly in appearance and stored in the heart. Some kings thought of themselves as having more than one *ka* Hatshepsut, female pharaoh of the Eighteenth Dynasty, claimed nine. After death, it was forcibly separated from the body and would inhabit the tomb in a constant effort to be close to the body in which it had spent its life. And since the *ka* needed everything that the person had needed during life – food, drink, clothing, perfume and shade from the hot sun – the goods placed in the tomb were primarily to satisfy its needs. The *ka* was distinguished from the dead person by being depicted with a pair of upraised arms on its head; or, in Ptolemaic times, by the pair of arms itself, shown to have grown legs and arms and carrying a feather fan behind the actual person.

The *ka* could be freed from the body during life when a person was asleep or in a coma. A story probably written in the last years of native rule in Egypt, around 800 BC, tells of a magician called Sa-Osiris. He read aloud a letter to his king, sent by a prince of Nubia, in which the prince had given permission to his magicians to inflict punishment on the king of Egypt. The *ka* of the pharaoh had thus been summoned to Nubia while the king slept. There, his *ka* was beaten 500 times with a stick in a public meeting place, and when the king awoke the next morning, he discovered the marks of the stick upon his bare back.

The *ba* was not a physical element, but like the body was unique to each person. It is perhaps best described as all the non-physical aspects that constitute an individual, what we might call character or personality. The *ba* was pictured as a human-headed bird. It was

When the ram-headed god Khnum *created a human being on his potter's wheel (above), he also created that being's* ka, *or double. The Egyptians represented the* ka *by means of a pair of upraised arms (below).*

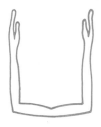

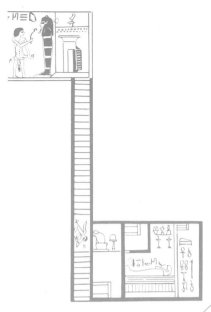

thought to have entered the body (described as its 'perch') at birth, together with the breath of life; both left the body at death.

Magical spells were said over the mummy (Chapter 5) to transform it into a form or entity that enabled the dead person to exist in the afterworld. This entity, the *akh*, and the gods inhabited the world of the afterlife. All funerary spells had one single aim – to allow the deceased to become an *akh*, to avoid the potential horror of dying again, a death from which there was no return.

The shadow and the name

In the Egyptian concept of human existence there were two other elements whose survival was essential. An individual was inseparable from his or her shadow, which mirrored every movement, although it was obviously incapable of any act of its own. If anyone behaved badly, there was the potential threat of their shadow being devoured by a demon known as the 'shadow gobbler'. To deprive a living human being of a shadow was to deprive them of existence itself.

But perhaps the most significant aspect of any person was their true essence, the spirit of individuality which distinguishes one being from another. This essence was encapsulated in the name given to the child at birth. So long as one's name was being spoken, so the Egyptians believed, immortality was being assured. So protection of the name of the deceased was vital. The tomb, the mummy, the equipment, the paintings and reliefs were all designed to help preserve the name of the individual. The greatest horror was to have your name destroyed, cut out from a wall.

As the Opening of the Mouth *ceremony is being performed by the priest at the entrance to the tomb (above), the* ba *is freed. Here it flies through the dark passages of the tomb to its new home in the burial chamber, where it will once again find an existence close to the body that in life had been its 'perch'.*

Death in ancient Egypt

Habitable land in Egypt is so severely limited that from earliest times the living chose to place their dead out in the hot, dry desert. Near urban areas, huge cemeteries sprawled over the sand to become necropolises, or cities of the dead, with rows of tombs forming wide streets. Fine buildings and sometimes trees and gardens lined them. Many of these large, well-built tombs have survived when the houses of the living have long vanished. For this reason alone people have tended to imagine Egypt as a death oriented society.

Burials of the god-kings

Neolithic burials, in the period before written Egyptian history, were simple pit graves in the sand of the desert fringes. People at this early time were buried with grave goods such as pottery, beads and tools. The body, at first simply laid in a shallow pit, came to be covered and the pit itself enclosed. These burials reflected the modest needs of a simple people. But as society developed, so too did aspirations for the next world.

Around 3100 BC, what had previously been loosely tied agricultural communities strung out along the Nile were united by the political will of a powerful chieftain. Perhaps a century later his descendants conquered the delta area of the north and the whole of Egypt was united. The first kings built their palace some 15 miles (25 km) south of modern Cairo, but they appear to have been buried in massive flat tombs, in Upper Egypt at Abydos, about 60 miles (100 km) north of modern Luxor (Thebes), for the first 400 years of pharaonic history.

Meanwhile, a great city, later called Memphis by the Greeks, developed around the royal court in the north. And here, for the following 4,000 years, many of the greatest and wealthiest of Egypt's people lived and died. They were buried closed by, in a giant necropolis, today known as Saqqara. Like those of the early kings, many of the tombs here were large, low, flat buildings. They resemble the stone benches often seen outside houses in the Middle East and are called by the Arabic word for a bench – *mastaba*.

By around 2700 BC, royal burials had begun to be made near the capital of Memphis. The king had achieved a divine status and this was reflected in his burial. For the duration of the Old Kingdom, a period lasting around seven centuries, pyramids were built to house royal mortal remains. The pyramid shape itself seems to have developed accidentally. The Step Pyramid at Saqqara began as the usual mastaba shape, which can clearly be seen in its lowest layers. But successive mastabas were added on top of the original, until a pyramid of steps was formed. The shape must have been pleasing to the Egyptians, reflecting as it did their belief in the 'mound of creation' upon which the gods had first created life, and where it was believed that the soul of their god-king would also be reborn. Experimentation with design and degree of angle eventually culminated in the three massive pyramids of Cheops, Chephren and Mycerinus at Giza. Around each pyramid, a city of mastaba tombs arose, each used by members of the royal family, or by a family promoted by the pharaoh.

Immortality within everyone's grasp
About 2200 BC, what was seen as royal failure to control the Nile brought about a loss of pharaonic authority and the decline of the Old Kingdom. Courtiers drifted away from Memphis and back to their home towns, where they consolidated their power and made themselves the focal point of their own small system, complete with courtiers. Their large tombs, hollowed out from rock cliffs, dot the banks of the Nile in Upper Egypt; and small shaft tombs at the foot of the cliffs are the burial places of their acolytes.

During these years the importance of mummification grew. It is likely that at the beginning of Egyptian history attempts had been made to preserve only the body of the pharaoh. During the Old

The three Giza pyramids *of Mycerinus, Chephren and Cheops dominate the view at the edge of modern Cairo. These great ancient funerary monuments stand as an awesome reminder of the power of the Fourth Dynasty pharaohs who built them over 4,500 years ago.*

Kingdom embalming of courtiers was undertaken, but in a perfunctory manner. Common belief was that the soul of a dead person would remain forever earthbound – only that of the king could expect to ascend to the company of the gods. But (during the so-called First Intermediate period that followed the fall of the Old Kingdom, beliefs underwent a radical change Now the soul of every Egyptian could expect to struggle towards the land of the gods, but the journey would be arduous and fraught with danger. The preservation of the body and the equipping of a tomb gave the soul of the deceased the strength and guidance it needed to reach its goal.)

About 2150 BC, two local rulers fought for total control of Egypt and a family from the south, from the region around Luxor, won and so began the Middle Kingdom. Through the Eleventh Dynasty and the first half of the Twelfth, the kings had to struggle to control the country. They eventually established a new city called Itj-Tawy ('Seizing of the Two Lands'), which seems to have flourished in the triangular area between the Faiyum Oasis and the main part of the Nile. And it was here that these kings built their pyramids. These structures, though large and imposing, were constructed around a core of stone walls and faced with locally made, sun-baked mud brick. At first, only members of the royal family were buried nearby, but about 1850 BC the courtiers came to be buried once again around the pyramids of their rulers.

HEROES OF THE MIDDLE KINGDOM

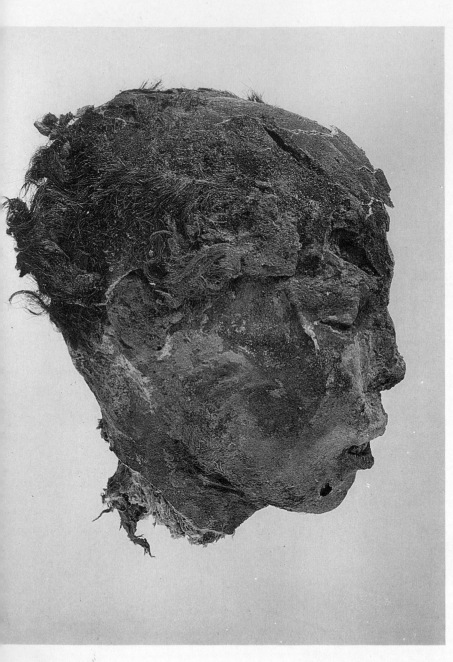

In 2040 BC, the ruler of Upper Egypt, Nebhepetre Mentuhotep, was engaged in a deadly struggle with the leaders of the north. He ordered his forces to confront the enemy in one, final, decisive battle. When the day was ended, Mentuhotep had triumphed and the enemy had been vanquished – and the throne of Egypt was his.

Almost 4,000 years later, in 1927, the American Egyptologist H. E. Winlock found the remains of sixty men in a tomb at Deir el Bahri, above the mortuary temple of Mentuhotep. On close examination, inscriptions on their wrappings revealed the bodies to be those of Middle Kingdom soldiers. Their poor condition and their proximity to the burial of the great pharaoh – a signal honour – seemed significant. Who were these men and why had they been interred at a royal funerary site?

Winlock reached what he felt to be the obvious conclusion: these were soldiers who had fought for Mentuhotep in that decisive battle. The poor condition of the bodies could be explained by the circumstances of war. After being slain, the corpses lay for a time on the battlefield, a prey to vultures and subject to a certain degree of natural desiccation, but beyond artificial mummification. Mentuhotep had acknowledged his debt to these valiant men and ordered the bodies to be collected, washed and swathed in the finest linen. They were then placed in a tomb overlooking the king's own mortuary temple.

The head of one of the soldiers found by H.E. Winlock at Deir el Bahri.

The New Kingdom: the Valley of the Kings

The Middle Kingdom was followed by what is known as the Second Intermediate period, a time when Egypt faced foreign rulers called the Hyksos, who established their own capital at Avaris in the northeast delta. Ultimately, another family from Luxor drove them out of Egypt and established the New Kingdom sometime around 1550 BC.

This new dynasty, the Eighteenth, produced some of the most brilliant rulers ever to hold the throne of Egypt. Powerful fighters, these pharaohs commanded loyalty throughout an empire that stretched from Nubia in the south to the borders of northern Syria; tribute filled the coffers of the Egyptian treasury. The monarchs sought greater security for their mortal remains – as well as for the gold and treasure with which they planned to be buried – and found it in a remote area on the west bank of the Nile near Luxor, a place we call the Valley of the Kings. Here most kings of three successive dynasties were buried in brilliantly painted tombs, and the hills to the east of the valley were honeycombed with smaller shafts built to house the remains of the courtiers who served them. Many of the exceptionally well-preserved mummies of these great rulers, and some of their queens and followers, have come down to us.

The pink-stained, yellow quartzite sarcophagus *of Tuthmosis III still lies in the king's tomb high in a narrow cleft in the Valley of the Kings where it has rested since 1425 BC. Like the burial chamber itself, the sarcophagus is in the shape of a cartouche, after the oval frames in which the pharaoh's names were contained. On the yellow plaster walls, painted buff to imitate papyrus, are the twelve sections of the Amduat (The Book of What Is in the Underworld).*

The New Kingdom began to decline thanks largely to the actions of a single king – Akhenaten. This heretic pharaoh questioned traditional patterns of Egyptian thought and rejected much that had gone before, especially the pantheon of gods. In trying to assert the authority of a single creator god, the Aten, the king virtually turned his back on state affairs at exactly the moment that the powerful Hittites, based in what is now Turkey, began to challenge Egyptian hegemony in the north of the empire. As Akhenaten devoted himself to his new philosophies, the empire weakened.

The Amarna period (so-called after the modern name of the location of Akhenaten's new capital city) was brief, but it was a time from which Egypt never fully recovered. By the Twentieth Dynasty, tombs were less well equipped and even the highest in the land were often forced to reuse burial equipment since the cost of providing new material was too great.

Mummification: peak and decline

During the Twenty-first Dynasty, mummification reached its height. Significant advances were made in the process and Theban mummies of this dynasty are truly fine. Their more life-like appearance was largely due to careful use of packing materials under the skin. But an unsettled time began in Egypt. Those employed to carry out mummification grew careless. Bodies, though on the outside as well wrapped as before, were speedily and ineptly embalmed.

From about 1085 BC, Egypt's throne was held by successive families of foreign rulers. Tombs were made in the same way as before and mummification continued, though with certain changes. During the sixth century BC, the first Greek settlers arrived, to be followed, in 332 BC, by the conquering army of Alexander the Great. From this time, any attempt at achieving the sophisticated results of the New Kingdom embalmers ceased and more and more effort was spent on making the outside of the mummy appear as elegant as possible. In the Roman period, narrow bandages were used, arranged in patterns, resulting in elaborate diamond-shaped effects on the outside of the mummies, with the face represented by a portrait on a board made using paints incorporating melted wax.

The introduction of Christianity in the first century AD, and the growth of the belief that death involved casting off the body, meant that fewer people were mummified. Coptic Christians were buried simply, their unprepared bodies dressed in everyday clothing. Only the 'pagans', followers of the old religion, were still mummified. Many of their bodies in the last years of mummification were crudely bandaged, and then wrapped in a linen shroud on which the image of the deceased was painted in watercolours.

Although we do not know exactly when mummification ceased, the temples and the ancient religious systems still existed in AD 515, when the Byzantine emperor declared them to be heretical. But even after this, pockets of the old worship survived, especially in Upper

This mummy portrait, *now in the Cairo Museum, is that of a Roman-period woman from the cemetery of Hawara in the Faiyum, one of the major sites where such portraits were found in great numbers. They owe their hauntingly life-like quality to the method of painting with wax impregnated with colour, which allowed detailed modelling of the features. The pictures of the deceased – which may well have been commissioned during life and kept in the home until death – were placed over the mummy and secured within its bandages.*

Egypt, until the arrival of Islam in AD 641. Today, vestiges of the old ways still remain. For most Muslim burials, the dead are cleansed and wrapped with bandages in the form of a mummy; three days after entombment, offerings of food and drink are brought to the graveside by the mourners. On each anniversary of the death and on religious feast days, offerings are given to the poor who gather around the tomb.

Mummies today

The aim of the Egyptian tomb was to provide a permanent house for the mummy. But greed and sheer curiosity over the centuries (Chapter 1) have taken their toll, and of all the hundreds of thousands of bodies which were prepared by the ancients only a few survive.

Over recent decades, museums have begun to awaken to the fact that mummies have their own stories to tell. Scientific methods and new technologies, when applied to ancient remains, often reveal as much as historical records or archaeological artefacts – sometimes perhaps more. Only 100 years ago little was expected from the examination of a mummy other than to be able to gaze upon the face of a person dead for over 2,000 years. Today, with a growing sense of responsibility towards the small number of mummies that still remain, we have become more demanding.

Museums all over the world are undertaking the analysis of their Egyptian human and animal remains and a vast field of new information is being made available. From the data gleaned by these projects, we can collate material on the daily lives of the ancient Egyptians and, for the first time, attempt to understand exactly how they looked, how they felt, the diseases from which they suffered and the food that they ate.

The examination of a mummy is a lengthy process. Much can be learned from X-rays, which leave the mummy intact. Actually unwrapping one should be only a last resort and done on the basis that as much information as possible is obtained. 'Dead men', Arthur Weigall, the English Egyptologist and author, once wrote, 'are not useless, and the excavator must not cheat the world of any part of its great perquisite. The dead are the property of the living and the archaeologist is the world's agent for the estate of the grave.'

Scientific examination of mummies *was in its infancy when the 'Two Brothers' were unwrapped in 1908 at Manchester University by Margaret Murray, the first full-time professional female Egyptologist. Here Dr Murray (third from left) and her colleagues pause as the historic moment is recorded by the camera.*

THE MUMMY OF A TANITE QUEEN

For a number of years scholars have been trying to sort out the complex relationship of the kings who ruled from Tanis in the delta during the Twenty-first and Twenty-second Dynasties. The discovery of six intact tombs from the period, in 1939 (Chapter 1), has helped considerably. Inscriptions in the tombs are providing information from which a family tree can be constructed. The bodies of the kings – Psusennes I, Amenemopet and Osorkon III – are still awaiting examination, but the remains of a Tanite queen found in 1881 at Deir el Bahri are interesting in their own right.

Queen Henttawy was the wife of Pinnedjem I, first king of the Twenty-first Dynasty, and the mother of his successor Psusennes, who ruled for fifty years and, like Tutankhamun, is known for the beauty of his gold funerary mask. Although her mummy appears to be that of an old woman, she was probably only thirty-five at the time of her death. Her mummy is grotesque, though, because subcutaneous packing pushed between the layers of skin to restore her to a life-like appearance introduced new sources of decay. This caused her skin to burst open. Her thin hair was supplemented, probably by the embalmers, with tight bundles of plaited, black-dyed string – a most inelegant coiffure. The embalmers of the Twenty-first Dynasty are known for having developed special techniques for restoration of body contour and features. It is unfortunate that their search for perfection led to Henttawy's mummy being not the image of the dead queen, but a caricature.

The mummy of the Twenty-first Dynasty queen Henttawy, found among the bodies of the 1881 royal cache. Her puffed and cracked face is sad evidence of the unreliability of the embalmer's art.

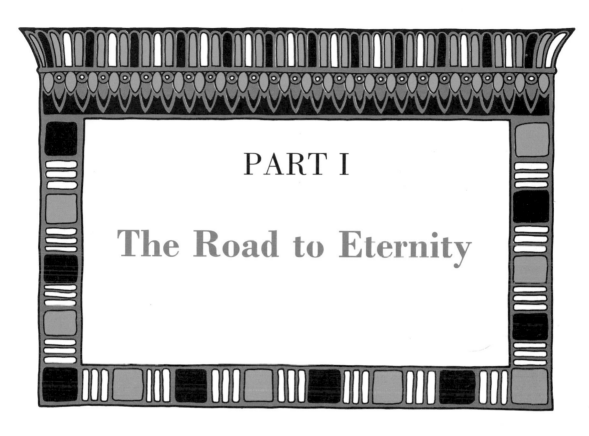

PART I

The Road to Eternity

Chapter One
Discovering the Mummies

THE AMBITION OF THE ANCIENT EGYPTIANS to provide a secure resting place for eternity has sadly been thwarted. Almost every type of burial has proved itself vulnerable either to the forces of nature or to the determined efforts of robbers. Precious items among the grave goods, such as jewellery, including the amulets within the wrappings of the mummy, and any stones or gilt on the coffin were often stolen first. Eventually, the very walls of the tomb and any statues might be broken up either to be reused or, in the case of limestone, burnt as fertilizer. Finally, if it had survived through all these intrusions, the mummy itself might be taken out and burnt as fuel or sold as a commodity. Some, very few, mummies, such as the royal mummies of the Cairo Museum, have been saved largely through the rescue attempts of ancient priests and modern archaeologists.

Ancient tomb robbery

All the archaeological evidence suggests that tomb robbery in Egypt is as old as the act of burial itself. The earliest graves – both simple pits and the later roofed-over style – of Neolithic Nile dwellers were often robbed and, although the bodies themselves might remain untouched, jewellery or precious possessions were frequently removed. As the Egyptians began to make the grave a more comfortable resting place and then to try to preserve the body, the wealthier among them, whose grave goods would have been a sure temptation to the greedy, also sought to make the burial more secure.

Robbery in the age of the pyramids
From 2600 BC, important courtiers chose to be buried in tombs of stone, which formed streets in the desert. The burial chambers were frequently placed at the foot of deep underground shafts. The Egyptians obviously felt confident that even if their possessions in the upper chambers were removed by robbers, at least their mummy would remain intact.

The tombs of these dead would have been well protected. Imagine a necropolis in the desert, its tombs sealed and in neat rows. Guards from a Nubian regiment of the army were frequently posted in the area, and mortuary priests would have visited the chapels in the tomb

This view of the interior of one of the passages of the Great Pyramid at Giza conveys what it must have been like for the ancient tomb robbers, making their way through the claustrophobic, pitch-black and forbidden inner chambers of the tombs.

superstructures at least once and perhaps three times a day. A robber would have had to approach the isolated desert spot unseen, and break into the tombs without being heard, and, once inside the claustrophobic darkness armed only with a flickering torch, be brave enough to face the penetrating stares of images painted or carved on the tomb walls. Moreover, ritual warnings were sometimes included on walls against anyone who violated the tomb. Typical is the inscription of Hetepherakhet, an official of the Fifth Dynasty, buried at Saqqara: 'I made this tomb on the west bank in a pure place in which no one had a tomb, in order to protect the belongings of one who has gone to his *ka*. As for anyone who might enter the tomb unclean and [intending to] do evil to it, it is the great god who will judge against him.'

If the prospect of entering an ordinary tomb would have been terrifying, then the robbing of a royal pyramid must have been perpetrated by some of the most determined and ruthless members of society. Pyramid entrances were always hidden, frequently sealed solid with blocks of stone. Once the robber got inside, through frighteningly narrow passages, he still had to find his way in darkness through numerous traps and false corridors to get to the burial chamber. Some of the later pyramids of the Twelfth Dynasty were so elaborately protected with secret passages that even experienced Egyptologists, who had entered many pyramids before, took months and sometimes years to find the one route that led to the chamber. Yet every pyramid proved to have been robbed. Even in the burial chambers where bones, bandages or human remains were found, the bodies had been ripped to shreds. The British army colonel Howard Vyse, who entered the smallest pyramid at Giza, that of the Fourth Dynasty pharaoh Mycerinus, during excavations in the late 1830s, did find a body within the sarcophagus. He shipped the remains back to England where analysis of them in the mid-1980s by the British Museum has proved that they are not from the period of Mycerinus at all, but are of Late period or Graeco–Roman date. So not only were the mummies of the kings despoiled but even their burial places were usurped.

The robbery of even the earliest of the royal burials must have occurred soon after entombment. Given the ease with which robbers penetrated the most complicated security system, they must have acted with the assistance of the builders themselves. The workmen who constructed the royal tombs and pyramids were well provided for and housed within villages or small towns that could be easily guarded. So did the workmen of the pyramid tombs corrupt those paid to watch over them? Or were they corrupted by the guards? Or did the workmen pass on their knowledge, for some form of reward, to criminals? It would seem likely that high government officials close to the king must have been aware of the existence of such a situation, but we have no direct knowledge of this from the records which have survived from the period.

The Valley of the Kings

By the start of the New Kingdom, around 1550 BC, the pharaohs finally despaired of finding security for their bodies by means of complex labyrinths within pyramids. The location of a pyramid could never be hidden and gave away the tomb's whereabouts, if not the easiest means of penetration. New methods were devised. The pharaohs decided to separate their burial places from their offering chapels (usually called mortuary temples), and to make the location of the tombs less obvious. It was probably Tuthmosis I, of the Eighteenth Dynasty, who ordered his architect, Ineni, to cut a tomb in a valley on the west bank of Luxor, '. . . no man hearing and no man seeing' – and so began the 500-year tradition of the Valley of the Kings. Throughout this period, nobles and courtiers cut their own small tombs in the cliffs in hills and valleys close by. But like the pyramids and mastaba tombs before them, these royal tombs and those of the great nobles were also robbed.

Ancient papyri record that around 1120 BC, during the reign of Ramesses IX, there were trials of tomb robbers in Luxor. Paser, the mayor of Luxor on the east bank, reported rumours of tomb robbing on the west bank to the king. Ramesses empowered his vizier (the king's appointed first minister) to investigate and set up a commission to visit the tombs to discover the truth. The commission reported that the tomb of only one pharaoh from the Seventeenth Dynasty had been found robbed: 'As for the tomb of King Amenhotep I which the mayor of Luxor had reported to the royal commission saying "Thieves had violated it", it was found intact.' On the tombs of the nobles, however: 'It was found that robbers had violated them all, dragging their owners from their coffins so that they were left on the sand, and stealing their funerary offerings which had been given to them, together with gold and silver fittings which were on their coffins.'

The tribunal continued its investigations and several workmen were brought forward on Paser's accusation to stand trial, largely for petty pilfering. According to surviving records of the testimony, in every case except one, their excuse was that the tomb was already open. Only one gang, led by a stonemason from Karnak called Amunpanefer, admitted to robbery of a royal tomb: 'We broke through . . . and we found the god lying at the rear of the tomb, and we found the burial place of his queen next to him. We opened their sarcophagi and the coffins in which they were and found the noble mummy of the king with a collar upon it and a large number of amulets. A collar of gold was around his neck, and a crown of gold. The noble mummy of the king was completely covered in gold and his coffins were decorated with gold and silver inside and outside, and were inlaid with every sort of precious stone. We collected the gold that we found on the mummy of the god, and we took all that was on the queen in the same way, and we set fire to their coffins. We took all the possessions of gold, silver and bronze and divided it between us.'

The granite sarcophagus *of Ramesses VI in the Valley of the Kings is a mute witness to the long history of violent tomb robbery whose beginnings date far back into ancient times. As royal power weakened towards the end of the Twentieth Dynasty, disturbance of the tombs of the pharaohs became commonplace. A papyrus fragment from the time of Ramesses IX tells of the confession of one band of thieves who spent four days breaking into the tomb of Ramesses VI.*

Ravage and reburial

Based on these ancient accounts, it was assumed until recently that all the royal tombs had unquestionably been robbed in a similar manner – by the workmen who built them. After all, the temptation must have been great: a single gold ring would have been the equivalent of several years' pay for one of these skilled men. But detailed excavation and subsequent study of the workers' village of Deir el Medina and records found there have recently cast doubt on the idea of wholesale robbery by the villagers. This settlement, over the hills from the Valley of the Kings, has now been shown to have been one of the most highly guarded places in Egypt. It was completely roofed over and walled on every side, with only one constantly guarded entrance to the north. Each item that left or entered the village was closely inspected. Everything the men carried out to the valley was weighed and noted; on their return, the procedure was carried out again to check for the slightest discrepancy. The distribution of all food, clothing, and even water was supervised from the royal warehouses on the east bank of the Nile.

The Twentieth Dynasty was an unsettled time for Egypt. Even the throne was not secure and its rightful ownership became the object of disputes. The region of Luxor experienced much of the political rivalry and actual fighting that resulted, and at the end of the dynasty the Valley of the Kings suffered violent incursions by Nubian troops who ran amok and violated the tombs of the pharaohs.

Many of the tombs now lay open and vulnerable to pilfering. In an effort to protect the royal remains the new high priest of Karnak,

Herihor, ordered many of the mummies to be rewrapped in simple bandages and had wooden dockets attached around their necks – these became their only method of identification. The bodies were then placed in ordinary coffins and secreted in several tombs. One group of mummies was relocated five or six times before finally finding its home outside the valley in the tomb of Queen Inhapi, at Deir el Bahri.

Robbery after the time of the Pharaohs

To those who came after the ancients, first the Christians and then the Arabs, the mummies became either symbols of a pagan culture or ancient relics that possessed special properties to be exploited. The Christians cast aside the bodies. The Arabs, with their concept of ancient Egyptian magic, saw in the mummies a substance that could be used to aid the living. In the Middle Ages, an Arab doctor in Cairo published a treatise on the use of bitumen, or pitch, as a medication. This was to be applied externally or taken internally, but he added, 'Where any difficulties arise from procuring bitumen, corpses may be substituted in their stead.' Whether mummies had been employed in this way earlier is hard to say, but from this time on, their use in medicine was prolific. Many thousands of ancient mummies were wilfully destroyed. Those in tombs that were easily entered, such as the Old and Middle Kingdom tombs along the Nile with their great open doorways, must have been speedily emptied.

Mummies as medicine

Around the twelfth century, mummies were divided by Egyptian doctors into four classes: Arabic mummies, being those prepared using aloes, balsam and myrrh (regarded as of little use); Egyptian mummies, being those of common people preserved in bitumen; artificial Egyptian mummy, a mixture of pitch and herbs sold as 'mummy' even though it had never been near a body; and corpses, those bodies buried in sand and dried naturally. The last group was considered as of the least use, and the naturally dried bodies were simply ground into powder to treat stomach upsets. The other three categories were imported into Europe by the ton. Often mummies were boiled and the melted oils were skimmed off to be used as ointments to stop bruising. Mummy could also be used as an ingredient in potions to cure a variety of ailments. During the fifteenth and sixteenth centuries, many people of note, including monarchs such as Francis I of France, relied on mummy as a cure.

Not everyone was impressed by the use of mummy, however. In the sixteenth century, the great French surgeon Ambroise Paré was so angered by the practice that he published his *Discours contre La Momie*, in which he stated that, 'It causes great pain in their stomachs, gives them evil smelling breath and brings about serious vomiting.' But despite opposition, so brisk was the trade and so great the prices at which mummies changed hands that contemporary Egyptians began to meet the demand for ancient mummies with modern copies. In 1564, Guy de la Fontaine, a French physician and doctor to the King of Navarre, was taken to a shop in Alexandria, where he was shown stacks of mummies. Voicing his amazement at seeing so many bodies in one place, he was assured by the keen salesman that these were 'fresh', none being more than four years old! By 1660, the English physician and author, Sir Thomas Browne, wrote that 'Mummy is become merchandise, Mizraim [the ancient word meaning 'Egyptians'] cures wounds and Pharaoh is used for balsam.'

Scholars and scientists

The number of visitors to Egypt began to increase in the years following the Renaissance as scholars sought to widen their experience. The French were especially drawn to things Egyptian. Nicholas Fouquet, Superintendent of Finances at the start of the reign of Louis XIV, the seventeenth-century Sun King, had among his treasured possessions several Egyptian statues, mummies and sarcophagi. After Fouquet's disgrace and imprisonment, the king inherited most of his treasures, including the Egyptian collection. In 1692, Louis XIV instructed Benoit de Maillet, his Consul in Cairo, to obtain more antiquities. De Maillet travelled far up the Nile collecting objects, among which was at least one mummy, which he unwrapped publicly before a French audience in Cairo in September 1698.

Philippe, Duke of Orléans, Regent of France from 1715 to 1723, decided to extend the royal Egyptian collection and to widen general knowledge about the country. He appointed Père Claude Sicard, a Jesuit who had lived in Cairo since 1707, to travel up the Nile valley. Père Sicard, who collected material and made maps as he went, was the first European since the Crusades to enter and describe the Valley of the Kings, a place then inhabited by ferocious outlaws. He entered ten tombs which he described as being 'of astonishing depth. Halls, rooms, all are painted from top to bottom.'

Egypt at this time was a dangerous place to be. Its Turkish overlords were suspicious of the intentions of foreigners, and the people of the Nile valley were afraid to speak to outsiders. They often turned to violence merely to survive. Napoleon's invasion of Egypt in 1798 changed the situation virtually overnight. The French government had appointed scholars to accompany the military expedition and record everything worthy of note along the Nile, from its flora and fauna to its monuments, and the manners and customs of its people. It was all with the aim of understanding the country, the better to control it. These scholars, or *savants*, protected by soldiers, freely wandered around temples and tombs.

By the time the British took control in 1801, the Egyptians were accustomed to the presence of Europeans. Egypt had become a

Curiosity about mummies *has a long history. In 1615, the Italian traveller Pietro della Valle employed local peasants at Dahshur to dig up mummies to send back to Europe. The exercise failed, but a worker supplied della Valle with already excavated Graeco-Roman bodies. Today the mummies are in the Dresden Museum.*

fashionable – and safer – place to visit. Many wealthy travellers were keen to see the sights and acquire souvenirs. From the mid-nineteenth century, as hotels began to open for trade and Thomas Cook sent his first 'package tourists', it became the custom for small groups of Victorian gentry to be led by guides to places where a pre-arranged 'tomb' awaited them. There, to everyone's delight, an ancient mummy would be withdrawn and carried in triumph back to the hotel. Here, after dinner, the mummy would ceremoniously and to great applause be 'unrolled' – and then, its usefulness at an end, simply discarded.

Many of the mummies were now exported to satisfy new 'scientific' appetites. In the first half of the nineteenth century, the eminent London surgeon Thomas Pettigrew arranged a series of lectures on mummification, to be followed by the public unwrapping of a mummy. Tickets to the lectures were sold out every night. Occasionally, because of the liberality of the application of resins and unguents to the body, the audience had to wait while Pettigrew rolled up his sleeves and resorted to a hammer and chisel to separate the body from its linen wrappings.

Egyptomania now swept the western world and the public demanded to know and see more. In 1814, two rival Europeans began to compete in the race to plunder Egypt. On behalf of England, the Consul-General Henry Salt was anxious to collect large antiquities for the British Museum, founded about sixty years before. Opposition over every piece was provided by the French consul, Bernadino Drovetti; and all the while, the bemused Egyptian authorities stood aside and watched in amazement. Bitter words and insults were frequently exchanged on sites as the collectors squabbled over their finds.

The Patagonian Samson

It was at this time that the most unlikely plunderer of mummies in modern times came onto the scene. Giovanni Battista Belzoni was a Paduan-born circus strongman. Although trained as an engineer and a more than adequate draughtsman, Belzoni – just over $6\frac{1}{2}$ feet (2 m) tall – earned his fortune on the stage at London's Sadler's Wells Theatre. Billed as 'The Patagonian Samson', he could carry between twelve and twenty people on an iron frame suspended from his shoulders. When he was rich enough to retire, he decided to travel in the Mediterranean. In 1814, at the age of thirty-six, he found himself in Malta. Here he was told that his experience in hydraulic engineering might prove useful to the Turkish ruler of Egypt, the Pasha Mohammed Ali, who was spending great sums of money modernizing the country.

Belzoni sketched out a new machine for raising water and set out for Egypt. He did not receive official backing for his machine and found himself penniless in a hostile land, and to make matters worse, isolated in a city suffering an epidemic of cholera. He and his English

Giovanni Belzoni *is a legend among Egyptologists. This memorial engraving commissioned by his widow shows her husband against the landscape of Luxor. Surrounding him are several of his major discoveries: the sarcophagus of Seti I, now in Sir John Soane's Museum, London; the head and arm of an unidentified pharaoh, and the colossal head known as 'the Young Memnon' (Ramesses II), both in the British Museum; and an obelisk from Philae, now in Kingston Lacey in Dorset. In the distance is a pyramid opened and entered by Belzoni in 1818.*

wife fled for aid to the consul, Henry Salt. Here they met the great traveller, Jean-Louis Burkhardt, who had been telling Salt of the many monuments and statues he had seen, some of which Drovetti's men had broken up into more portable pieces. Salt, unexpectedly presented with a poverty-stricken strongman, seized his chance and immediately hired Belzoni as his agent.

And so it was that Belzoni travelled south with an extraordinary shopping list of many of the finest pieces of sculpture that still lay on the banks of the Nile. After a successful mission, he was dispatched by Salt a second time, and arrived in Luxor in 1817, hoping to work in the temples there. Drovetti's agent, however, had already secured these rights for the French and Belzoni was offered the opportunity of working in the Valley of the Kings, where he had found two tombs on his previous visit. He met with resounding success, and in just ten days he found six previously unknown tombs. On his return to England in 1821, Belzoni published an account of his work in an autobiography which was well received by the general public and he was lionized by London society.

In his book, Belzoni described the tomb passages through which he had to bend his oversize frame: 'Of these tombs many people could not withstand the suffocating air which often causes fainting . . . In some places there is not more than the vacancy of a foot left which you must contrive to pass through in a creeping posture like a snail, on pointed and keen stones that cut like glass. After getting through these passages, some of them two or three hundred yards long, you generally find a more commodious place, perhaps high enough to sit. But what a place of rest! Surrounded by bodies, by heaps of mummies in all directions; which, previous to my being accustomed to the sight, filled me with horror. The blackness of the walls, the faint light given by candles or torches for want of air, the different objects that surrounded me, seeming to converse with each other, and the Arabs, with candles or torches in their hands, naked and covered with dust, themselves resembling living mummies, absolutely formed a scene that cannot be described.'

In the light of the thousands of mummies that we have lost, what follows perhaps seems of minor importance – but consider that some of this took place in the Valley of the Kings. Belzoni reports: 'I sought a resting place, found one and contrived to sit; but when my weight bore on the body of a dead Egyptian, it crushed it like a band box. Naturally I had recourse to my hands to sustain my weight, but they found no better support; so that I collapsed together among the broken mummies with such a crash of bones, rags and wooden cases as kept me motionless for a quarter of an hour, waiting until it subsided again. I could not remove from the place, however, without increasing it and every step I took I crushed a mummy in some place or another . . . Thus I proceeded from one cave to another, all full of mummies piled up in various ways, some standing, some lying and some on their heads.'

This mid-nineteenth century engraving *was described as 'an interior of a mummy pit or sepulchral chamber at Thebes with a fellah woman searching for papyri and ornaments.' Looking at it, one can easily visualize the mummy-packed tombs through which Giovanni Belzoni made his way, eagerly helped by local peasants seeking financial reward from the determined and enthusiastic European giant.*

Mummies as industrial fodder

The depredation of Egyptian mummies was still not at an end, nor the ingenuity of mankind to find new uses for them. The nineteenth century saw the dawn of a machine age activated by the Industrial Revolution – and new functions for mummies. An American paper manufacturer from Maine, Augustus Stanwood, struck a deal for tons of linen mummy wrappings to be turned into paper. Unfortunately, so discoloured were they that, unable to make them into white paper as he had planned, he turned them into brown wrapping paper instead. When a cholera epidemic later broke out and was seemingly traced to Stanwood's wrappings, the production of it was halted. Today it is known that such infectious material is unlikely to have survived for hundreds, and certainly not for thousands, of years.

The final indignity was perpetrated, though, in the last years of the century. In his tongue-in-cheek account of foreign travel, *Innocents Abroad*, the American writer Samuel Clemens, better known as Mark Twain, recorded the last insult to mummies, when he watched stokers shovelling spadefuls of them into the fireboxes of locomotives. Twain states that he heard an engineer call out 'D..n these plebeians, they don't burn worth a cent! Pass out a King!'

Modern discovery and rescue

It would hardly be surprising if not a single mummy had survived this ghastly treatment into the current century. Yet some have. The founding of the Antiquities Organization in Cairo in 1858 by Auguste Mariette resulted in the first control ever exerted over unofficial excavations and the export of Egyptian antiquities. Henceforward, anyone of any nationality who wanted to dig in Egypt had first to obtain a signed agreement from the Antiquities Organization. Excavators had to agree to allow inspectors on site at any time and not to enter any tomb they might find without an inspector present. In addition, the contents of any violated tomb were to be presented first to the newly founded Egyptian Museum, which was entitled to make its own selection of the finest pieces; the rest were to belong to the excavator. Only in the case of an unviolated tomb would everything remain the property of the Egyptian government. But the chance of finding an intact tomb then must have seemed quite remote.

The legendary Abd el Rassuls

Despite the existence of the Antiquities Organization, however, illicit excavations continued. In 1873, the English writer Amelia Edwards encountered just such an unorthodox excavation on the west bank of Luxor. 'The diggers were in the pit', Miss Edwards recorded. 'We were just in time, for already, through the sand and rubble with which the grave had been filled in there appeared an outline of something buried. The men, throwing spades and picks aside, now began scraping up the dust with their hands and a mummy case came to light. It was shaped to represent a body lying at length with the hands crossed upon the breast. Both hands and face were carved in high relief. The ground colour of the sarcophagus was white, the surface covered with hieroglyphed legends and somewhat coarsely painted figures of the four lesser Gods of the Dead [i.e. Four Sons of Horus].'

Miss Edwards recorded her reaction to the pathetic appearance of the mummy: 'Once they are lodged and catalogued in museums, one comes to look upon these things as "specimens" and forgets that they were once living beings like ourselves.' And she also went on to mention that rumours were rife in Luxor of 'a tomb that had been discovered on the western side – a wonderful tomb, rich in treasures . . .' These rumours by and by assumed more definite proportions. Dark hints were dropped of a possible papyrus.

The rumours heard by Amelia Edwards about a new tomb proved completely true. One had indeed been discovered at Luxor. In 1871, the Abd el Rassuls, a family from the west bank village of Sheikh abd el Qurna (often known simply as Qurna) had chanced across the concealed entrance to a tomb, along the cliffs north of Deir el Bahri. After lowering themselves down a rope into the shaft, they found themselves standing in a passageway filled with mummies. They had discovered mummies and coffins before – enough to realize that these were no ordinary burials. The anthropoid coffins, though for the most part simple and crude, bore the serpent headdress (the uraeus) on their brow, the sign of kingship. The Abd el Rassuls must have felt a curious mixture of fear and elation. To discourage the curious, they dropped a slaughtered donkey down the tomb shaft, and continually renewed it; the festering smell of decay in the hot sun was certain to keep tourists at bay. They told tales of their meeting with an *afrit*, a troubled spirit or ghost, a story guaranteed to keep out other villagers.

Over the next few years, the family removed objects only rarely, knowing that otherwise the fine illuminated papyri of superb quality and the inscribed statuettes would attract unwanted attention. But people eventually began to gossip as the Abd el Rassuls prospered. The objects they sold found their way to collectors, and eight or nine years later, some of the objects began to appear in the major European auction houses. They proved indeed to be royal, belonging to kings and queens of the late New Kingdom. What is more, their near-perfect condition was a clear indication that something new must have been found.

The first royal cache
In 1881, Gaston Maspero, head of the Antiquities Organization, sailed south to Luxor to investigate. Here he traced the rumours with little difficulty to the Abd el Rassuls, who revealed nothing, despite an interrogation by the police that included beating on the soles of the feet (the bastinado) so severe that one of the brothers was never able to

walk easily again. The police released the men and, defeated, Maspero left the area.

The village of Qurna found itself under virtual siege, so tightly policed that normal life was impossible. Accusations were levelled against the Abd el Rassuls for being the cause of the misery, and within the family itself, violent arguments broke out. On 5 July 1881, Mohammed Abd el Rassul, the eldest brother, decided that peace must be restored to the village at all cost, and walked into the police station and gave himself up. The police telegraphed Cairo and the following day Emil Brugsch, Maspero's assistant, arrived. He was led by the silent, angry brothers up the cliff to the tomb and was then himself let down on a rope. Maspero later described the event: 'The first object which had presented itself to Brugsch's gaze when he reached the bottom of the shaft was a white and yellow coffin inscribed with the name Nesikhonsu . . . A little further on was a coffin of Seventeenth Dynasty style, then the Queen Tiuhathor Henttaui, then Seti I . . . The entire length of the corridor was so similarly obstructed and disordered that it was necessary to advance on all fours, not knowing where to put hands and feet. The coffins and the mummies, all glimpsed by the light of a candle, bore historic names: Amenhetep I, Tuthmosis II in the niche near the steps, Ahmose and his son Siamun, Sequenre, Queen Ahotpe, Ahmose Nefertari and others . . . Where I had expected to find one or two minor kings, the Arabs had dug up a vault of pharaohs. And what pharaohs!'

For the next five days, the bewildered villagers of the west bank watched as the excavators, sweating profusely in the full heat of the summer sun, emptied the chamber. The mummies often had to be laid outside on the sand until caskets could be found to hold them. The mummy of Ramesses I lay there so long that his wrappings and resins grew warm and his arm began to lift, apparently of its own accord, terrifying the workmen nearby. Eventually the chamber lay empty, and the mummies, in coffins and on biers, were carried slowly in procession to the river. 'From Luxor to Quft [sic] on both banks of the Nile the wailing fellahin women with dishevelled hair followed the boat, and the men fired off their guns, just as they do at funerals.'

Method replaces mayhem
Royal tombs aside, in the years following the establishment of the Antiquities Organization, the random looting of graves and tombs was replaced slowly by the methodical and scientific techniques of archaeology. One man, Flinders Petrie, was responsible for establishing many of the new procedures for examining cemeteries and for studying the remains within them. In 1894, outside the town of Tukh, 20 miles (32 km) to the north of Luxor, Petrie was given permission to examine a large necropolis. It contained 2,149 graves of men, women and children who had been buried at the dawn of Egypt's history. By setting his men to work slowly and carefully on every grave, recording

RESTING PLACE OF KINGS:
THE 1881 ROYAL CACHE

The mummy identified *as that of Tuthmosis I (right) is the body of a young man. History indicates that the king died at about fifty, leading scientists to question the accuracy of the original identification.*

On 6 June 1881, Mohammed Abd el Rassul led a group, including Emil Brugsch of the Egyptian Antiquities Organization, along the cliffs immediately south of Deir el Bahri. Once Mohammed had cleared the debris that filled the base of a shaft entrance, Brugsch descended and made his way through a corridor and then an opening under 3 feet (1 m) high. Successive passageways contained coffins and artefacts strewn about by robbers. But a chamber at the end of the tomb – for this had originally been a tomb, made in the Eighteenth Dynasty for Queen Inhapy – was packed with coffins. Inscriptions on them listed the names of many of the New Kingdom rulers.

The mummies were carefully removed from the tomb in which they had lain for some 3,000 years. Together with the artefacts from the tomb, they were taken across the Nile to Luxor. On 15 June, a steamboat sent by the museum in Cairo arrived, and the royal party was loaded on board to make its way slowly north. Since then the mummies have rested in the peace and security of a special room in the Cairo Museum.

The wrapped mummy of *Tuthmosis III (above) was broken into by robbers looking for precious amulets and jewels. The photograph of his mummy lying on a bier (above right) shows the king after unwrapping in Cairo over a century ago.*

Queen Nodjmet's mummy *(left) shows the results of the packing techniques introduced during the Twenty-first Dynasty. The face is so padded that it has become round out of all proportion.*

The mummy of Seti I *is well preserved, the face showing dignity even in death.*

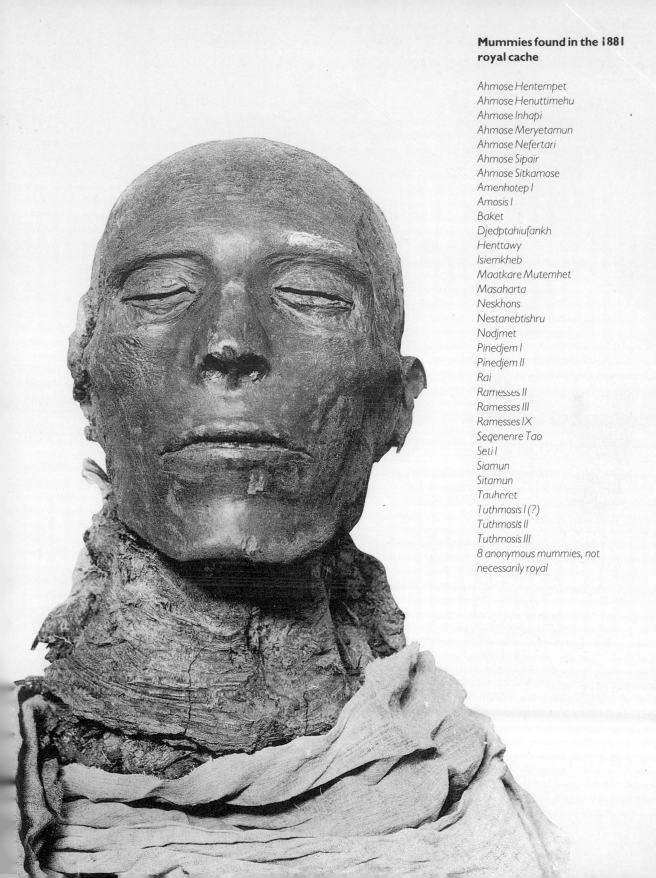

Mummies found in the 1881 royal cache

Ahmose Hentempet
Ahmose Henuttimehu
Ahmose Inhapi
Ahmose Meryetamun
Ahmose Nefertari
Ahmose Sipair
Ahmose Sitkamose
Amenhotep I
Amosis I
Baket
Djedptahiufankh
Henttawy
Isiemkheb
Maatkare Mutemhet
Masaharta
Neskhons
Nestanebtishru
Nodjmet
Pinedjem I
Pinedjem II
Rai
Ramesses II
Ramesses III
Ramesses IX
Seqenenre Tao
Seti I
Siamun
Sitamun
Tauheret
Tuthmosis I (?)
Tuthmosis II
Tuthmosis III
8 anonymous mummies, not
necessarily royal

the exact contents and positioning of everything, and then correlating the results, he was able for the first time to establish a sequence of styles and fashions (Sequence Dating) that gave a glimpse of Egypt's emergence from the Neolithic era.

But not all nineteenth-century archaeologists were as methodical as Petrie. The first archaeologists to work at Giza on the Old Kingdom tombs surrounding the Fourth Dynasty pyramids discarded many of the mummies they found virtually unrecorded. Only their skulls were retained, in keeping with the late nineteenth-century belief that everything – race, age, sex, stature, and even intelligence – could be determined from them. Only in recent years have these begun to be scientifically examined and published.

Hidden burials of the high priests

It was scarcely to be expected that such a discovery as that of the 1881 royal cache could be matched, but the quiet hills of Egypt are ever full of surprises. Mohammed Abd el Rassul, who had learned his lesson, started to work as foreman for the Antiquities Organization. In 1891, he led the inspector to another likely site at Deir el Bahri. Here lay the bodies of almost 160 successive high priests from the Temple of Karnak, many from the family of the high priest Herihor, who had restored and reburied many of the bodies of the kings and queens at the end of the Twentieth Dynasty, some 3,000 years before. There were far too many mummies for the Cairo Museum to handle, and many were donated to museums around the world. There was some suspicion that the Abd el Rassuls had long known of this tomb – and taken what they could – and the authorities dismissed Mohammed from their service. It was an event that was to have great repercussions.

The second royal cache

In 1898, the inspector of antiquities, Victor Loret, was working in the Valley of the Kings when he came across a previously unknown tomb entrance cut into the rock floor in a quiet recess. The passageway led steeply into the earth, pitch black, and scattered with rubble and debris. Having negotiated the slope, and traversed a pit beyond, Loret found himself in a large columned chamber, again filled with debris. Against one wall lay a curious wooden boat. 'A horrible sight', he wrote, 'a body lying there upon the boat, all black and hideous, its grimacing face turning towards me and looking at me, its long brown hair in sparse bunches around its head.' The body was that of an unknown teenage prince, perhaps the son of the tomb owner, Amenhotep II. The prince's mummy appeared to have been unwrapped by robbers when the oils on the body were still wet, for the body was stuck to the boat.

A passage led further downwards into the darkness. At the end of the tomb was a huge columned hall, the floor thick with broken funerary equipment. 'The sarcophagus in the middle of the room was

MUMMIES IN THE KING'S TOMB: THE 1898 ROYAL CACHE

In 1898, Victor Loret discovered the tomb of Amenhotep II in the Valley of the Kings. What lay inside was not just the mummy of the pharaoh but those of eight other kings, one unknown – but presumably royal – woman, and the remains of six more bodies. Like the royal mummies found in 1881 at Deir el Bahri, these too were immediately sent to Cairo, where they rest among their royal brothers and sisters.

Amenhotep II (right below), in whose tomb the 1898 cache was found, was left in his sarcophagus in the Valley of the Kings. Sadly, his mummy was destroyed and this photograph is all that remains of the discovery of his body.

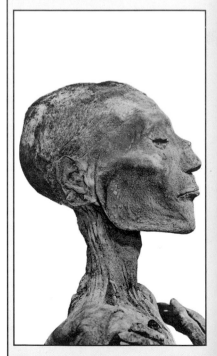

The face of Ramesses V shows evidence of a rash of small pustules.

Mummies found in the 1898 royal cache

Amenhotep II
Amenhotep III
Merenptah
Ramesses IV
Ramesses V
Ramesses VI
Seti II
Siptah
Tiye (?)
Tuthmosis IV
6 anonymous human remains, not necessarily royal

The identity of *the body of this elderly woman (right) from the 1898 cache is uncertain. She has been identified as Queen Tiye, wife of Amenhotep III, but this has been challenged.*

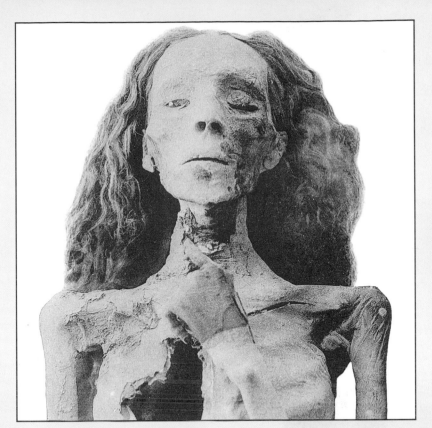

open, but was it empty?' Loret wondered. As he peered inside, he received a shock. 'A coffin lay at the bottom, having at its head a bunch of flowers.' It later proved to be the body of Amenhotep II, the first pharaoh ever to be found in his own burial chamber. As if that were not enough, side-chambers proved to be stacked with twelve more mummies. Finally, inside another walled-up chamber, Loret discovered a further pile of coffins. Like Brugsch before him, he read with trembling hands the names of more of Egypt's great pharaohs. Here lay the remains of eight kings and an unidentified woman.

In the years following the discovery of the first two caches, feelings within Egypt perceptibly changed. Archaeologists, far from being seen as saving Egypt's royal dead from tomb robbers, were regarded as little more than tomb robbers themselves. The government gave orders that the mummies Loret found should not be removed, but should be left where they were. It was to prove a sad mistake. In the first months of 1901, men guarding Amenhotep II's tomb were overcome and it was robbed. The mummy of the little prince in his boat vanished, together with many other pieces, including the pharaoh's great long bow. As for the mummy of Amenhotep II, it was unceremoniously unwrapped, its amulets and jewels stolen and one arm torn off in the robbers' haste. While arrangements were made to remove the rest of the mummies to the Cairo Museum, the new inspector of the Valley of the Kings, Howard Carter, managed to identify the culprits – the Abd el Rassuls. But although proof was found in their home leading to their arrest and trial, they were eventually freed.

So the last of the royal mummies, like their predecessors, were now shipped from Luxor to Cairo. Far from being mourned on the way, however, the cases containing their bodies were swiftly and anonymously removed to the north – with one last hitch. At Cairo, customs officials were required to find a classification for the mummies for taxation purposes before they could be released to the museum. Finding no suitable tariff, the nearest equivalent description of the 'goods', was chosen. As a result, eight of Egypt's greatest pharaohs entered the capital city as dried fish!

Tutankhamun

Howard Carter, the inspector who had traced the robberies from the second royal cache to the Abd el Rassuls, resigned from the Antiquities Organization in 1903, but stayed on in Luxor. And it was here that he was introduced to Lord Carnarvon, who was having no success in digging on his own. In 1907, Carter and Carnarvon formed what was to be the most famous partnership in Egyptian archaeology.

Also in 1907, archaeologists working for the American Theodore Davis, in the Valley of the Kings, found a small pit containing a number of large pots and a quantity of linen. One of the pots bore the coronation name of Tutankhamun. The entire find was later identified by the Metropolitan Museum of Art's H.E. Winlock as the

I The mask of Tutankhamun –
one of the great treasures of the Cairo Museum. It is almost 2 feet (54 cm) high, made of solid gold, and weighs $24\frac{1}{4}$ pounds (11 kg). The mask is inlaid with lapis lazuli, carnelian, quartz, obsidian, turquoise and coloured glass.

Overleaf
II The north wall of Tutankhamun's burial chamber, above the sarcophagus, is richly painted with scenes that illustrate the royal transition from the world of the living to that of the dead. At the far right stands Ay, Tutankhamun's successor and already wearing the crown of kingship, who performs the ceremony of the Opening of the Mouth on the body of the dead ruler in his form as Osiris, king of the underworld. In the middle, the sky goddess Nut, mother of Osiris, welcomes the young king as her own son. Finally (left) the ka of the king, with the ankh or symbol of life in his left hand, is shown accompanying Tutankhamun to the underworld where he embraces Osiris.

remains of a funerary banquet. The bundles of linen had been used in the mummification process, perhaps carried out somewhere near the pit. What was now clear was that the tomb of Tutankhamun was still to be found – and Howard Carter thought he had a fairly good idea where it might be.

Carnarvon took up the concession to dig in the valley, in 1915, and over the next few years, on his behalf, Carter excavated many tombs in the valley, but was prevented from working in his area of first choice because it disturbed the tourist traffic. Eventually, Carnarvon's patience and willingness wore thin and he agreed to back only one final season. Carter then chose to dig in a small triangular patch of ground in front of the tomb of Ramesses VI, within a short distance both of the cache found in 1907 and of a mysterious tomb (Tomb 55), also found by Davis that year, which was linked with the reign of Tutankhamun.

By the morning of 4 November 1922, Carter's men had exposed a step, which proved to be the first of sixteen. At the bottom, Carter saw the top of a doorway bearing the seals of the ancient necropolis guards. In a fever of excitement, he cabled Carnarvon: 'At last have made a wonderful discovery in the valley; a magnificent tomb with seals intact; recovered same for your arrival. Congratulations!' Seventeen days later, the whole doorway was cleared, and at the base was the seal impression both men had waited over ten years to see 'Nebkheprure' (Tutankhamun).

On 26 November, Carter made his way to the door sealing the inner chambers: 'Slowly, desperately slowly, it seemed to us, the remains of the passage debris that encumbered the lower part of the door was removed, until at last we had the whole door before us. The decisive moment had arrived. With trembling hands, I made a tiny breach in the upper left-hand corner . . . Candle tests were applied as a precaution against foul gases and then, widening the hole a little, I inserted the candle and peered in. At first I could see nothing, the hot air escaping from the chamber, causing the candle flame to flicker, but presently, as my eyes grew accustomed to the light, details of the room within emerged slowly from the mist, strange animals, statues and gold – everywhere the glint of gold. For the moment – an eternity it must have seemed to others standing by – I was struck dumb with amazement, and when Lord Carnarvon, unable to stand the suspense any longer, inquired anxiously, "Can you see anything?" it was all I could do to get out the words, "Yes, wonderful things."'

The initial excitement quickly subsided in the face of difficulties with the Egyptian government over who should have control of the tomb's contents. Eventually, after a hostile legal battle, the government won. From this time, all objects excavated in Egypt would be the property of the Egyptian government. The archaeologists had to accept defeat and, in an uneasy atmosphere, the work of clearing the tomb went on – it was to take ten years. Although the burial chamber had been opened in 1923, the detailed examination of the contents –

III In this image *from the outside of the second of the gold shrines surrounding the burial of Tutankhamun, a mummiform figure of the king stands with his head and feet encircled by two serpents – Mehen, the Enveloper, encompasses the head. The whole of the panel is inscribed with descriptions of the gods depicted, and chapters from the Book of the Dead.*

sarcophagus, coffins and mummy – was to wait until the 1925–26 season, when, in poor conditions and with limited technology, it was examined by two doctors from Cairo. In 1968, using modern X-ray equipment the mummy was examined again (see feature).

The gold of Tanis

In 1939, a further small group of six tombs was discovered under a temple courtyard at Tanis in the delta. Three of the burials belonged to kings of the Twenty-first and Twenty-second Dynasties. The French archaeologist, Pierre Montet, made little fuss about his find in the hope of not attracting the attention of robbers. But it was to no avail, for in early 1943, his storehouse was broken into and many of the smaller objects stolen. Much of this material appeared on the antiquities market, including bronze figurines from the burial of the pharaoh Psusennes and some of the jars which had contained internal organs of the mummies. The bodies themselves were not removed by the robbers and the remains were taken to Cairo.

Current work in Egypt

The change in the law resulting from the discovery of Tutankhamun's tomb has meant that fewer major excavations funded from outside Egypt have taken place; in addition, the cost is higher than most universities, museums or governments are willing to subsidize. Attention has been turned to threatened sites in Egypt, perhaps most notably the resiting of the temples of Abu Simbel during the 1960s and early 1970s. Work is constantly going on to conserve the monuments and record inscriptions that are being eroded away. One major project, being carried out by the University of California at Berkeley, is creating a detailed topographical survey of the necropolis area of the west bank at Luxor. But evidence concerning mummies and ancient burials is still being produced – sometimes when least expected.

Since 1975, one major series of excavations has been undertaken by a joint British–Dutch team, led by Professor Geoffrey Martin of the Egypt Exploration Society and Dr Jacobus Van Dijk of the Leiden Museum, southeast of the Step Pyramid at Saqqara. Their initial aim was to locate a series of tombs known to have been open to view in the 1840s, when the great German archaeologist, Karl Lepsius, visited and recorded the monuments of the ancient necropolis. The team was especially interested in finding the tomb of Maya, a high official in the time of Tutankhamun. The tombs themselves had long since vanished under the soft sands of the Saqqara plateau, but using the sketch map made by Lepsius' architect, mud-brick walls emerged within minutes of digging. What emerged was the tomb of Horemheb – last pharaoh of the Eighteenth Dynasty – built for him when he was a general. (His tomb as pharaoh lies in the Valley of the Kings.)

Successive seasons of excavation have revealed more tombs, providing new and exciting information. In the tomb of Tia, a sister of

THE MYSTERY OF TOMB 55

In 1907, two Englishmen, Arthur Weigall and Edward Ayrton, digging on behalf of the American Theodore Davis, discovered a tomb in the Valley of the Kings whose door bore seals with the name of the pharaoh Tutankhamun. The location of this sealed tomb, later called Tomb 55, was to provide one of the clues for Howard Carter when he narrowed the area of his search for Tutankhamun's own tomb. In the entrance passage of Tomb 55, a gilded panel from a shrine carried the figure and name of Queen Tiye, mother of Akhenaten, pharaoh during the intriguing Amarna period of the Eighteenth Dynasty. In the burial chamber itself lay a coffin containing a mummy. Davis called on the services of a doctor who happened to be touring in the Valley, telling him that the mummy was that of a queen. The doctor, who had never seen a mummy and had no training as a pathologist, did not challenge Davis' view. The remains were sent to Cairo where the anatomist Elliot Smith declared that, on the contrary, they were those of a man, possibly around twenty years of age. And so a heated controversy over the identity began that still continues.

Today only a handful of bones, including the skull, is left. Analysis of these skeletal remains indicates that they belonged to a person about 5 feet (1.52 m) tall, and with a blood group A2 MN (i.e. type A, sub-group 2, with antigens M and N) – the same type as that of Tutankhamun.

But whose remains are these? Are they those of a man or a woman? Davis' idea that the mummy might be Tiye's must be discounted on grounds of age alone. Early suggestions that the mummy was Akhenaten's are surely called into question when one considers that he ruled for seventeen years and was a father of three children by his fifth regnal year. One long-held notion is that the body belonged to one Smenkhkare, possibly a brother of Tutankhamun. Another suggestion is that it may have been the mummy of Kiya, a little-known queen of Akhenaten, now thought to have been Tutankhamun's mother. The mystery of Tomb 55 remains unresolved.

The mysterious *coffin, lying amid the debris that filled Tomb 55. Dampness caused the coffin's bier to collapse and the mummy was reduced to bones and bits of dried skin.*

Panels from *Queen Tiye's gilded shrine dominated the small chamber, partially obscuring the coffin at the rear. Canopic jars stood in a wall recess.*

REVEALING TUTANKHAMUN

'A great day in the history of archaeology – I might say in the history of archaeological discovery – and a day of days for one who, after years of work excavating, conserving and recording, has longed to see in fact what had previously been only conjectural.' So Howard Carter records the events of Wednesday, 11 November 1925, the day on which the mummy of the boy-king Tutankhamun began to be unwrapped, some three years after the discovery of his tomb.

When the lid of the solid gold innermost coffin was removed, Carter saw for the first time the celebrated mask that had preserved in gold the king's youthful features since 1323 BC. With great difficulty, he then set about freeing the mummy from its coffin and its poorly preserved linen wrappings. A post-mortem, limited by lack of equipment, was carried out the next day.

The mummy

When the king's mummy was revealed, it could be seen that the body had been badly damaged by the liberal oils and resins, leaving the skin and tissue brittle and blackened; many of the joints broke apart. Only the face, shielded by the gold mask, escaped real damage. The feet were fitted with gold sandals, and the toes and fingers were covered with gold caps. The arms and chest were adorned with jewels.

Tutankhamun was estimated to be between seventeen and nineteen years of age. This was confirmed later by X-rays of his epiphyseal joints – allowing for the earlier maturity of people in ancient Egypt, the younger age seems the more likely. The face was well preserved. His head had been closely shaven, and no regrowth of stubble was visible.

The king was found to have been 5 feet 8 inches (1.7 m) tall, of slim build, and narrow-shouldered. He had long eyelashes, slightly protruding teeth, and ears pierced with unusually large holes, about ½ inch (12 mm) in diameter. His eyes were present, but it was not possible to say what colour the irises had been. Two wisdom teeth had erupted shortly before his death. There seemed to be no signs of disease or injury.

The second examination

In 1968, permission was given for a limited analysis of Tutankhamun's mummy to be carried out in his tomb in the Valley of the Kings. X-rays revealed a thinning of the bone behind the left ear. This could possibly have been the result of a blow, but there is no conclusive evidence. The X-ray also showed what appeared to be a small bone fragment in the skull; it was assumed that this was a piece of bone broken from the nasal cavity when the brain was removed. Two distinct layers of resin in the skull cavity were also evident, one along the top of the skull and a second at right angles to the first.

A tiny portion of rehydrated tissue analyzed in England proved that Tutankhamun's blood was Group A, subgroup 2, with antigens M and N present, the same type as the body in Tomb 55.

When the lid *of Tutankhamun's quartzite sarcophagus was removed, the outermost of three coffins (below) was revealed. The first two were of wood, overlaid with gold and inlaid with faience and coloured glass. The third, innermost, coffin was of solid gold and weighed 296 pounds (110.4 kg). Each of the coffins bears the visage of the king and shows him as the god Osiris holding the crook and flail. Within the third coffin was the royal mummy (right), over its head the famous gold mask.*

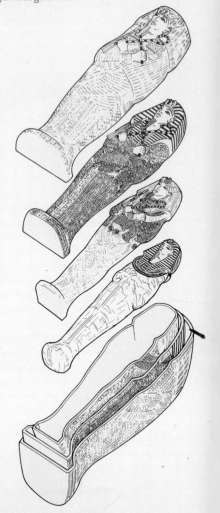

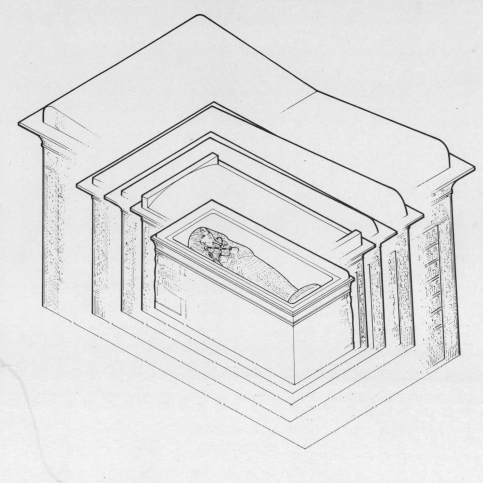

The stone sarcophagus containing
*Tutankhamun's three coffins lay within a
nest of four gilded wooden shrines.*

MUMMIES IN THE TOMB OF IURUDEF

In 1984, the British-Dutch team excavating at Saqqara, under the directorship of the Egypt Exploration Society's Professor Geoffrey Martin, found a burial shaft in the tomb of the Princess Tia, sister of Ramesses II. The shaft belonged to one of her aides, Iurudef. Several chambers off the main passage contained coffins and a large number of mummies. Like many New Kingdom burials, that of Iurudef had been set to the torch and completely incinerated – freeing the rooms for burial of more mummies.

The excavators had expected that these subsequent mummies, as usual in such circumstances, would prove to be a cache of Late-period, or more probably of Graeco-Roman date. To everyone's surprise, the seventy-five mummies were found to be of New Kingdom date, placed there perhaps within a few decades of Iurudef's own burial. Had space in the Saqqara necropolis become so precious by the Nineteenth Dynasty that even in Ramesside times multiple burials had to be made?

Most surprising of all, a high proportion of the bodies were those of children, a category hitherto believed to have remained unmummified because of the high cost of the process. The coffins were of a very low standard; many were little more than crudely nailed together fragments of wood. Several of the coffins that had been finished, painted and inscribed were covered with meaningless jumbles of pseudo-hieroglyphs and pictures.

The face from one of the coffins found in the tomb of Iurudef – the powerful yet serene visage of an Egyptian who left this earth over 3,000 years ago.

Ramesses II, a pyramid base was identified and in the nearby burial shaft of one of her courtiers, a man named Iurudef, several dozen burials were found (see feature). On 6 February 1986, the efforts of the team were finally rewarded with the discovery of the tomb of Maya itself, a tomb so far unique at Saqqara with its beautiful wall paintings. All these tombs had been robbed in antiquity and there were few remains. Horemheb's tomb contained the bones of a woman thought to have been his wife Mutnodjmet, possibly the sister of Queen Nefertiti; only fragments of the remains of Maya and his wife Meryt were found.

The future

The physical discovery of mummies in the sands of Egypt may now be drawing to a close, but in museums all over the world a new search is under way. Archaeologists have now realized that the search for the secrets of mummification need not take them any further than their own collections. The mummies that have survived are, therefore, undergoing many scientific tests and trials, and by using all the means that technology can provide, a different, more intricate form of discovery is now taking place.

Chapter Two
Making a Mummy

EGYPTIAN MUMMIES REPRESENT a marriage of spiritual thought and practical experimentation over thousands of years. Both the earliest beliefs and the reasons for artificially preserving the bodies of the dead are lost in the mists of time. But an increasing wealth of evidence is shedding light on this mysterious practice, allowing us to delve into the minds of the ancient people to whom it was so important.

Early beliefs in an afterlife

Around 450 BC, the Greek historian Herodotus sought to discover the reasons for mummification. The Persian rulers, he recorded, had exhumed the body of the last native pharaoh, Amasis, who died about 526 BC, and ordered it burnt. This was regarded as a great insult for, as Herodotus was told, 'Egyptians believed fire to be a living creature which devours whatever it gets, and when it has eaten enough, dies along with the food on which it has fed. It is wholly contrary to Egyptian custom to allow dead bodies to be eaten by animals; and that is why they mummify them, to prevent them being eaten by worms.' If this were true, then it would seem that mummification developed for purely practical reasons. But is this the whole story?

Why preserve the body?
The collection of ancient funerary spells known as the Pyramid Texts gives some indication that preservation of the body was linked with life hereafter. Spells urged the dead to 'secure your head to your bones [Spell 13] . . . collect your bones, gather together your limbs, throw the sand from off your flesh [Spell 373].' The earliest examples of these texts date to royal burials of the Old Kingdom, but they contain beliefs that certainly predate that time. Although the exact meaning of the spells in the Pyramid Texts is difficult to interpret, it certainly appears that the Eyptians considered it important that the body remain intact – this may have had something to do with the deceased's entering the next life.

The shallow, desert graves of the Predynastic Nile dwellers contained funeral goods; simple pots, beads and offerings of food and drink, for the most part. But the fact that the burials contained these things at all seems to imply that the ancients believed the deceased

This natural mummy *is the body of a Predynastic man, buried at Gebelein about 3200 BC. His body was dried and preserved solely due to the action of the hot, dry sand which quickly absorbed any moisture. Once drying was complete, there was nothing that could decay. Today this mummy can be seen in the British Museum, still surrounded by the typical black-topped red pottery with which it was buried.*

might have some use for them in an afterlife. The hot, dry sand around these bodies quickly absorbed the water that constituted seventy-five per cent of their weight – and without which decay could not take place. The remains of even the recently dead would have been some three-quarters lighter, hard and rigid, with a leathery skin – but perfectly preserved. These 'natural mummies' would surely have been noticed out in the desert, as winds or animal activity disturbed the original burials, and perhaps eventually encouraged the notion that artificial preservation might be possible.

Growth in wealth meant that the simple graves gave way to lined pits, eventually roofed over, the inclusion of more elaborate grave goods, and the use of coffins to protect the body. One direct result of this was that the body was removed from the desiccating effects of the sand, and decomposition set in, reducing the remains to skeletons. This obviously proved undesirable because the next development in burial methods involved early attempts to preserve the body – in a contracted, or foetal, position – by wrapping it tightly in linen bandages soaked in resin. This method later became more elaborate and during the Archaic period (the first three dynasties), attempts at a more lifelike appearance were made. Details such as genitals were added in linen padding.

If the body itself were to survive, something had to be done to counter the effects of decomposition, and it was eventually realized that decay somehow originates in moisture. This led to the removal of the soft internal organs, or evisceration, for decay in these organs quickly spread to the rest of the body. The change in position of the body from contracted to extended – necessary for removing the organs through the side of the abdomen – indicates that this must have happened during the Third Dynasty.

During the late Fifth Dynasty and the Sixth Dynasty the wrapped body was covered in a layer of plaster or resin and features of the deceased were moulded and painted. One such mummy, that of Waty, found at Saqqara in 1966, has achieved the distinction of being known as 'the oldest mummy in the world'. The body, including the genitals, had been finely moulded, even a callus on one of Waty's feet is clearly visible; features – eyes, eyebrows and moustache – had all been picked out in black paint; the torso appears slightly green. But the body within the wrappings still decayed and the eventual result was a hollow shell, within which remained only bones. But moisture must be extracted from the whole body to stave off the process of decomposition and soon the ancient embalmers began to work on methods to achieve this. A drying medium was found in natron, or *netjeryt* (meaning 'divine' or 'of the god'), used in purification or cleansing rituals. With evisceration and drying of the body, or desiccation, the basis for true mummification was established.

Preserving the dead

Although the first attempts at artificial preservation of the dead occurred as early as 3000 BC, no satisfactorily detailed Egyptian description of mummification has ever been found and there are few depictions of it – perhaps because it was considered too sacred to be shown to the uninitiated. For the only written accounts of the process, we must leap ahead some 2,500 years to the writings of Greek historians. According to Herodotus, writing in the fifth century BC, there were three methods of mummification: 'The most perfect practice is to extract as much of the brain as possible with an iron hook, and what the hook cannot reach is rinsed out with "drugs". Next the flank is laid open with a flint knife and the whole contents of the abdomen removed. The cavity is then thoroughly cleansed and washed out with palm wine and again an infusion of pounded spices. After that it is filled with pure bruised myrrh, cassia and every other aromatic substance with the exception of frankincense, and sewn up again, after which the body is placed in natron, covered over entirely for seventy days – never longer.

'When, for reasons of expense, the second quality is called for, the treatment is different; no incision is made and the intestines are not removed but oil of cedar is injected into the body with a syringe through the anus, which is then stopped up to prevent the liquid from escaping. The body is then dry-salted in natron for the prescribed number of days, on the last of which the oil itself is drained off. The effect of it is so powerful that as it leaves the body, it brings with it the stomach and intestines in a liquid state.

'The third method, used for embalming the bodies of the poor, is simply to clean out the intestines with a purge and keep the body seventy days in natron.'

THE FATHER OF A QUEEN

In 1904, an excavation team in the Valley of the Kings discovered a virtually intact tomb containing two mummies, that of Yuya and his wife Thuya. This old couple were not royal and so their bodies were not subjected to the gallons of resin, poured over the mummies of the kings and queens, that often damaged the royal remains. The result is two exceptionally well-preserved mummies.

Yuya and Thuya owe their place of burial among royalty to their daughter, Tiye, chief wife of Pharaoh Amenhotep III and mother of Akhenaten. Whether Tiye was one of the mourners at her parents' funeral, perhaps with Akhenaten and his wife Nefertiti, by then living far to the north in their new city dedicated to the worship of the Aten, one can only speculate. It is a fair assumption that the Princess Sitamun, sister to Akhenaten, was present, for among the burial goods were many given by her, including a chair specially made as a funerary object; on it is a scene that shows her making an offering to her grandparents.

The bodies

Yuya had been Master of the King's Chariotry and a priest of Min, the god of Coptos (modern Qift) associated with Amun of Karnak. He was about sixty-five to seventy at his death; a tall man, almost 6 foot (1.8 m), with a thin face, an aquiline nose and white hair. Thuya was approximately the same age and had a fine head of auburn hair – the same colour as the growth of beard on her husband's chin. Both Yuya and Thuya appear to have suffered from bad teeth.

The face of the mummy of Yuya, found in the Valley of the Kings. Although he himself was not of royal blood, his daughter Tiye married Amenhotep III. So Yuya became father of a queen and grandfather of the pharaoh Akhenaten.

55

As we shall see, Herodotus' account raises a number of controversial issues. The following description of the process draws on his version together with the few depictions and inscriptions known from tombs and coffins, and mummy analyses.

Purification

As soon as death took place, the embalmers would have been called in by the family to carry the deceased away on a bier to the *ibu*, the 'tent of purification'. Here a lengthy prescribed ritual, taking seventy days, began. The chief embalmer was the 'Controller of the Mysteries', who represented Anubis, the jackal-headed god of cemeteries and embalming. He was assisted by the 'God's Seal Bearer'. The lector priest was present to read appropriate spells throughout the procedure. In addition, there were a number of *wtw*, minor priests who carried out ordinary tasks such as the bandaging.

At the *ibu*, the body was thoroughly cleansed, using water containing the purifying agent natron. This ritual cleansing, the first

Depictions of the different stages of the embalming ritual, *such as these three scenes on the coffin of Djed-bast-iuef-ankh in the Hildesheim Museum, showing the process in stages, are rare. Here one can see (above left) the corpse being purified; (above) the body being dried in a bed of natron on a lion-headed bier, while priests, the chief of whom wears the mask of the god Anubis, carry out sacred rituals; and finally (above right) the canopic jars, containing the prepared internal organs, stand beneath the mummy which has been completely bandaged, its head covered with a funerary mask.*

In this painting *from the Nineteenth Dynasty tomb of Nekhtamun at Deir el Medina, near the Valley of the Kings, the god Anubis presides over the embalming ritual. In his hand is an adze, the instrument used in the Opening of the Mouth ceremony. The protective goddesses Isis (left) and Nephthys (right) stand at the ends of the bier assisting in the ritual.*

of many, may have symbolized the rebirth of the deceased. Several depictions survive, including one on the Late period coffin of Djed-bast-iuef-ankh in the Hildesheim Museum, West Germany, showing the deceased being cleansed as a blackened corpse.

Removal of the organs

Once cleansed, the body was taken to the *wabet*, the 'place of embalming', for removal of the internal organs. Herodotus' description of this process, largely duplicated some 400 years later by another Greek author, Diodorus Siculus (who perhaps copied parts of it from the earlier work), is still far from explicit. Several points are made clearer from examination of the bodies themselves. In most cases, a long incision was made on the left side of the abdomen, the position changing around the time of Tuthmosis III from one running down the side to one from the pubis to the hip bone. The exact line of the cut was marked by a priest called a 'scribe' and another known as a 'slicer' or 'ripper up' performed the operation with a flint knife. Evidently, as part of the ritual the priest who carried this out was chased away with abuse and the throwing of stones. But once the cut had been made, the lungs, stomach, intestines and liver were removed (kidneys were often left in place, or overlooked as if they were thought to have little significance). Based on examples found in embalmer's caches and now in New York's Metropolitan Museum of Art and the Boston Museum of Fine Arts, a wooden instrument shaped like an adze was probably used for the removal. After this, the cavity appears to have been cleansed and then filled with temporary stuffing.

From the late Middle or early New Kingdom onwards, according to the available evidence, the brain was also regularly removed. This may have been done at the *ibu* and was effected either through a hole punched in the thin bone at the top of the nostrils (the ethmoid bone), or through an incision at the nape of the neck. At this time a coating of resin was also applied to the face.

A very few mummies, especially from the Late Period, still have their viscera intact within the body, in keeping with the least expensive method of mummification. Others, including one mummy from the first century AD in the University Museum, Philadelphia,

The position of the incision
through which the internal organs were removed varied slightly through Egyptian history. One major change occurred in the Eighteenth Dynasty, when the incision shifted from one running vertically down the side of the body to one slanting from the hip bone to the pubic area.

appear to have had their internal organs removed through the anal passage. This method seems to have begun during the period of Persian occupation, and could prove to be the hallmark of one particular embalmer or workshop. Perhaps this method was used for the poor, especially when mummification was no longer practised as a fine art.

If, as specified in Herodotus' second method, some fluid were injected into the corpse to dissolve the viscera, the identity of that fluid is still in doubt. (The English analytic chemist, Alfred Lucas, suggested that a better translation of Herodotus' phrase 'oil of cedar' would be 'oil of juniper', though neither is particularly destructive of tissue. Lucas, in fact, believed that the organs within the body lying in natron would have decomposed and, at the end of the process, emerged as a thick fluid anyway – an effect Herodotus might mistakenly have thought due to a fluid.) Diodorus' account of mummification states that the oil was not injected but simply used for anointing the body. Any moisture introduced into the body before it was placed in natron for the lengthy drying process would have encouraged internal decay.

The heart was seen as the seat of wisdom, of intelligence, and it was essential that it be kept with the body of the deceased. There were even powerful spells in the Books of the Dead to ensure that body and heart were not separated; a powerful amulet (the heart scarab) protected it. This organ, therefore, was an exception to the evisceration process and was not removed from the body. If the heart was taken out accidentally, while the other internal organs were being removed, it was later put back.

Drying of the body and the natron controversy
Probably on the sixteenth day after death, following cleansing, evisceration and temporary packing of the body cavity, desiccation began. Both Herodotus and Diodorus agree on natron as the drying agent. From analysis of several embalmers' caches, this material has been identified as a natural salt of sodium carbonate and seventeen per cent sodium bicarbonate, with some additional sodium sulphate and sodium chloride, that occurs mainly in the western delta in the Wadi Natrun, some 40 miles (64 km) northwest of Cairo. (Na, the modern chemical symbol for sodium, comes from the Latin word for natron.) Experiments performed on dead white rats in the Manchester Museum showed that the high percentage of sodium bicarbonate is the optimum for effective desiccation. On the other hand, Lucas tested the material found on the skins of several mummies and found the crystalline substance to be simple salt (sodium chloride), so it is possible that a variety of salts could have been used.

One of the great debates in Egyptology arose over just how the natron was employed. On one side were those who believed that it was used wet, in solution; on the other, those who thought it was used dry, in a bed. The dilemma stems from a comment of Herodotus. What for years was mistakenly understood as 'pickled' is now more properly translated as 'dry salted' – the closest Herodotus could get to a word for preserving, i.e. mummification. 'Pickling' seemed to imply that the salt was used in solution as brine. The discovery of the Fourth Dynasty Queen Hetepheres' viscera in a three-per-cent brine solution seemed to support this, and for many years scholars universally believed that the liquid method was the correct one for all of Egyptian history. Experiments carried out on amputated human limbs at the University of Glasgow proved that natron had to be used dry. In later work at Manchester University, when a brine solution was tested in preserving the bodies of rats, however, it was found that the decaying process appeared to be speeded up and the bodies disintegrated. It seems far more likely, then, that the body was placed in a bed of dry natron or salt.

The accepted view of desiccation now is that the body was laid on a bed which sloped gently towards the foot, where a basin caught anything draining from the body. The finest versions of the bed itself may have been made of stone with lions carved down the sides, as in the embalming tables of the Apis bulls at Memphis; or wood; or, in the case of the poor, perhaps simple mats laid on the ground. The thoracic (chest) and abdominal cavities were cleansed, and then were filled with natron so that the drying process acted from within as well as from without. Finally, the corpse was totally covered in piles of dry natron.

How long did embalming take?
Herodotus states that embalming, which he took to mean the desiccation in natron, occupied seventy full days, but he seems to have misunderstood that the drying of the body was just one part of a ritual that usually took seventy days in total. In several accounts of royal burials, a period of forty days is mentioned for desiccation. The account of the death of Joseph's father Jacob in Genesis refers to forty days for his mummification and seventy days for the period of mourning, which ended in his burial. (Experiments conducted at Manchester University confirmed that after forty days the body was indeed totally desiccated, stiff, hard and virtually beyond all further natural decay.)

It has been noted that the significance of the seventy-day lapse between death and burial – or death and rebirth – could reflect the seventy-day period when Sothis, or Sirius the Dog Star, vanished, eclipsed by the sun. Its reappearance heralded the Egyptian New Year, the time that the annual inundation of the Nile was expected to begin. So in some way the ancient Egyptians may have linked seventy days with the time necessary for rebirth.

There is evidence that certain bodies were removed from the natron before the full forty days thought to be necessary for desiccation. Many mummies were anointed with hot, melted resins after completion of the drying process, most probably as an additional means of preserving the body. Inside several skulls, including that of the pharaoh Tutankhamun, two distinct layers of resin can be seen to have formed – the first in the top of the skull implying that the head was hanging vertically downwards; the second when the head was horizontal. If the body were left in natron for forty days, it would be rigid, and the only way for resin to form a solid layer in the top of the skull would be to stand the body on its head or to suspend it by its feet – one questions whether this would have happened in the case of a pharaoh. Alternatively, the neck and head may have been free enough to be tilted backwards over the edge of the embalming table. During the Third Intermediate period, mummies began to have linen swabs or other substances packed under the skin to restore a more lifelike appearance. To achieve this successfully, the skin must have been soft and pliable and not fully dried. Finally, some mummies, including a mummy examined in Lyons, appear to have been bandaged when still flexible, in other words when still containing moisture.

The use of resins alone, once solidified, would have resulted in a stable body – even if the body itself were not completely dry beforehand. It is possible, therefore, that the embalmers deliberately shortened the drying period, perhaps to make the body easier to deal with, knowing that the melted resins would complete the process. It is also possible that the natron was reused so often that its effectiveness at drawing out moisture was reduced and, even if the body had remained in it for forty days, full drying would not have been accomplished.

Preservation of the internal organs

Like the body, the removed viscera were treated, anointed with oil and resin, and wrapped individually in linen, to be placed in the tomb. Where they were placed in the tomb varied through Egyptian history. Most often, they were placed in pots, called canopic jars (Chapter Four). During the Twenty-first Dynasty, they began to be wrapped in linen and replaced inside the body cavity; in the Late period, the wrapped viscera were placed between the legs of the mummy. Herodotus' account of the organs' removal tells of packing the empty cavity with spices, but Diodorus writes only that the viscera were simply washed with palm wine and spices. It has been believed that the viscera were placed in the natron with the body. But, if this were true, it may not have been common practice, for microscopic examination of tissue sections from the internal organs of the Lyons Late-period mummy showed no trace of natron or any other salt. The analysis team concluded that Diodorus' account could reflect the truth. If a palm wine, heavily laced with a variety of herbs and spices, were used, it would be the equivalent of a disinfectant, flushing away all sources of decay. The subsequent application of bandages and resin to the viscera would have been enough to preserve them.

IV **The coffin** *of the Twelfth Dynasty warrior Userhet, found at Beni Hasan, now at the Fitzwilliam Museum, Cambridge.*

Overleaf
V **A painted coffin** *of the Eighteenth Dynasty.*

VI **This heavily** *decorated cartonnage coffin lid of the priest Nekhtefmut is from the region of Lukon and dates to the middle of the Third Intermediate period.*

V   VI

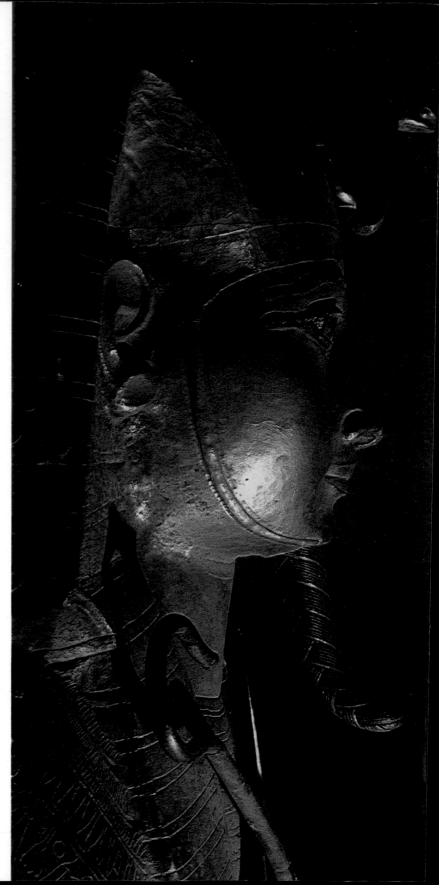

VII   VIII

Anointing and decorating the body

Once the preservation of the body had been completed, it was removed from the natron, carefully washed to remove all traces of salt and, when dried, taken to another area. This may have been called the *per nefer*, literally 'house of beauty'. (*Per nefer* could, alternatively, have been the generic name for the whole embalmer's complex, with the *wabet* simply being a building or tent where evisceration and desiccation took place.) The body, shrunken and much reduced in weight, was then emptied and restuffed with materials, which might include resin-soaked linen, more natron, lichen, onions, mud, or sometimes sawdust mixed with other substances. The material with which the body had been stuffed during desiccation was removed and kept aside. In later periods even the embalmer's tools, which might contain some minute portion of the corpse, were saved to be placed with or near the body. Often such materials (the swabs used for cleaning, for example) were thought to be unclean and unfit to be inside the tomb, but were buried near it.

In the *per nefer*, perfumes and oils (juniper oil, beeswax, spices and natron, milk and wine) were rubbed over the dried, leathery skin to make it supple – the quality and quantity of these unguents depended on the ability of the deceased person's estate or family to pay. The embalming incision, rarely sewn, usually either was sealed with wax or had a metal plate placed over it. This plate was decorated with a magical symbol for protection. Orifices, such as the nostrils, were plugged with wax or linen. In later periods, the body was filled out to restore natural contours, pads under the eyes, in the cheeks, and so on. The process had to be carried out with great care to ensure good results. The unfortunate mummy of the Twenty-first Dynasty royal lady, Henttawy, had her cheeks packed when not quite dry. When they shrank upon drying, the skin cracked. Sometimes the eye orbits were left in place; in other cases, the eyes are missing or simply flattened in their sockets. In later times, artificial eyes were often introduced into the sockets. Female breasts, which lost all shape during desiccation, often had padding placed over them to simulate natural appearance. Linen pads would also be placed around the mouth, although in some burials from the Graeco–Roman period, small thin sheets of gold shaped like a tongue were placed between the lips, perhaps as a magical device to restore the power of speech in the hereafter. When anointing was complete, the body was covered with molten resin.

The bodies of men were often coloured with red and women with yellow ochre. The embalmers would have applied henna to the feet and hands. In the Graeco-Roman period, gold leaf was applied to parts of the body, the nipples of women, for instance; female mummies began to have their faces rouged and eyes highlighted. Often before bandaging, jewellery given by the family and frequently made specifically for the purpose of being used as grave goods was placed on the body.

VII The mummy of *a young boy found at Hawara in the Faiyum. It dates to the Roman period, about the end of the first century* AD.

VIII The gilded mask *of the Twenty-first Dynasty pharaoh Psusennes, found at Tanis in the delta by Pierre Montet.*

THE UNKNOWN MUMMY

The unknown mummy *from the 1881 cache is a horrifying sight. Whether he died in convulsions and was hastily interred, or was buried alive is something we may never know. Meanwhile, his mummy with its agonized expression lies among those of the New Kingdom pharaohs in Cairo.*

Among the anonymous mummies from the 1881 Deir el Bahri cache was one of the strangest ever to be discovered in Egypt. In the underground corridor which led to the burial chamber lay a plain, white-painted wooden coffin without a single inscription. Inside was a complete sheepskin which had shrunk and become shrivelled. When it was cut open, in Cairo, in 1886, this sheepskin revealed an unwrapped body that gave off a repulsive smell, unlike most mummies which tend to have a sweet odour. One witness described the moment that the face of the deceased appeared: 'It is difficult to give an adequate description of the face thus laid bare. I can only say that no countenance has ever more faithfully recreated a picture of such affecting and hideous agony. His features, horribly distorted, surely showed that the wretched man must have been deliberately asphyxiated, most probably by being buried alive.'

Closer examination seemed to support this view. The man had had his hands and feet bound together. The body bore no sign of injury and no attempts at mummification had been made – all his organs were intact. (Some natron had been put around the skin.) The remarkable state of preservation had been achieved by the exclusion of air from the sheepskin and by the dry condition of the tomb.

Who was this man? Had he been a criminal, even one guilty of as heinous a crime as treason, he would undoubtedly have been executed and his body destroyed. But the high priests responsible for organizing the cache must have dictated a punishment to fit his crime: the miscreant was sealed alive inside a soft sheepskin – a material it is believed the Egyptians considered ritually unclean – shutting out all air, and as the horrible shroud gradually shrank, the man within would have died a hideous death.

In any event, the anonymous young man lay, and still lies, among kings. But by destroying his name, his identity has been lost and he has been denied the immortality for which every Egyptian yearned.

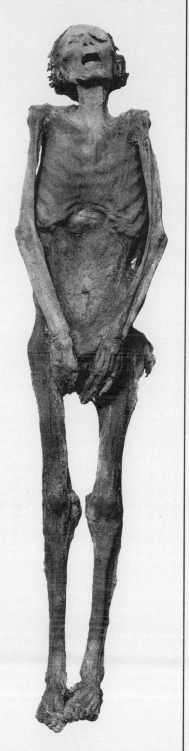

STYLES AND USES OF CANOPIC EQUIPMENT

The internal organs removed during mummification were placed in four containers. The Greeks called them canopic containers because of their human- or animal-headed stoppers thought to resemble the local god of Canopus in the delta, who was represented as a human-headed pot.

In the early days of experimentation to try to preserve the body, the internal organs were removed, wrapped and placed in a pit in the burial chamber. The oldest canopic jars known were found in the burial of Queen Meresankh, and date from the reign of Mycerinus. After this time, such containers, often made of limestone or alabaster, are quite common.

In the Old Kingdom the jars had simple convex lids, but during the First Intermediate period these lids gradually gave way to the human-headed variety, made of stone, wood, pottery, or even cartonnage. In the late Nineteenth Dynasty some of the lids began to have

The heads of *the canopic jars represented the Four Sons of Horus: (left to right) Hapi (a baboon) guarded the lungs; Duamutef (a jackal or wild dog) the stomach; Imseti (a human) the liver; and Qebehsenuef (a falcon) the intestines.*

animal heads. The jars themselves were placed inside a painted wooden chest.

In the Third Intermediate period, 'dummy' canopic jars were often provided even though the organs themselves were now put back inside the mummy – each organ often accompanied by a small figure of the appropriate Son of Horus. Often these packages were put between the legs of the mummy.

The use of canopic jars as containers for the preserved organs re-emerged briefly during the very late Twenty-fifth and the Twenty-sixth Dynasties. In the Late period the organs were usually placed between the mummy's legs.

Wrapping the mummy

At least fifteen full days were set aside for the meticulous process of encasing the mummy in layers of linen. The entire process was punctuated with prayer and ritual. Linen was supplied by the family or by the embalming workshops. For wealthier clients, bandages may have been specially woven, made of the finest fabric and many yards in length. These were sometimes also decorated with painted inscriptions from one of the magical books in order to assure the protection of the body. It was even possible to obtain linen which had been used in the local temple for the daily dressing of the cult figure of the god in the shrine. For the most part, though, sheets of ordinary household linen were handed over, often fabric that was well worn. (In the case of the Lyons mummy, a sail was provided – and the embalmers did not even bother to remove all the wooden rigging loops.) This linen was torn roughly into strips, often more than 16 yards (15 m) in length and varying between 2½ and 8 inches (6 and 20 cm) in width. Pads of linen and more complete sheets were also held in readiness. The wrapping of a mummy required vast quantities of linen. The Eleventh Dynasty mummy of Wah, when unwrapped and carefully examined by the Metropolitan Museum of Art, proved to have had more than 1010 square yards (845 sq m). On some occasions, especially in the later periods, some of the linen was dyed. Popular colours were red (from a dye extracted from the roots of the madder plant), yellow (using saffron, or onion skins) and blue (from a native variety of indigo).

The head was first tied in place, with one band around the face holding the jaw firm, and another wrapped around the head and shoulders to fix the neck. Then the toes and fingers – and genitals, in the case of men – were wrapped individually using narrow fabric strips. The arms and legs would be bandaged next, each limb separately. This was followed by the torso. Over this and every subsequent layer of wrappings, amulets or pieces of jewellery would be placed and then brushed over with melted resins. These included a variety of resins from coniferous trees native to Egypt, and gum resins based on myrrh. The resins would have varied in colour from gold to dark brown, but after drying and hardening, they became black and pitch-like. Interaction between residues of salt on the body and the resins resulted in a brittle glass-like material that produced rock-hard flesh beneath the bandages. The resins penetrated right through to the body tissues themselves, and the glassy substance has been identified within many of the body tissues.

Now the prepared remains were bandaged from head to foot in layer upon layer of linen, the arms and legs wrapped close to the body to form the usual mummy shape. The position of the arms varied greatly from period to period. Sometimes those of men were extended and the hands placed over the genitals; while women's arms might be straight along the sides of the body or crossed over the chest. Each layer of bandages was secured by strips either running from head to

The preparation of a mummy *was a painstaking process, dictated by established ritual and carried out by specialists. (Left to right) One embalmer marked where the incision (whose position could vary as shown) was to be made; another actually made the cut. Bandaging involved yards of linen wrapped strips. Each finger and toe, and arm and leg were covered separately. Special care was taken to preserve the features of the face. The whole was covered with a shroud secured by more strips of linen. Finally, a mask with the features of the deceased was laid over the head and shoulders. The mummy was then placed in a coffin, such as this elaborately decorated example, which is typical of the Twenty-first Dynasty, about 1000 BC.*

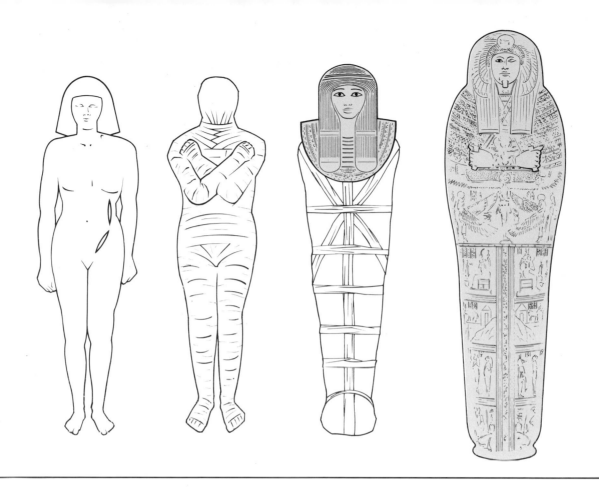

foot, or crossed around the shoulders and hips in a figure of eight arrangement. Smaller strips were bound around the legs and arms. (Many of the coffin lids were painted with what appear to be simulated mummy bands.) At each stage, pads of linen were inserted to ensure that the finished shape would be satisfactory. Often, the final layer of bandages was covered with a single large sheet, or shroud, wrapped around the body and secured in place by yet more linen bands. From the New Kingdom this final shroud was sometimes dyed red. During the Twenty-first Dynasty, red leather straps crossed over the shoulders of the mummy. In the Late period, the body was covered by a net of tubular blue faience beads.

The mask

From the time of the Middle Kingdom, during certain periods, a mask was placed over the face and shoulders. The majority of these were made of cartonnage, a substance created out of linen or papyrus reinforced with plaster or resin, and not unlike papier mâché. Once it had been shaped and hardened, it was painted. In the case of royal burials, the masks were probably always of gold, sometimes inlaid with precious and semiprecious stones. Perhaps the most famous object ever to have been recovered from Egypt was the mummy mask found over the head and shoulders of Tutankhamun, and a similar, though less elaborate, one was discovered on the mummy of King Psusennes when his burial came to light at Tanis. After the mask was set in place, perfumes, unguents and more resin would be poured over the mummy. In the case of Tutankhamun, it has been estimated that about 4 gallons (19 litres) of fluid were used.

Finally, the mummy was placed inside a coffin at the time of burial. The coffin which held the body might perhaps be only the innermost of a series. It is possible that the relatives of the deceased were allowed to see the mummy in the coffin before the lid was put into place, for often on the outermost shroud floral garlands, posies or larger bouquets made of full flowers, berries and petals would be laid. It could well have been the mourners who completed the anointing of the mummy, once it was in its coffin. In the case of Tutankhamun, chemical interaction between various elements of the ointments resulted in a sort of combustion which carbonized the tissues of the body – only the face, protected by the mask, escaped being affected.

After rituals were carried out at the *wabet*, the mourners and priests made their way to the *sekh*, a temporary structure set up outside the tomb in which the last stages of the funerary ritual, described in Chapter Four, were carried out.

Late developments

During the Late and Graeco-Roman periods, more emphasis was placed on the bandaging than on the contents. In the Greek period, the dead had increasingly lurid face masks placed over intricately criss-crossed bandages. The masks, often heavily gilded and using colours seldom used by Egyptians – pinks, pale greens, purples and oranges – depict the dead person as if resting on a pillow, with the face at an angle from the body.

According to both Herodotus and Diodorus, mummies were often kept in the houses of the living. Wooden cupboards with stable, or Dutch, doors have been found, and it is believed that the mummies would have been stored upright in them. This would have enabled members of the family to open the upper door and make offerings of food and drink, as well as kind words for their ancestors. Many mummies that have survived from this era do, in fact, show weakness in the bandaging around the ankles that could have been caused by years of being propped upright.

Herodotus goes even further, for he records that models of mummies in their coffins were produced at the end of banquets or other celebrations in the homes of the rich, and paraded before the guests. The 'body' was shown to each person, in turn, with the words,

This striking portrait *of a woman named Demos, who died aged thirty-four, about* AD *100, was found by Flinders Petrie in 1888 at Hawara, the cemetery of the ancient town of Arsinoë in the Faiyum. It is now in the Cairo Museum. The portrait may have been commissioned during the deceased's lifetime and, at death, placed over the mummy's head, its edges enclosed by the outer layer of bandaging. Like most of the Faiyum portraits, this one is of encaustic (a paint made from pigment and beeswax) on wood, and was created by using a brush and a metal instrument called a cestrum, similar to a modern palette knife. Because of the wax medium the panel could be subjected to heat and reworked a number of times; this allowed a fine detail to be achieved and also resulted in a very thick layer of paint.*

'Look upon this body as you drink and enjoy yourself; for you will be just like it when you die.' This Epicurean philosophy certainly sums up the old Egyptian belief that life was brief, a transitory time that must nevertheless be enjoyed to the full before one was forced to leave it.

In the Roman period, people had portraits painted during their lifetime. Executed on thin board panels, the paints were mixed not as before with water, but with melted wax. This wax, or encaustic, method of painting created images that are strikingly lifelike. Paint drips on some of the boards indicate that they were painted while the board was vertically upright – the oldest surviving paintings showing the use of the easel in fine art. After death, the boards were trimmed to shape and handed over to the embalmers. The boards would be placed over the head of the mummy and enclosed within further layers of bandages. Narrow strips of linen were used, often coloured blue, red and white. These were wound around the body until a striking multicoloured diamond pattern resulted. A small gilded stud was fixed in the centre of each diamond, making the overall effect extremely eye-catching. A cartonnage case often covered the mummy's wrapped feet, and feet or sandals were painted on the top and bottom surfaces.

Christianity and after

The Coptic Christians were generally buried wearing their ordinary clothes. These take the form of simple linen or wool-and-linen mix tunics or chitons (a long woollen garment worn by the ancient Greeks). The bodies, placed in low, barrel-vaulted, brick tombs on the surface, were preserved naturally by the drying effects of the air. Several of them can be seen in the Musée des Beaux Arts, Grenoble. The tunics worn by these bodies were often brightly decorated with bands of tapestry lying over each shoulder and caught with a roundel, or small decorative medallion.

'Pagan' practices continued alongside the newer burial methods for several centuries. A number of burials have been found near Deir el Bahri, some of which have been dated to as late as the fourth century A D. Bodies were given only the most cursory of treatments before being completely covered in linen; a plastered and painted bust was then placed over the mummy and sewn in place. The face was moulded so as to appear startlingly three-dimensional. These painted images showed the deceased wearing Greek- or Roman-style clothes, often with a goblet of wine or a bunch of grapes in their hands, symbols of the cult of Isis. The dead are generally shown in the presence of the old Egyptian gods of the dead, especially Anubis and Osiris.

Examination of some of the bodies preserved from different periods has led many archaeologists to believe that bodies may have been rewrapped from time to time for a whole variety of reasons. What is clear is that communication between the mummified dead and the living did not cease entirely at the time of burial, but at some stage the living descendants may have inspected the mummies to check them for damage.

Our understanding of the mummification process is still far from complete, but as the analysis of those few mummies that have survived continues more of the ancient methods will undoubtedly be revealed.

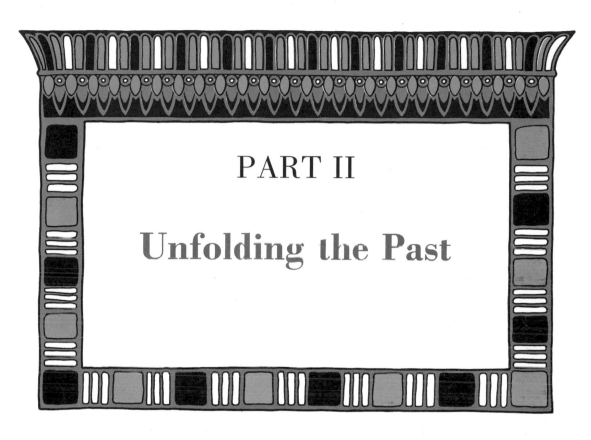

PART II

Unfolding the Past

Chapter Three
Analyzing the Mummies

SERIOUS AND WIDESPREAD interest in the analysis of mummies began after the discovery of the two major caches of Egyptian royal mummies on the west bank of Luxor a century ago. The recovery of the bodies of some of the ancient world's greatest rulers inevitably prompted speculation. People wanted to know what, for instance, Ramesses II looked like, how tall he was, the colour of his eyes and hair, the state of his teeth and from what diseases he might have suffered. At first, efforts were concentrated on these royal mummies. More recently, many museums have been examining their non-royal mummies, some for the first time. Almost three-quarters of these projects have involved X-ray analysis, the first step to understanding the ancient remains. And some of the most up-to-date modern technology is helping to reveal numerous details – details that are small in terms of individual mummies, but when looked at in the broader context of many analytical results help to create a clearer picture of ancient Egyptian life and death.

Mummies: from collection to CAT scan

A number of the European and American tourists who visited Egypt following the Napoleonic occupation acquired mummies which they 'unrolled' either on the spot or back in their native countries. After the original owners died, their heirs often donated the mummies to local museums. These remains, unwrapped and without satisfactory provenance (i.e. no clear indication of their exact source), form a large proportion of current museum stocks of mummies. But there were already a few mummies in national institutions. When the royal surgeon Sir Hans Sloane left his collection of artefacts from all over the world to the British nation in 1753 – the acquisition of which formed the basis of the British Museum – one mummy was already in their possession. This was to be followed thirteen years later, in 1766, by another, said to be from the great necropolis of Saqqara. In the same year, the Ashmolean Museum, Oxford, obtained the mummy of a small child, although details of its original source are unrecorded.

First steps in analysis
One of the earliest recorded examinations of a mummy, performed out of historical and scientific interest rather than sheer curiosity, was

undertaken by the Champollion brothers early in the nineteenth century. The elder, Jacques-Joseph, had had a lifelong passion for everything Egyptian, a love which he imparted to his brother and student, Jean-François, the famous decipherer of hieroglyphs. Where the brothers acquired the mummy, that of a young man of the Ptolemaic period, is unknown, but an account of the unwrapping was published by the elder brother in 1814. The body, which had intact finger- and toe-caps, made of gold, was in good condition at the time of the examination. When it was rewrapped, the brothers crossed the arms over the chest, a position the body apparently was not in earlier. The strain of this together with a rather ineffectual attempt at rebandaging, has resulted in severe erosion around the arms and chest, and the loss of the mummy's feet. Today, the mummy is in the Musée des Beaux Arts, Grenoble.

The arrival of the first cache of royal mummies in the Cairo Museum in 1881 heralded the new era of mummy examination. It is reported that within half an hour of their arrival, many of the mummies had been unwrapped. Photographs taken at the time of the unwrapping of the body of the pharaoh Ramesses II show that the linen bandages, most of which were free from resin (the wrapping was probably done during the Twentieth Dynasty by the High Priest Herihor when he rewrapped and moved the mummies of the royal dead to safety), were simply cut through from head to foot. There was no attempt to record how the wrapping had been done. The mummy of Amenhotep I, a particularly finely wrapped body with floral garlands still intact over the bandages, was left untouched, and today remains the only pharaoh among the Cairo royal mummies who is still wrapped as he was found over a century ago.

In 1889, the mummies were examined closely by Gaston Maspero, director of the Antiquities Organization; and the results were published in 1895. Maspero described the mummies' external appearance at length, remarking upon such features as their height and build. In the same year that his report appeared, Konrad von Röntgen discovered X-rays, a technique that would in time make the examination of mummies more fruitful.

X-ray: the new technology
The first mummy to be X-rayed was one held by the British Museum. In the 1890s, Flinders Petrie, by this time one of the world's most celebrated Egyptologists, was able to take plates only of the feet and legs because of the size and weight of the equipment available to him. But it was enough to prove the efficacy of the method. At the same time in Vienna, a doctor called Bloch managed to take two fine plates of an Egyptian mummy for medical rather than for archaeological purposes. The pictures, published in 1897 in Leipzig, were authenticated by the great German Egyptologist Georg Ebers, and were significant because they covered the whole of the body, enabling scholars to study internal bone structure and packing.

Maspero suggested in his first report on the Cairo royal mummies that X-rays would prove of immense value in the study of the bodies and, in 1903, Dr Khayat performed a single X-ray on the body of the pharaoh Tuthmosis IV in order to try and establish the cause of death. The analysis of this X-ray by the pathologist Grafton Elliot Smith for the first time gave clues as to the true age of the king at his death. From the state of the king's bones, Elliot Smith was able to determine that Tuthmosis was a relatively young man at death, far younger than earlier historical estimates had suggested.

In the early 1900s, Elliot Smith and a team of doctors were given permission to examine the royal mummies in Cairo in closer detail – but not with X-ray equipment. Perhaps it was considered that not enough was known about the after-effects of such an analysis – that the mummy might develop problems in later years as a result of the bombardment of the bodies with X-rays. The team found the exercise frustrating, because the heavy resins that coated the bodies were so solid that, apart from the use of X-rays, only the total destruction of the remains would have made a thorough study possible. So, only cursory estimates of the ages could be formed and, since only a small number of the mummies showed any external evidence of the cause of death, few were reached. But publication of Elliot Smith's results in the Cairo Museum catalogue of *The Royal Mummies*, in 1912, excited great interest.

In the decades that followed, museums around the world began to study the mummies in their own collections – but with X-rays – although their efforts were often severely hampered by the lack of detail about origin and accurate dating of their specimens. The Belgian Frans Jonckheere and the British scholar P.H.K. Gray, both Egyptologists and doctors, between them published reports of over 200 mummies in Britain, France and Holland. The Civico Museo di Storia ed Arte in Trieste published the report of their study in 1951. Fifteen years later, the X-rays taken of all the mummies in the collection of the City Museum in Liverpool showed exclusively how valuable this method of analysis could be.

Finally, in 1967, permission was given to a team of scholars from the University of Michigan, backed by Alexandria University and the United States Health Service, to X-ray the royal mummies in Cairo. The publication of their findings aroused great controversy, since the ages of the bodies frequently proved to be inconsistent with the number of years the pharaohs had apparently ruled. Today, the actual identification of several of the royal mummies is being questioned.

The next steps in technology
In the mid-1960s, another form of radiological machine came into wide use. This was the computed tomography scanner, known familiarly as the CAT scanner. This machine into which the mummy was passed enabled pictures to be taken of 'slices' through the body. Now, instead of simply having horizontal views of mummified

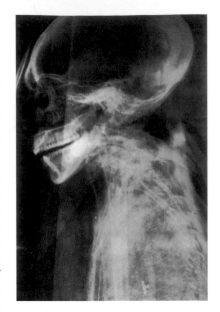

X-rays provide a method *of investigation that does not involve destroying the coffin, mummy or wrappings. In 1967, Amenhotep I (above), the only one of the pharaonic mummies to remain fully wrapped, was X-rayed in Cairo. The remains were those of a healthy man, with protruding teeth, like those of many of his family.*

In 1966, the Egyptian Museum of Turin X-rayed the mummy of Kha (right), whose intact burial had been found in 1906, at Deir el Medina, by Ernesto Schiaparelli. The X-rays revealed hoop earrings and a collar made of a series of gold rings, possibly the 'gold of honour', an award presented by the king himself. An amulet known as 'the girdle of Isis' is under the collar. The long, thin chain supported a heart scarab (not shown). The dark area in the middle of Kha's forehead is a snake's head amulet.

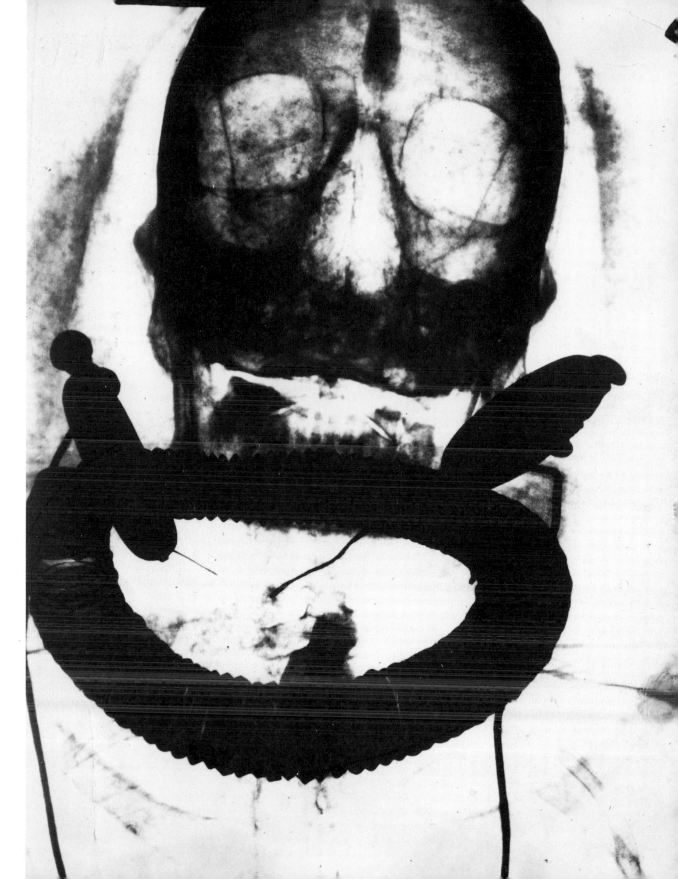

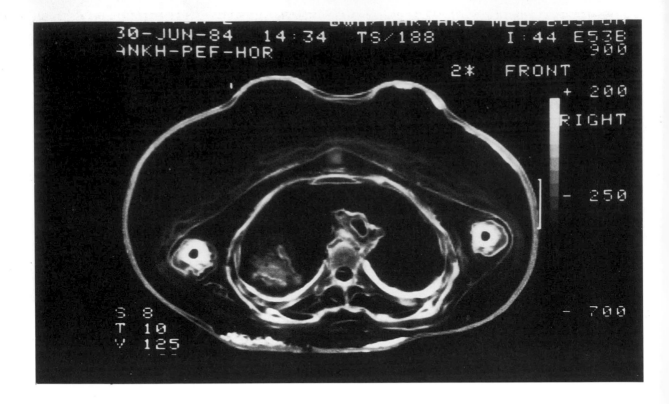

30-JUN-84   14:34   TS/188   I:44 E538
ANKH-PEF-HOR   900

2* FRONT
+ 200
RIGHT
- 250
- 700
S 8
T 10
V 125

bodies, cross-sectional pictures allowed scholars to see exactly what lay within the wrappings. CAT scanners reveal differences in density much more easily than X-rays, so that soft organs can be viewed.

Projects in Philadelphia in 1973, in Manchester in 1975, and in Boston, Minneapolis, Lausanne and Lyons during the 1980s have all used this technology with great effectiveness. But these last projects have gone further than the previous ones in their aims and researches. Instead of simply recording the findings from the X-rays and CAT scans, teams from all over the world have attempted to extract ever more detail. The use of endoscopes, either metal viewing tubes or glass fibre rods, have enabled pathologists to look inside the mummies while causing minimal damage to the body itself.

In order to study the structure of cells under a microscope, tissue must be rehydrated and cut into thin sections, but the actual rehydration is often still a very difficult procedure. Many samples of tissue have simply collapsed into a sludge-like mass while undergoing the process. Those attempts that have succeeded have allowed slide sections to be taken that have shown still intact basic cell structures. In Cambridge in 1983, further tests on some rehydrated mummy tissue samples proved that even the DNA structure (the basic genetic structure within each cell) could be identified. Sensationalized speculation in the press at the time mooted the possibility of cloning

This CAT scan *of Ankhpefhor (above) – a male of the early Third Intermediate period, probably from Luxor and now in Boston's Museum of Fine Arts – shows a 'slice' through the chest cavity. The outer white perimeter is the line of the cartonnage coffin. Inside this are the bones of the arm, seen as two white circles on either side of the chest. Inside, remains of the heart can be seen in the middle.*

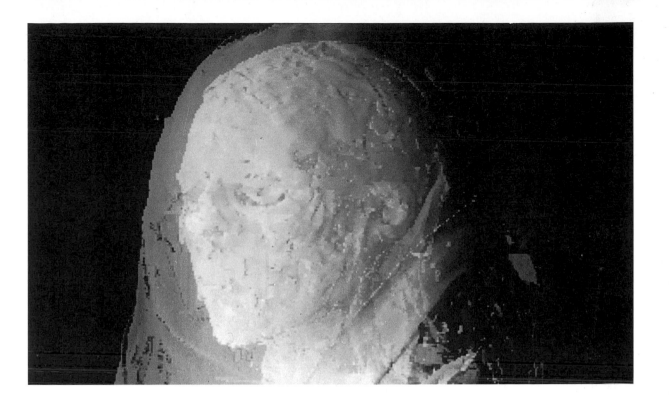

This three-dimensional
*reconstruction of the head of
Boston's mummy Tabes (above) –
a female from the Third
Intermediate period – has been
created from CAT-scan images.
The head is startlingly clear
through the wrappings, even the
hair, which has been matted
because of the resins used in
mummification. Tabes' nose has
been pushed out of shape by being
wedged against the cartonnage
covering her face.*

from such tissue samples – but speculation is all it is, for these cells are not truly 'living' or capable of life. The thought of long-dead tissue being regenerated has also given rise to speculation that diseases, such as smallpox, could be contracted from mummies. But scientific research has proved that although bacteria and viruses are a minor problem, there has never been a viable smallpox bug found older than 200 years. Exciting though they may be, such ideas must remain the stuff of science fiction.

Other tests have been carried out on samples of materials from on and around the mummies – such things as crystalline deposits, resins, packing materials and wrappings – by applying spectroscopy and, more recently, chromatography. Both methods are based on the weight (i.e. atomic weight or mass) of elements. Spectroscopy identifies the elements because each has a different, specific weight. Chromatography sorts the elements by the difference in the speed of movement. These methods not only allow the composition of the materials to be identified with great accuracy, but also, in some cases, for the place of origin to be specified. Some metals, the volcanic glass obsidian, and most clays bear a chemical 'fingerprint' that makes them unique to one particular area which may, given sufficient information, tell us more about where the mummy was prepared or where the material used in the process came from. We are still unsure,

In 1916, the Minneapolis Institute of Arts acquired the Late period mummy of a woman. Details of the original location of the body had been lost, but the two elaborately painted coffins record that the occupant was the 'Lady Teshat, Lady of the House, Daughter of the Doorkeeper of the Gates of the Temple of Amun, Djehutihotep'. On stylistic grounds, the coffins themselves can be identified as coming from Luxor (ancient Thebes).

X-rays taken during the 1920s have unfortunately been lost, but the mummy was X-rayed again in 1975. It was plain that the mummy itself was damaged, and that between its legs lay a second adult skull. It is not unusual to find stray body parts in a wrapped mummy, but to find such a skull was indeed a rare occurrence. Eight years later, the mummy of the Lady Teshat was subjected to computed tomography scanning (known as CT or CAT scanning), first in Minneapolis and then at the world-renowned Mayo Clinic, Rochester, Minnesota.

The scans showed that damage to the body was extensive, with broken ribs, upper arm and collar bone. There were also curious creases on the soles of the feet. The damage had been done after

death, presumably by robbers. The lines on the feet are thought to have occurred during the embalming or wrapping of the body. One conclusion reached on the basis of the scans was that the mummy had been rewrapped in antiquity and that the second skull, also badly damaged, had been inserted at this time. It may well have been from a nearby burial, perhaps of a relative, also disturbed by robbers.

In spite of the damage to her body, Lady Teshat's legs were intact, and it was determined that she had been in her mid- to late teens when she died.

Despite another scan in 1988, we still have no proof of how this young wife died, and no clue to the identity of the owner of the second skull. Each analysis leaves unanswered questions.

The mummy of *the Lady Teshat has been analyzed with the most modern equipment, allowing the maximum of detail to be extracted from her remains with no damage to them at all. In 1975, the mummy, still in its coffin (far right) was X-rayed (right). In the 1980s, the body was the subject of two CAT-scan analyses (above).*

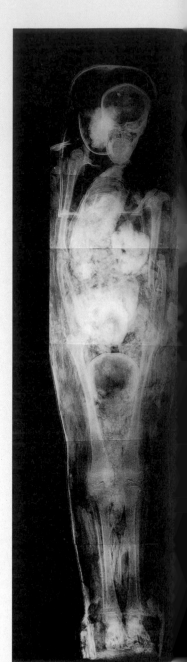

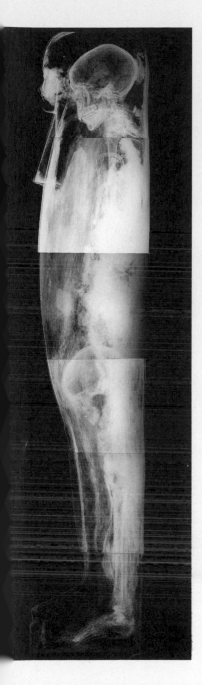

for example, how much of the linen used in the bandaging came from materials supplied by the family (i.e. from local sources) and how much was provided from a centralized, royal store. Analysis may one day reveal the answer.

Methods for calculating the ages of the mummies

In the case of the royal mummies, historical sources provide some information that can serve as a rough guide by which ages can be estimated. In nearly every case, it is known almost exactly how long the kings ruled, and the events they celebrated at various stages of their reigns. The dates of such events as their marriages, the birth of their children, the dates at which they held major festivals and their military campaigns fill the long texts on tomb and temple walls. This historical assessment naturally coloured the first visual examination of the mummies. The body of Ramesses II, for example, a man who is thought to have ruled Egypt for sixty-seven years and who was capable of fathering a child in the first year of that reign, was estimated to be at least ninety years of age. When the archaeologists and, later, the pathologists, examined the body, therefore, it was always with these dates in mind.

When scientists come to examine the bodies of ordinary people, however, such milestones in their lives simply do not exist. In no case is the age at death of any individual clearly stated, and so other methods must be applied to try to assess this.

Skeletal examination

An individual's age at death can be estimated by studying their skeleton. This estimate is much easier and produces a more accurate age range in children and adolescents than it does in adults. During childhood and adolescence, the permanent teeth develop and erupt, displacing the deciduous (milk) teeth. This occurs within reasonably well-defined age ranges concluding with the eruption of the third molars (wisdom teeth), usually in the early twenties. At the same time, under normal conditions of nutrition, the juvenile skeleton grows and develops. It is able to do so because many of the bones have growth plates, known as epiphyses, at their ends. Each epiphysis consists of a plate of cartilage, which is X-ray opaque, whose purpose is to keep the end 'of the bone (joint) apart from, although still connected to, the main part of the bone. This separation allows the bone to expand in size during the growth period and when growth ceases, by the age of about twenty-five, all the epiphyses have fused and turned to bone. The epiphyses undergo fusion at different rates for different bones; there is also a different rate for the two sexes, which is why girls stop growing earlier than boys. Epiphyseal fusion occurs in every case within a fairly small age range. Fusion itself varies from joint to joint; those in the hands and feet are the first to join, the last to join are in the collar bone. It is important to understand that whenever attempts are made to estimate an individual's age at death, only an age *range* may be given, and never a specific age.

In the case of adults over the age of twenty-five, the estimation of age at death is much more difficult. Specialists working with human skeletons from archaeological contexts use as many age-related changes as they can in order to build up a picture of the adult's age. In the past, people ate a much coarser diet than is the case today, at least in the Western world. Cereals for flour were, literally, stone ground even for the pharaohs, and this technique inevitably incorporates small fragments of stone into the flour. The coarser the diet, the more attrition (wear) is induced on the crown of the tooth. Various schemes have been produced for assigning age ranges to the wear patterns formed on the molar teeth in adults. These schemes, however, should not be applied generally to age people, since we can never be sure about the diets of individuals or populations in the past. The nature of these diets affects the attrition rates. In order to produce age ranges based on tooth attrition, the specialist must have a large group of skeletons with all ages represented, from foetuses to the elderly. Examination of Egyptian mummies has shown that many pharaohs suffered from caries (decay) and abscesses of the jaw, suggesting that diet in ancient Egypt was high in sugar and, possibly, carbohydrates.

Recession of the gums and the consequent loss of the bone of the jaw and of the teeth is a condition that increases with advancing age and the 'pocketing' (small gaps that occur around the teeth, into which food can accumulate and cause infection, as the gums grow flaccid with age) and failure of the soft supporting tissue; hence the phrase 'getting long in the tooth'. It can be seen in the skeleton as a recession of the jaw line and, when it occurs, suggests an older person. Equally, an increase in osteoarthritis, particularly of the spine and other major joints, occurs with ageing, often starting in the thirties. Age changes occur at the pubic symphysis where the two sides of the pelvis meet, although these must be used with caution. Not only do they give very wide ranges with increasing age (e.g. 34-86 years for the oldest phase), but they can only be applied safely to males. In women, pregnancy and childbirth affect this symphysis and obscure the patterns.

It can thus be seen that ageing an individual at death with any accuracy, from the skeleton, is only possible in the young. There is no evidence to support the idea that people reached skeletal or sexual maturity at a different age in the past. As is the case today, these maturations occurred within an age range. Although the pharaohs appear to have married young, this is not an exclusively Egyptian phenomenon, as our own history will confirm. During the Middle Ages, for instance, it was common for the nobility to marry as children although the marriage could not be consummated until sexual maturity was achieved. This may well have been the case in ancient Egypt.

THE PROJECTS AND THEIR RESULTS

The royal mummies

The mummies of many of the kings and queens of ancient Egypt are held in the Cairo Museum and come from the two caches found in the late nineteenth century. The first, discovered in 1881 at Deir el Bahri, contained forty royal mummies; the second cache, from the tomb of Amenhotep II in the Valley of the Kings, contained thirteen mummies including an unknown woman. Many of the rulers are identified either from inscriptions on their coffins or from tags, or dockets, placed around their necks.

Although most of the mummies were undisturbed within their wrappings, a number of the bodies appear to have been badly damaged. The body of King Merenptah, for example, the thirteenth son and heir of the great Ramesses II, was covered with the marks of axe cuts. Most of these were the result of post-mortem damage. It seems that when the royal tombs in the valley were first robbed, the mummies were torn, or hacked, apart to remove whatever jewellery was on them. A prime example is the terrible state of the mummy of Ramesses VI.

Injury and violence

None of the mummies showed any clear evidence of long bones fractured during their lifetime. This is surprising in view of the fact that historical records indicate that many of these pharaohs were great warriors. Although some pictures of fighting pharaohs, such as those found on the furniture and burial equipment in Tutankhamun's tomb, can be dismissed as idealizations, other depictions are considered totally credible. Some of these kings must have fought in several series of campaigns, and the idea that all of them escaped unscathed demonstrates great ability – or luck – or the age-old idea of the leaders of battles directing events from far behind the line of battle.

Only one king, Seqenenre Tao of the Seventeenth Dynasty, clearly died a violent death. The skull of his mummy, the least well preserved of all the royal mummies, bears the marks of a number of wounds made by axes, clubs and maces. At least one shows signs of healing, so the king must have lived for some time after this blow, which may have resulted in brain damage leading to the paralysis that seems indicated in his body. There are two theories to account for the rest of the wounds: the first, that the king was attacked while asleep, perhaps by several assassins; the second, that he died in battle. The latter theory finds some support in the poor condition of the body. Examination of the wounds and damage to the skin suggests strongly that the king may have died while kneeling, and the body may later have been attacked by carrion as it lay on the battlefield.

Seqenenre Tao *was a ruler of Upper Egypt, in the south. He rebelled against the foreign Hyksos kings who ruled Egypt from their capital in the delta. That Seqenenre died a violent death is all too apparent from his mummy. Looking at the damage to his skull, one can imagine the ferocity of the blows he must have endured that resulted in his death.*

THE BRAVEST FIGHTER OF THEM ALL?

Among the cache of royal mummies found in 1881 at Deir el Bahri was the damaged and poorly embalmed body of Seqenenre Tao, a ruler in Luxor during the troubled Seventeenth Dynasty. One of his sons, Kamose, is credited with the final expulsion of the foreign Hyksos rulers; another, called Ahmose, founded the Eighteenth Dynasty and became the first pharaoh of the New Kingdom. The Austrian scholar Manfred Bietak and his Czech colleague Eugen Strouhal studied the wounds in Seqenenre's skull in the 1970s and demonstrated to their own satisfaction that the injuries were inflicted by bronze weapons of a purely Hyksos design. Did Seqenenre therefore meet his death in battle?

Historical records are helpful, but not conclusively so. We know that Seqenenre Tao came into open conflict with the Hyksos king Apophis, who wrote a letter to the Luxor ruler saying that the hippopotamuses in Luxor were making such a commotion that he could not sleep. 'Hippopotamus' is thought to have been intended as a derogatory term that referred to Seqenenre himself and his two sons. Military confrontation was inevitable. And not only his sons, but also his wife, Queen Ahotep, appear to have been involved, for one of the sons later gave her the award of three golden flies, the highest honour for military valour.

The exact sequence is unclear, but Seqenenre's wounds must have been inflicted at two different times – and the second resulted in his death. One of his arms was paralyzed, which could well have been caused by the injury to his head where the skull showed evidence of healing. But did Seqenenre die at the hands of an assassin, as some argue, or on the field of battle? Manfred Bietak's theory holds that the angle of the various wounds confirms that the king died in battle, on his knees, no doubt fighting to the last.

85

From historical evidence, we can imagine that other kings may have been forcibly removed from the throne. Ramesses III, for instance, may well have been murdered following a well-documented conspiracy of his wives to place someone else in his stead. His body shows no sign of violence, but it is possible that he may have been poisoned. Others, such as Ramesses IV, reigned for only a short time. Once again, the mummy of this king may one day suggest more of the real story of his demise.

What the mummies reveal about heredity

One long-held, and now outdated, theory about the pharaohs was that inheritance passed through the female line and it was essential that a male heir must marry the chief royal heiress to ensure his right to the throne. In other words, kings married their sisters, and their sons and daughters married each other, and so on. Historical records in recent years have shed more light on this. Many kings did marry their sisters or half-sisters, presumably for state reasons; and these queens stood before the goddesses as the king stood before the gods. We do not know if all these marriages were actually consummated or resulted in offspring. What does seem to be the case is that only a small number of such unions produced children who became the next rulers.

Armed with only superficial knowledge, it is often mistakenly assumed that inbreeding, or close genetic reproduction (i.e. reproduction between close blood relatives), would quickly result in children with deformities. In fact, there is as much chance of producing 'good' genes as 'bad' ones. The problem is that, because the gene pool eventually – after generations – becomes so restricted, genetic defects have more opportunity of recurring. The so-called incest taboo is the method that has evolved of maintaining a good, mixed gene pool, and greatly reducing the frequency at which abnormalities occur.

The Seventeenth Dynasty and early Eighteenth Dynasties consisted of several generations of rulers who apparently interbred. The family line ended with the reign of Amenhotep I, who married two of his four sisters, and died in his early twenties, apparently leaving no heir. It is a strong probability that one or both of those wives may have been sterile as the result of constant close genetic reproduction – perhaps nature's way of dealing with a restricted gene pool.

Some family traits can easily be observed in the mummies of this royal line. A prime example are the bodies of the queens, which appear very similar to each other. The first of them, Queen Tetisheri, mother of King Seqenenre Tao, was the grandmother of Queen Ahmose Nefertari and great-grandmother of Queen Ahmose-Meritamun. These ladies appear to have been of a similar build, and all had pronounced protruding teeth. All three also had very thin hair, but this does not necessarily reflect what their hair was like in life. Ahmose-Nefertari also had scoliosis, a sideways curvature of the spine, a defect shared with both her daughter Ahmose-Meritamun

The mummy of Amosis *(right), founder of the Eighteenth Dynasty and the New Kingdom, shows him to have been uncircumcised. He suffered from arthritis and died while relatively young. The embalmers removed his brain not through the nose, but at the base of the skull, a method occasionally employed during the Old Kingdom.*

and her son Amenhotep I. One learns to question artistic depictions of royalty when Ahmose-Meritamun's mummy, that of an obviously physically handicapped woman, is compared with wall paintings, which show her as tall, slender and straight.

X-rays of the body of Amosis, second son of Queen Tetisheri and the victor over the Hyksos kings, show that the young king (he died in his mid- to late-twenties) suffered in his knees and back. His vertebral column also shows some evidence of arthritis, surprising considering his youth. But arthritis is perhaps the commonest complaint shared by the royal mummies of several dynasties. Another victim – and another king renowned as a fighter – was Ramesses II. He suffered osteoarthritis in both hips, although in this case it was probably due to his advanced age.

The bodies of the pharaohs show them to have varied a great deal in height. Most were in the region of $5\frac{1}{2}$ feet (1.7 m) tall. A marked exception was the Eighteenth Dynasty's Tuthmosis III. Perhaps the mightiest ruler Egypt ever knew, he fought for, won and controlled an empire of immense size, that stretched from Sudan to Turkey in the north. His mummy shows that he was only about 5 feet (1.5 m) tall. His son Amenhotep II was markedly taller than his father, but he appears to have inherited his father's muscular frame. The kings of the Nineteenth Dynasty were also quite tall. Seti I was about $5\frac{1}{2}$ feet (1.7 m) tall; his son Ramesses II was over 6 foot (1.8 m). Both men were slender in build, and must have been remarkable in life for their hook noses – a strong Ramesside trait.

Illness among the pharaohs

Several of the royal bodies show conclusively that they suffered ill health during life. Tuthmosis II, brother-husband to Hatshepsut, seems to have been a weakly individual, and his skin appears covered in patches, the cause of which remains unidentified. X-rays of his grandson Amenhotep II demonstrate some evidence of the early stages of rheumatoid arthritis. The neck and trunk of his mummy are covered with tiny nodules, but it was impossible to identify their cause. Amenhotep's son and successor, Tuthmosis IV, was about thirty when he died, a fact belied by his appearance – that of a balding, extremely emaciated individual. His state is not solely attributable to mummification and, although the cause is unknown, it is considered likely that the great wasting and loss of body weight is somehow tied to his cause of death.

Perhaps the unhealthiest of all pharaohs is that of the mummy identified as Amenhotep III – though that designation is not universally agreed. The body itself was badly damaged, having been attacked by robbers in antiquity. But from what remains it can be determined that this individual suffered from severe obesity and appalling teeth, covered in tartar and ridden with holes, caused by caries. The caries resulted in abscesses in his jaws which must not only have given him pain but also constant stomach troubles. One might

The Tuthmosides

Tuthmosis I

FAMILY TREES OF THE PHARAOHS

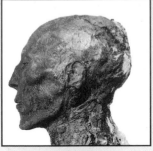

Seti I
|

Ramesses II
|

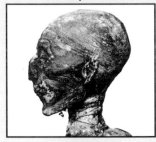

Merenptah

The identity *of Tuthmosis I (above) has been questioned, but the strong resemblance between his mummy and that of his son Tuthmosis II (right) argues in favour of the original identification.*

Tuthmosis II

Tuthmosis III

Amenhotep II

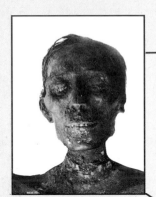

Tuthmosis IV

Tuthmosis IV (left) *brought peace to Egypt at the end of his ten-year reign after a time of turbulence. His son Amenhotep III (below) had a long, peaceful reign that was followed by the brief Amarna period. The use of resins has caused the darkened appearance of both mummies and is commonplace among prepared bodies of this time.*

Amenhotep III

The family resemblance *among the Ramesside kings of the Twentieth Dynasty is the most distinctive of any Egyptian royal family. The father, son and grandson above (top to bottom) all share the hooked nose that is their hallmark.*

RAMESSES
THE GREAT

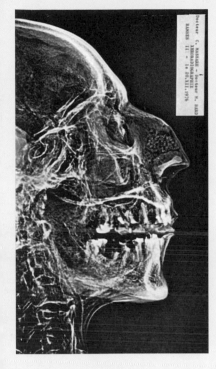

During the summer of 1977, Cairo airport witnessed an amazing sight. As a plane waited, shimmering in the heat, a guard of honour saluted a coffin that was being wheeled towards it with the utmost solemnity. A few hours later the mysterious cargo was discharged in Paris where it was greeted with similar ceremonial. The 'cargo' was none other than the pharaoh Ramesses II, dead for more than 3,000 years, and travelling under a passport listing his occupation as 'King (deceased)'.

The body of Ramesses II was one of those discovered in the royal cache at Deir el Bahri in 1881. Known to history as the builder of Abu Simbel and the hypostyle hall at Karnak, victor over the Hittites, husband to almost 100 wives, and father of at least 200 children, Ramesses has earned his epithet, 'the Great'.

In 1974, deterioration had been noticed in the skin around the king's neck. The subsequent appearance of larvae was evidence of beetle invasion, a condition that could quickly have turned Ramesses' mummy to dust if not checked. Several such affected mummies had been successfully treated at the Musée de

l'Homme, Paris, and the French president himself now offered the museum's expertise to the Egyptian authorities for the treatment of the great pharaoh. The offer was gratefully accepted and a team of twenty scientists devoted their energies and skills to saving the body of Ramesses II.

The mummy, wrapped in layers of plastic and still in its wooden crate, was placed in a sterile chamber and its temperature was steadily lowered. The scientists then removed the mummy, first from the crate and then from the plastic. The examination, isolation and identification of the invading organism took some time, since it was important to have little physical contact with the body itself so as not to cause more damage or contamination.

The treatment proved a success. The invader was destroyed, and the damage to the mummy repaired. Afterwards, as part of a major exhibition about the life and times of this great ruler, his mummy was placed on display. Today, the body of Ramesses II once again lies in its permanent home in the Cairo Museum among the kings and queens of pharaonic Egypt.

The X-ray of the head of Ramesses II (above) showed the contrast between the condition of his back and front teeth. Judging simply from the appearance of his mummy, where the front teeth were visible, the state of his teeth seemed remarkably good. X-rays of the full mouth revealed that those at the back were very worn.

The mummy of Ramesses II (right) lies in state in his coffin in front of a wall relief showing the pharaoh triumphant in his chariot.

think of this as a predictable outcome for a pharaoh who, after a brief blaze of glory in his youth, is supposed to have spent the rest of his life in a most hedonistic fashion in the midst of his sizeable harem. A letter, sent to King Tushratta of Babylonia during the later years of Amenhotep III's reign, requested the visit to Egypt of the 'healing statue of the goddess Ishtar', and it is tempting to think that this deity was being summoned to try to relieve a king who was being sorely tried by health problems.

Siptah, possibly a descendant of Ramesses II, ruled at the end of the Nineteenth Dynasty, taking the throne after Seti II. A minor when he became pharaoh, he ruled only seven years, dying in his late teens or early twenties, a fact demonstrated by the excellent condition of his teeth. But it is the condition of his legs which stimulates most interest in his mummy. The left foot was severely deformed and was thought to be an indication of a club-foot. But, during the Michigan X-ray analysis, it was pointed out that when taken in context with the severe shortening of the right leg and atrophy of the soft tissues, the presence of a neuro-muscular disease, such as polio, was a strong possibility.

How long did the pharaohs live?

Although the ages of the royal mummies have been hard to establish, few of the pharaohs seemed to have survived much beyond the age of fifty. X-ray analyses of these mummies show no clear reason for death, and evidence of disease suggests that several of them probably died as the result of some illness. Two individuals that cheated death for longer, however, were Ramesses II and his son and heir, Merenptah.

The mummy of Ramesses bears such a strong physical resemblance to the body of his father Seti I, and grandfather Ramesses I, and his son Merenptah, that his identity seems unquestionable. His body is that of an elderly man, serene in an eternal sleep. His skin is light in colour, his eyes closed as if sleeping, and his fine white hair, tinged slightly yellow during the mummification process, billows behind his neck. His mouth is slightly open, revealing healthy white teeth at the front of his mouth. To all appearances he is indeed the eighty- or ninety-year-old gentleman that history describes: a king who ruled for sixty-seven years. The analysis of the X-rays showed him to have suffered from badly eroded teeth, abscesses in his jaws, severe arthritis in his hips and widespread arteriosclerosis in the lower extremities, a condition that might have given rise to circulatory problems and rendered movement difficult.

Merenptah was born in the seventh year of Ramesses' reign and was his father's thirteenth son, making him between fifty and sixty years of age when he finally succeeded to the throne, from which he ruled for ten years. His mummy is that of an old man, balding and obese, and, like his father, with bad teeth and gum disease. Severe degenerative arthritis is obvious in the vertebrae in his neck, and the

soft tissues of his upper leg indicate the possibility of arteriosclerosis. His thigh bones show evidence of fracture. All in all, a man showing considerable wear – but this was compounded after his death by robbers who caused much damage when they broke the body open in the search for valuables.

Two things about the mummy of Merenptah are especially notable. The scrotum was missing, evidently removed during the embalming process, for resin covered the open flesh. This castration may have taken place during the excision of an inguinal hernia, but there seems little reason to do this after death. And, second, when the body was initially seen, observers remarked on the great incrustations of salt. Since Merenptah was then regarded as the pharaoh of the Biblical Exodus, when the Israelites departed from Egypt supposedly across the Sea of Reeds, this was taken by some writers as evidence that he had drowned in the Sea of Reeds – the Bible never states that the pharaoh died, only his army. In fact, natron and the mummification procedures could easily account for the salt deposits.

Future analysis of the royal mummies
The analysis of the royal mummies has already shown us a great deal about the ruling families of the New Kingdom. And it is interesting, and to some degree sobering, to realize that unlike the images carved on the walls of temples and painted on the walls of their tombs, they were often physically relatively unprepossessing. But there are so many questions yet to be answered. Identities of mummies are being challenged, relationships between some individuals are matters of great controversy, even ages are in doubt.

Permission has still not been given for any more detailed analysis to be carried out, and whether it ever will be given is a moot point. These are, after all, the mortal remains of some of the ancient world's greatest rulers and, as a result, are not only unique in the world of archaeology but are also entitled to the deepest respect. Few of the living were ever permitted even to gaze for long upon the face of a pharaoh – so perhaps it is presumptuous to demand more of them dead than they gave when alive. But the temptation is strong. Examination by endoscope for example could, with minimum damage, allow the inside of the bodies to be examined for further clues to the state of their lives and the cause of their deaths.

The left foot of Siptah, *last male ruler of the Nineteenth Dynasty, was for a long time interpreted as a club foot. Analysts in the 1960s determined that when taken in context with the rest of the pharaoh's body, the condition is more likely to have been polio or a similar affliction.*

Mummy projects around the world

Museums tend to possess few mummies with documented histories and fewer still are known by a specific name or have any recorded genealogy. Unlike Cairo's royal mummies, therefore, analysis of these bodies takes on an entirely different perspective. Museums must first try to establish even the sex and period of a mummy before they can consider its age or the cause of death. Because many of these

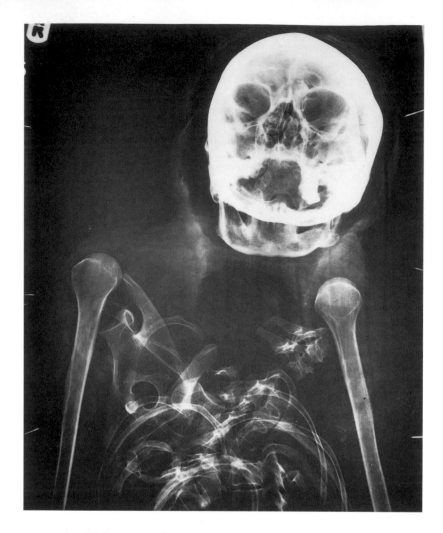

mummies lack any indication of their origin, even the smallest details, such as the type and weave of linen wrappings, the mode of preservation and the position of limbs within the bandaging can be of vital importance. A number of institutions have organized quite comprehensive projects – but in isolation from each other. At some future date the collation of, for example, types of linen wrappings or styles of embalming may lead to the identification of the work of varying establishments.

X-ray surprises

Many of the X-ray projects carried out have been on wrapped mummies, and the results have been fascinating. Often even the determination of sex has proved difficult because of the bad condition of the bodies. X-rays have confirmed the general belief that the standards of mummification dropped considerably during the Late and Graeco-Roman periods. A number of the bodies from these periods have been found to have been in an advanced state of decay even before the mummification process began. Some mummies reveal themselves as little more than a jumbled mixture of bones.

One mummy in the Liverpool City Museum (No. 16.4.1861.1) proved to be a disjointed muddle of bones that nevertheless does appear to have belonged to a single individual. Another mummy, apparently of a child, in the City of Bristol Art Museum, was also exposed as a fake, made up of a number of bones – albeit children's. A rather macabre discovery revealed by X-ray lies in Liverpool University: a Graeco-Roman child's coffin containing the bodies of two large mummified cats.

Exposing the dead

The unwrapping of mummies – often brought back by intrepid nineteenth century travellers – has also provided much interesting information. In 1851, Edmund Hopkinson, a wealthy English

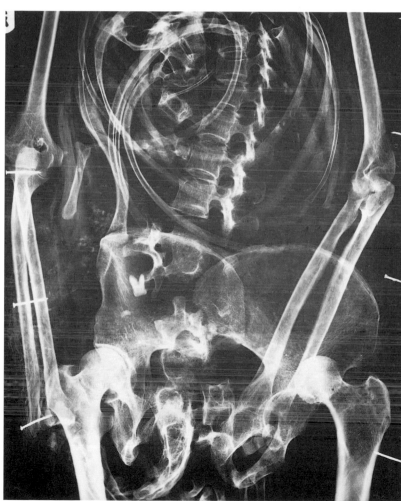

landowner, invited a large audience to witness the unwrapping of a mummy which he had acquired after it had been brought to Britain by Robert Hay, a Scottish traveller and collector, earlier in the century. The actual unwrapping was carried out by Mr Rumsey, a prominent surgeon. From the many layers of bandages emerged the body of a young man in a fine state of preservation. Curiosity satisfied, the mummy was partially rewrapped and handed over to a local museum, from which it was transferred, in 1953, to Liverpool to replace mummies lost there during World War II. In 1966, when it was X-rayed, a long metal instrument was seen inside the mummy's skull. When this was carefully removed through the mummy's nose, it was found, with great amusement, to be a scoop lost by Mr Rumsey over a century earlier!

In 1885, a mummy was acquired by Edwin Simond, a traveller and enthusiastic amateur Egyptologist, who helped to found the museum in Alexandria. Documents and the inscription on the mummy's coffin identify it as that of Nes-shou, an embalmer and the son of an embalmer. It was doubtless in no small measure due to his calling that the mummy was in a superb state of preservation. Eleven years later, Nes-shou was given to the museum at Yverdon, where Simond had studied in his youth before moving to Egypt. And there, before the assembled village, the mummy was publicly unrolled.

Unwrapping is brought up to date

Nearly a century after the discovery of Nes-shou, in 1982, the Yverdon museum authorities decided to undertake a study of the mummy using the most modern equipment. And, in November of that year, Nes-shou was subjected to a full radiographic examination, involving the use of a CAT scanner. With his own interest in preserving the bodies of the dead, no doubt his *ka* would have been gratified by the attention it received that day.

The body proved to be that of a man around fifty years of age, mummified during the Ptolemaic period. The CAT-scan images of his skull proved that his brain had been removed by the normal route, through the bone at the back of the nostrils. The cavity had then been filled with resins. The teeth seemed to be in a reasonably good state, considering his age. Tomographic pictures also showed packages inside the chest cavity, containing the viscera; and also a number of amulets distributed in the layers of wrapping still over the mummy. The heart scarab was seen to be still in place.

Even modern examinations, however, are not without their problems, as was discovered in 1973, when the late, distinguished palaeopathologist Aidan Cockburn suggested the 'autopsy' of a number of Egyptian mummies in North America. The unwrapping of the first mummy PUM I (i.e. Pennsylvania University Museum mummy 1) caused some problems, but a great deal was learned about how to approach the analysis of a mummy effectively. The second mummy proved no less difficult.

During the 1970s, a large-scale mummy analysis took place in North America. Several of the mummies were from the University Museum, Philadelphia, among them two known as PUM III and PUM IV. Both mummies were unidentified, their origins unknown, and they had no coffins. They both illustrate the type of embalming the remains of ordinary or poor Egyptians might have undergone. In each case the desiccation process had not been completed and tissue breakdown had resulted. Also the packing and wrapping methods employed had been cursory and crude.

PUM III

The head of this mummy was already unwrapped and separated from its body, damage perhaps done during an earlier recorded examination. After being X-rayed, PUM III was carefully unwrapped. Most of the outer bandages had been torn from a single large sheet of worn fabric. They were also heavily stained with materials used in the mummification process. The mummy was in a fragile state, and tissue broke away from the bones with the least touch.

The team determined the remains to be those of a woman in her mid- to late thirties, who had lived in Egypt during the Late period. Carbon dating of the wrappings at the Smithsonian Institution, Washington DC, gave a date of approximately 835 BC. (She may have lived through the time in which the pharaoh Sheshonk I defeated Rehoboam and sacked the temple of Jerusalem as recounted in the second book of Chronicles in the Bible.) Resin was not used on the body itself in any great quantity. There was no embalming

THE PENNSYLVANIA PROJECT

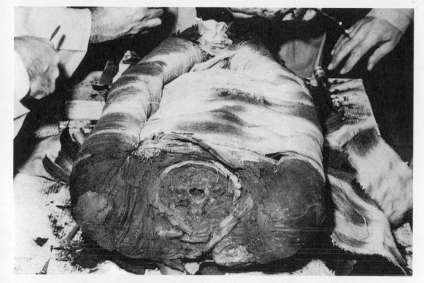

incision and many of PUM III's internal organs were still present. The abdomen, however, was empty and stuffed with linen soaked in resin – except for the liver, most abdominal organs could not be identified; the bladder and uterus had been removed, evidently via the anus, through which the linen packing had then been pushed.

The analysis team determined that PUM III had been 5 feet 6 inches (1.56 m) tall and weighed about 91 pounds (41 kg), a low weight for her height. She had a healed rib fracture and poor teeth, which must have given her pain. A small tumour was found in her left breast, but this does not seem to have caused her death, since it proved to be benign.

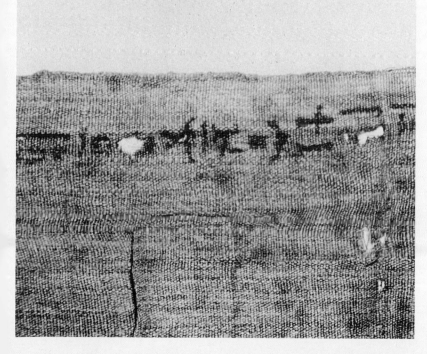

This view of the mummy of PUM III (above) shows how the head had become detached from the body. The hole is the trachea, or windpipe. The hasty and haphazard wrapping of the body is also apparent; the bandages around the body enclose one arm, but not the other. The stains on the bandages are from the fluids used in the embalming process.

A section from the wrappings of PUM III (left). The hieroglyphs indicate that the owner of the cloth was not PUM III but named Imyhap, the son of Wah-ib-Re.

THE PENNSYLVANIA PROJECT

PUM IV

When the analysis team X-rayed this mummy, which dated to the first or second century AD, they judged it to be that of a boy, aged about eight. The skull was fractured in several places, but this probably occurred after death.

Material used for bandaging was worn and the mummy was carelessly wrapped. Loose cord was wound around the body as if to hold the wrappings in place. There had been little effort at creating a lifelike appearance by padding. The body packing was sawdust, mixed with some sort of oily substance. The body itself was tied to a board. The boy was dressed in an outer decorated tunic, which he may have worn during life, but under this were three full-length gowns, perhaps made specifically for the burial.

The boy was approximately 3 feet 6 inches (106 cm) tall; it was not possible to determine his weight. His skin was dark and badly preserved. It was a mass of holes, and covered with beetles and insect larvae. The hair was dark and matted. Like PUM III, internal organs appear to have been removed via the anus. The body cavities were filled with a granular material. Both halves of the brain were still within the cranial cavity.

The team found no evidence that could point to this young boy's cause of death.

The upper body *of PUM IV contains the remains of granular packing material, and shows numerous holes in the skin. The whole mummy was poorly preserved and covered with larvae from insects.*

The mummy of Wah *was found in his intact Eleventh Dynasty tomb during Metropolitan Museum of Art excavations during the 1919–20 field season. The wrappings were as they had been since the embalmers put them in place on the estate manager's body and they afforded Egyptologists an excellent opportunity to study Middle Kingdom bandaging techniques. Around the mummy was a fringed kilt (right, above), though this carried the name of someone else. Under this were: a dozen bandages a handspan wide circling the mummy – one was almost 40 feet (12.3 m) long; large sheets and pads of linen filling the shape out to that roughly of a cylinder; a layer of bandages streaked with resin; twenty sheets and pads; the mask (right, below) over ten more sheets and pads; a layer of thick, black resin; another layer of wrappings wound around the mummy; a further dozen sheets and pads; Wah's jewellery; six more bandages and pads; more jewellery; six large sheets and twelve more pads and sheets; each thickly covered with resin; more jewellery; more bandages, within which was a dead mouse and lizard, a cricket, and swabs used to apply the resin. The amount of linen used came to a staggering 1,010 square yards (845 sq m) – an indication of a very prosperous man.*

This mummy, PUM II, was first X-rayed, at which time it was noted that the brain had been removed and four packages were present in the abdomen. When the mummy was examined prior to unwrapping, it was discovered that the lavish application of molten resins throughout the bandaging process had caused the whole mass to become so hard that even hammers and chisels proved to be totally useless. Eventually, the wrappings had to be cut open using a Stryker saw, a diamond-edged blade usually used for cutting only the hardest stones. It took nine people seven hours to cut away all the bandages – the team found that the mummy had been wrapped in twelve layers of linen. Once this major hurdle had been overcome, the tissue was subjected to carbon dating and gave a death date of around 170 BC (plus or minus 70 years).

Looking at wrappings
The linen bandages of the mummies often prove to be of almost as much interest as the mummies inside. In the case of PUM II, a small ball of cotton was found within the wrappings, having been included accidentally during the embalming. The only cotton previously found in Egypt had originally come from the Indus valley, and had been brought into Egypt in Roman times, some 400 years after PUM II. It has been suggested that cotton was considered so rare and valuable that it might, in fact, have been introduced deliberately as a sort of amulet or precious gift.

In 1940, at the Metropolitan Museum of Art, a mummy was unwrapped. The body was that of a man called Wah, discovered in an intact tomb in Luxor in excavations in 1920. It was found that approximately 1010 square yards (845 sq m) of linen had been used as wrappings. This included at least one piece of linen, complete with a fringed edge.

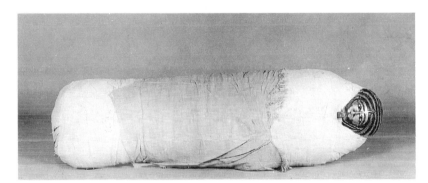

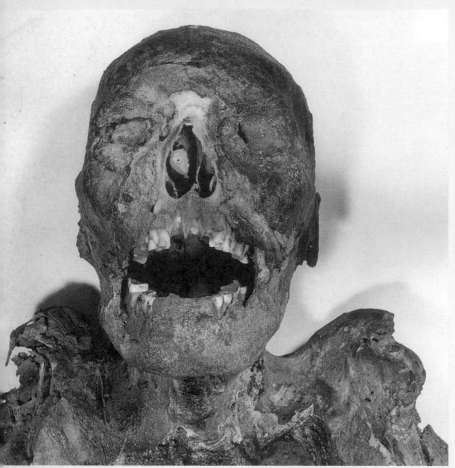

THE BRISTOL PROJECT

Horemkenesi was a minor priest in Ramesses III's mortuary temple and the foreman of a group of workmen in the Valley of the Kings. He held his positions just after the last of the royal burials in the Valley, that of Ramesses XI, was made about 1085 BC. His own burial in the tomb of one of the royal ladies at Deir el Bahri was undistinguished, with no grave goods or amulets, and no decoration save a beaded network over his wrapped mummy. For nearly 3,000 years, his remains lay undisturbed until they were discovered and excavated by the Egypt Exploration Fund during the 1904-05 field season. The mummy was sent to the Bristol Museum, which as one of the subscribing institutions of the Fund, was entitled to a share of the finds. In 1976, during an exceptionally hot summer, the surface of the linen wrappings became heavily encrusted with white alkali salts that had migrated from the packing in the

The unwrapping of *Horemkenesi,* whose head is shown above, was treated as an archaeological excavation. The body was placed on a surface surrounded by a marked grid so that each bandage could be numbered and plotted. The body had been wrapped in a long bandage (right) which went in a figure of eight from the head around the feet and back. Bits of loose mud and natron can be seen under this wrapping. The embalmers used a twisted bandage to tie the arms in place (opposite left), in front of the body. They also tied Horemkenesi's legs together both at the knees and the ankles, with pads of linen to keep the legs slightly apart.

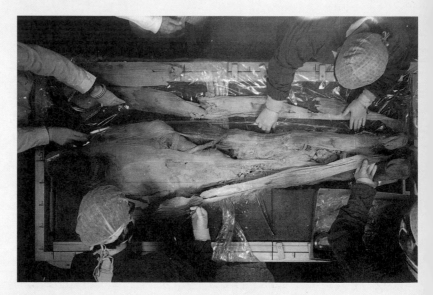

body and bandaging. The high humidity affected the natron salts in the packing and they literally started to 'eat' the cloth in which the mummy was wrapped.

The Bristol Museum had not unwrapped any of its mummies since the 1830s. But in the 1970s a project was undertaken to utilize modern X-ray techniques to examine all the mummies in the collection. During the project the damage to Horemkenesi's wrappings became obvious and his mummy was deemed a special case. In March 1981, it was decided to unwrap and examine the body in detail – if its loss was inevitable, at least some knowledge would be gleaned.

The examination

The mummy proved to have been wrapped in a variety of strips torn from worn, used household linens. Mud containing stray pieces of straw had been packed into the body cavity to restore the body's shape; the inner bandages contained a packing of mud and natron. The body of Horemkenesi, his head shaven, was revealed to be that of a stout man in his mid- to late fifties. The feet had been badly eaten by carrion beetle larvae, so toe-prints could not be taken. The two fingerprints that could be made showed no sign of calluses, suggesting that he had

not been a manual worker. Arthritis was clearly present in his shoulder joints. X-rays of his spine showed evidence of a thickening and degeneration of the vertebrae, in technical language diffuse idiopathic skeletal hyperostosis (D.I.S.H.). This condition usually occurs in the middle-aged and elderly, and sufferers tend to be obese; it can cause bad posture and a resultant pronounced stoop.

One intriguing aspect of the mummy was that the jaw had been moved down – possibly deliberately – leaving him open-mouthed. There are only a small number of such instances known and speculation as to the reasons for this vary. One possibility is that the mouth was opened to create a channel through which poisons could escape.

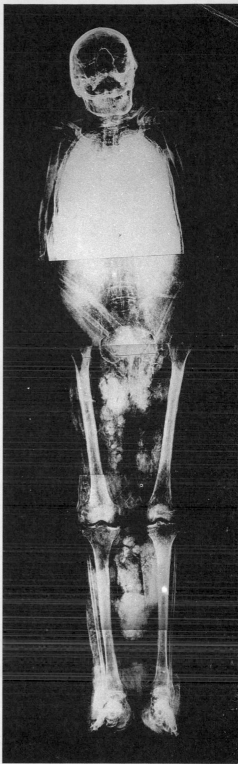

A composite X-ray *of the mummy (right). The mud packing of the chest cavity shows as a dense area. The packages between the legs were pads of cloth.*

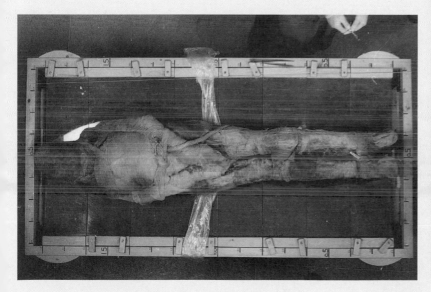

In 1974, a mummy was studied by a team in Toronto. The mummy Nakht, or ROM I (i.e. Royal Ontario Museum mummy 1), was a poor weaver buried in a reused tomb chamber at the funerary temple of Mentuhotep II, at Deir el Bahri, and found in the 1904-05 excavation season. Nakht's body, in its coffin, was probably placed there sometime between 1150 and 1100 BC. Although he was not well-off, his wrappings were unusually fine, no doubt due to his trade. Many of the basic bandages had been torn from a well-worn cloth, probably a piece of bed linen. Some bandages used in the outer wrappings, however, were patterned with blue stripes woven into the fabric. An outer shroud was wrapped around the body as a tunic with a kilt tied over the top – one of the few examples of surviving evidence for dress in ancient Egypt. The basic garment was ankle-length with a simple circular hole for the head. It was held in place by another piece of linen rather like a wide sash, but which was in all probability a kilt. A piece of linen laid over the legs proved to be a complete child's tunic, of very fine linen and with decorative edges of patterned weave.

These wrappings, with results from other unrollings of mummies, suggest that most mummies were prepared using household linens, presumably provided by the family. Many of these were heavily used, some shrunk through excessive washing over many years, others repaired time and again until beyond use. This contrasts strongly with the wrappings of the royal mummies, most of which, not surprisingly, seem to have been specially woven for the purpose. This suggests that the provision of linen was the responsibility of the estate of the deceased, and that even where the person was of a high rank, little could be expected to be provided by the state, the embalmers or by the royal treasury.

What do mummies of commoners reveal?

The remains that have been examined worldwide cover the whole range of ages, from foetus through to that of elderly person. Every museum's collection will differ in what it contains; some may have only one mummy, or even just a fragment of one. But like the mummies of their rulers, those of the ordinary Egyptian reveal a number of physical problems – some of them the normal results of the ageing process. Together with attrition of the teeth, due to the high amount of sand and stone in the diet, there was also considerable evidence of poor dentition. Bad and missing teeth would have made their jaws appear collapsed. And stomach troubles, the result of such dental problems, would have caused discomfort, and perhaps listlessness. Again, like the pharaohs and queens, arthritis was a very common problem indeed, and many of the older members of the population would have walked stiffly and in some pain.

Several mummies revealed problems that occurred as the result of trauma or injury. A woman of the Late period, now in the Liverpool

City Museum, had damage to her spine, apparently from her youth, that may have left her virtually unable to walk at all. Two others in the same collection had suffered broken bones. That of a woman was found to have a compound fracture of the right arm, while that of a man, called Nesmin, shows evidence of a well healed broken rib.

Lung-related diseases

X-rays demonstrate that illnesses of the lung appear to have been widespread. When the four mummies in the Pennsylvania University Museum were examined, tissue sections from the lungs of all of them revealed pneumoconiosis, due to dust in the lungs. When the mummy of Nakht was examined in Toronto, it had not only sand particles in the lungs, but also a sooty, carbon deposit. Since we know that the ancients did not smoke, this must have been caused by prolonged periods of sitting in smoke-filled enclosed spaces. This may have been indicative of their working conditions.

In 1901, Dr Margaret Murray examined two mummies (known as 'the Brothers') in the Manchester Museum. Tissue sections from the bodies were kept until the 1970s, when they were re-examined as part of a major mummy survey, initiated by Manchester's Dr Rosalie David. When rehydrated and looked at under a microscope, these sections revealed evidence of severe pneumoconiosis, or silicosis. The result of such conditions would have been constant shortness of breath and severe bouts of coughing. Interestingly, medical papyri contain a large number of prescriptions to deal with coughs.

Heart and circulatory problems

Two mummies – one in Yverdon, the other in Pennsylvania – are both of elderly men, and prove to have suffered from arteriosclerosis (hardened arteries) and heart disease. One should bear in mind that these two mummies were elderly, and most instances of heart disease among the Egyptians are found in remains of the elderly. Perhaps the physical symptoms were simply the result of a long life.

Parasites

Another problem shared by many ordinary mummies and yet indiscernible so far in the royal mummies is parasitic infestation. A whole variety of intestinal worms infected the irrigation canals of ancient Egypt and, when these flooded the fields, the infestation was transferred to the sodden soil. The body of the young weaver Nakht, in Toronto, was heavily infected. When tissue from his body was rehydrated and stained to form sections for microscopic examination, the intestines proved to have the remains of parasites attached to them – the eggs of schistosoma and tapeworms. The tapeworms would have resulted in severe weight loss, and would have been acquired through eating undercooked meat. In Nakht's muscle tissue, a cyst was found, which is thought to be that of *trichinella spiralis*, commonly found in pork. This meat, now known to have

THE MANCHESTER MAIDEN

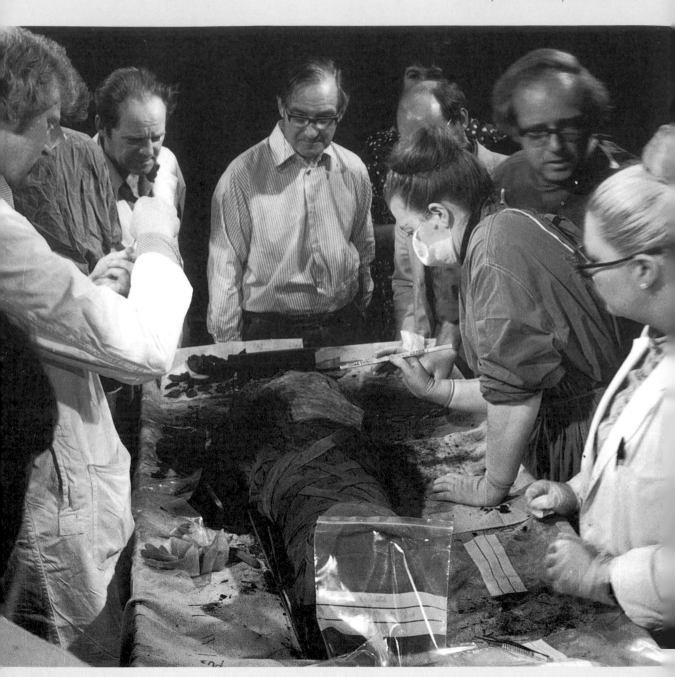

X-rays revealed it to be the body of a child or youth, and also showed that part of the legs were missing. When the museum decided to unwrap a mummy from the collection, 1770 was chosen.

The examination

Paint on the skull, and provision of both male and female features, suggested that even at the time of mummification the body was so badly decayed that its sex could not be determined. The bones of the legs had been broken, and both feet were missing. The left leg had been broken below the knee and the right above the knee. The embalmers had attempted to make the length of the remaining bones equal by tying pieces of wood to the right leg. After this a bundle of reeds and mud had been used to create 'artificial legs'. A study of the bones suggested that 1770 had, in fact, been a young girl. So how had she lost her legs? Suggestions of an injury that brought about her death seemed possible, but comments by Herodotus and Diodorus Siculus also allowed for the possibility that her corpse had been retained by the family long enough after death for decay to set in before the body was sent to the embalmers. Alternatively, the body may have had to be transported some distance to be mummified.

X-rays of the skull showed that the girl had been born with the sinuses on the left side of her head blocked. This would have made breathing a continual problem. When the Manchester scientists later 'moulded' the skull in plaster, with layers of 'flesh' added over the face to allow the image of 1770 to live once more, the lips were left parted to indicate her breathing problem.

Dr Rosalie David *gently probes mummy 1770, during its unwrapping in June 1975, at the University of Manchester's Medical School.*

been a staple source of protein for the poor, may well have been the source of the tapeworm as well.

Nakht died in his teens, and the cause cannot be determined. But it could have had something to do with the side-effects of the parasites in his body. Examination of his liver also showed that he was suffering from the early stages of cirrhosis, which may well have been the result of the schistosomiasis, since schistosomal ova were found in his liver.

In the Manchester project, in 1976, the stomach and intestines of a female mummy – Asru, called a 'Chantress of Amun' – were tested and it was shown that she had suffered from an infestation of strongyloides, a worm which enters through the skin, travels to the lungs, matures, goes on to the pharynx from where it enters the stomach and intestines. Asru would no doubt have had constant stomach upsets and, perhaps, wheezing.

Further evidence of infestation was found in the body of the unfortunate Manchester mummy Number 1770. A hard nodule attached to the intestinal wall proved to be the remains of guinea worm, a particularly virulent type. The female grows to great lengths before finally emerging through ulcers, usually in the lower legs. If this worm dies before it is removed, severe inflammation can set in, and ulcers may develop.

But such problems did not stop at death. Microscopic examination has shown that a good number of the mummies showed evidence of insect infestation which took place during the embalming process, and stopped with the application of the hot resins. Since the drying process, where the body was laid for days in natron to preserve it, would have destroyed the larvae, it must be assumed that the eggs were laid and the larvae hatched after the body was withdrawn from the salt but before the resins were poured over it.

Glimpses of the past

Examination of the mummies has revealed more, however, than simply medical details concerning the dead. X-rays of the body of a young man called Nes-shutefnut, in Liverpool, showed that his legs and hips had been badly broken about the time of death, and both his feet were missing. There is speculation about whether or not he may have been beaten to death, or tortured, or perhaps the embalmers deliberately stretched the body for some reason. Why the feet are missing is mysterious, but could simply be due to carrion beetle larvae as was the case with the Bristol mummy. Thus it is possible that the damage to the body was caused after death in some way.

Much is known of ancient Egyptian titles, but little about exactly what those titles meant in terms of duties performed in life. The Manchester mummy Asru, for instance, was called 'Chantress of Amun', as we have seen. It has always been assumed that this involved singing and dancing in temple ritual. But examination of the soles of her feet showed none of the wear that would be expected from constant contact with the surface of the floor. So what did her title mean? And what of the other dozens of titles borne by Egyptians?

Many of the bodies that underwent the full mummification process are, understandably, from the higher ranks of Egyptian society, because the cost of the best kind of mummification was prohibitive for all but the very well off. Yet a good number of the mummies of the rich also show evidence of intestinal parasites, and this has given rise to speculation that even people of high status may have carried out the same forms of work as peasants, who walked in sodden fields or worked up to their waists in the river. But this is not necessarily so, for most intestinal parasites are acquired by ingesting the ova, i.e. by eating or drinking, not by absorption through the skin, usually from its annual host, which varies depending on the type of parasite. To have taken such parasites in through the skin would have meant standing daily in infected water or constantly treading barefoot in heavily sodden and infected soil. So although we can question the nature of the lifestyle of these well-placed people, we cannot infer that because they shared the diseases of the poor they lived like them.

THE LYONS SAILOR

In 1985, a team of medical experts, led by the Egyptologist Professor Jean-Claude Goyon, undertook a minute examination of an anonymous mummy in the Guimet Museum of Natural History in Lyons. The main aim of the project was to assess the mummy in exacting detail, with a view to analyzing every action of the embalmers, both in terms of the physical preparation of the body and the wrapping of the prepared corpse. All would be carried out with due reference to the embalming texts. At every stage, the proceedings could be stopped and the appropriate expert could carry out specific tests.

The wrappings
The bandages that wrapped the Lyons mummy – who proved to be a man – may provide a slender clue as to his occupation. The examining team decided to piece together the bandages, much as the original embalmers had torn them

apart to form narrow strips suitable for binding. They proved to have been ripped from a large square piece of material that had been heavily repaired. On one side a fastening loop was still attached to part of a wooden ring. What the team had in their hands, in fact, was a sail from a small square-rigged vessel, and the wooden ring was part of the rigging. So perhaps our mummy was that of a boat owner or sailor.

The body
The features of the man were well preserved. Probably around forty at death, of slender build and high cheekbones, he had been reasonably fit, and though his teeth were worn, they were not badly damaged. His lungs show marks typical of pneumoconiosis, or dust in the lungs, suggesting a prolonged exposure to the elements – just the sort of life a sailor might have had.

IX Analysis of the *head of the Lyons mummy yielded information on removal of the brain and the method of preserving the skull.*

X **The Lyons mummy** *enters the CAT scan machine.*

Overleaf
XI **In this scene from** *the Book of the Dead, the deceased, Here-ubkhet, has reached the end of her perilous journey and arrives at the Fields of the Blessed.*

XII **The face of** *Amun, from Deir el Bahri. The god's face is black, symbolizing rebirth.*

XIII **Anubis leads** *the deceased Hunefer to the scales where his heart is to be weighed against the feather of the goddess Maat. The ibis-headed god Thoth records the result, and the ferocious monster Ammit stands by to eat Hunefer's heart should it prove to be laden with sin. But Hunefer is vindicated and the falcon-headed Horus leads him to Osiris.*

XIV **On this wooden stela,** *now in the Louvre, a harpist plays before Re-Horakhte – Horus of the Horizon – the god of the morning sun. At the top of the stela are two wadjet eyes, powerful symbols of protection.*

Final colour page
XV **This detail from** *the tomb of Sennedjem at Deir el Medina shows a priest wearing the mask of the god Anubis tending to Sennedjem's mummy.*

XVI **Female mourners in** *the funeral procession of the Eighteenth Dynasty vizier Ramose express their grief on the walls of his tomb at Luxor.*

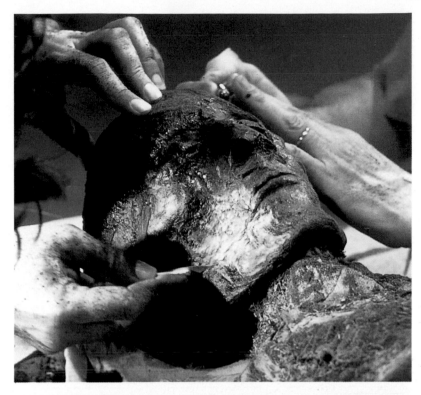

X

IX

XII   XIII

XI

XIV

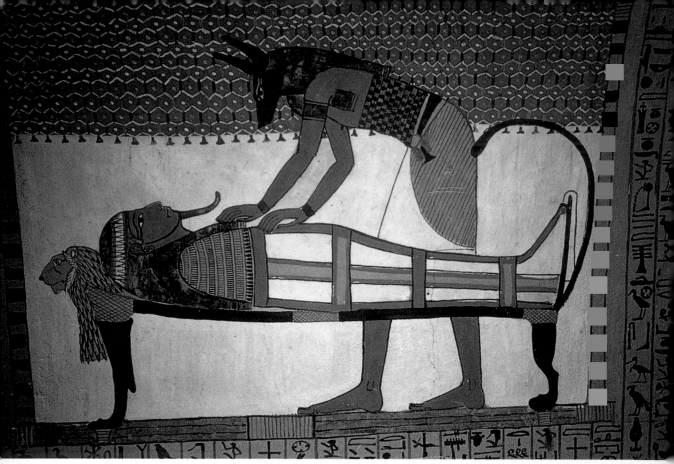

XV

XVI

PART III

Myth and Magic

Chapter Four
Burial in Ancient Egypt

THE ELABORATE RITUALS of mummification culminated on the seventieth day when the prepared body in its coffin, surrounded by priests, professional mourners and grieving friends and relations, was taken to the place of burial. This was a day of sadness for the loss of the living, but it was also one of great joy for the *ka*, or life force of the deceased, which was about to enter a rich afterlife.

Another kind of ritual now took place, composed of spells to protect the tomb and mummy; to release the *ka* and restore the senses (the so-called 'Opening of the Mouth' ceremony); and to smooth the transition to the afterlife – a hazardous journey for which even the pharaoh needed supernatural assistance. The embalming priest (*wt*) had supervised mummification. Then it became the duty of the *sem* priest, in charge of the funerary ceremonies, to oversee the rites which sustained the *ka* or life force of the dead person, so that it could be reunited with the *ba*, the aspect that had made the deceased an individual in life – his character or personality. At death the *ba* journeyed to join the *ka*. Once the union had taken place in the safety of the next world, the Egyptian could become an *akh*, the state in which the dead existed among the gods.

These magical rituals were centred around the tomb. The Opening of the Mouth took place outside, the offering rituals inside. So that the deceased would continue to be remembered – and, therefore, to live eternally – his or her name was inscribed on the tomb, both in areas open to visitors and in parts sealed from view.

A funeral in Egypt

There are examples of burials from virtually all periods of Egyptian history, from the earliest pit graves, which occur throughout Egyptian history and was the way in which the vast majority of the population was buried, to mastabas, pyramids and rock-cut tombs. And carved or painted on the walls of many tombs, beginning with those of the Old Kingdom, are scenes of the funerary rituals which date back to the first kings – and perhaps to the time of the legendary superheroes who became the gods of Egyptian mythology. The ritual varied slightly through history and the meaning of some of the detail is lost or unknown, but a clear sequence of events can be

This **Nineteenth Dynasty** *relief (right) is from the tomb of an unknown man and shows part of his funeral procession. Women and girls dance excitedly to the music of castanets and tambourines. They are facing towards the coffin, which is being carried by the men wearing long kilts; some of these pallbearers are shaven, others wear long wigs. The relief block itself was used in the building of the Serapeum and is now in the Cairo Museum.*

This **exquisite cosmetic** *chest and equipment (above), now in the Metropolitan Museum, formed part of the grave goods buried with the Princess Sit Hathor Yunet about 1890 BC. The chest is of inlaid ebony with gold mountings; the cosmetic jars are of obsidian and would have held eyepaint and ointments, the small rouge dish is of silver. The chest also contained razors and whetstones for sharpening them. The mirror is a copy of the original in the Cairo Museum.*

reconstructed. One should bear in mind that these depictions record the funerals of royalty, courtiers, high officials and the wealthy; of the funerals and spiritual expectations of the ordinary Egyptian little is known.

A day of sorrow dawns

On the day of burial, family and friends assembled at the house of the deceased to give vent to their grief and begin the long procession which would take them to the cemetery. There is some evidence that, at least in the Old Kingdom, men mourned outside and women inside the home. At some point those who were to be part of the procession joined the waiting professional mourners, who wore pale garments denoting mourning. They were streaked with dust, and they pulled at their hair and beat their breasts. Raising their arms and fists, they gesticulated wildly as if totally abandoned in grief – for someone they may never have known.

In addition to those attending the burial rites, servants assembled to carry the grave goods: food, wine and beer; fresh bread, fruit, nuts and vegetables; jars of perfumes and unguents; flowers, vases and lamps; furniture, some specially made for the tomb, some which had been used by the deceased; clothing, sandals and bolts of linen – the *ka* would lack for nothing. Special possessions relating to the life or profession of the deceased were included in the grave goods. In the case of a military man, for instance, there might be weapons and chariots; for a carpenter or a mason, tools; for a scribe, a favourite ink palette and a supply of materials. A woman would normally have been buried with her cosmetics, mirrors and jewellery; a child with the toys and games that had given pleasure in life. It was not unusual to be buried with musical instruments as well.

Behind this troop of servants came others bearing very special things indeed. Some carried the canopic jars and chest into which the internal organs of the deceased were to be placed. Others the chests containing the _ushabti_, small figures placed in the tomb which would magically carry out any tasks the deceased was requested to perform in the afterworld.

Next came a statue of the deceased, followed by the _sem_ priest, wearing his traditional panther skin; the coffin, brilliantly painted in primary red, blue, yellow and green colours, placed in a boat and accompanied by two female mourners. In the Old Kingdom, these mourners were denoted in accompanying inscriptions as kites (_djeryt_), or hawks, and in later times they dressed as such, representing the goddesses Isis and Nephthys. The wife of the dead man may fittingly have represented Isis, for Isis was the sister–wife of the god of the dead, Osiris. (From the time of the New Kingdom, the deceased was said to become an 'Osiris'.) It is unclear whether at this point the coffin actually contained the mummy, which may have been kept in readiness at the embalmer's workplace on the west bank.

At the edge of the Nile, the whole procession boarded boats. The mourners' was first; the second carried the coffin, the _sem_ priest and the two kites. Other members of the funeral party, servants and grave goods filled the remaining boats. The wails of the mourners filled the air as they constantly turned back proclaiming their grief towards the bier on the second boat.

From Nile to necropolis

On arrival at the opposite side of the river, the entire party disembarked and, once again, formed a procession. They first went to the _wabet_, where additional purification ceremonies may have taken place. If the mummy had not already been brought back to the home of the deceased, it may have been here that the body was placed in its coffin. And from the _wabet_, the final earthly stage of the journey began. The mummy in its coffin, under a canopy that looked like the night sky, and accompanied by everything needed to sustain it in the much longer journey through eternity, made its way over the hills to the cemetery. (During the earliest dynasties, when pharaohs died they were thought to join the 'stars' (some deities, such as deceased pharaohs, were thought of as 'stars', or 'Imperishable Ones') and there is little doubt that the design of the canopy recalled that belief.)

Somewhere along the way, the procession was met by _muu_ dancers. Curious performers known only from depictions of funerals, they characteristically wear short pointed kilts and tall feathered headdresses. From representations ranging over the whole of Egyptian history, these dancers appear to have been male and female, although it appears that some dances could only be performed by males. It is thought that the movements of the dance they performed were laid down early in Egypt's history.

Muu dancers were _part of the traditional funeral. They performed sacred dances whose origins appear to go back to the earliest periods of Egyptian history._

The Opening of the Mouth
ceremony was evidently an innovation of the New Kingdom and took place outside the entrance to the tomb. The priests carried out rituals and touched instruments to the mouth of the mummy or a statue of the deceased. When this was completed, the senses would be magically restored. Behind the coffin here stands the figure of the god Anubis.

The Opening of the Mouth ceremony

On the way to the tomb, perhaps at the tomb itself, various rituals took place, including the symbolic re-enactment of journeys made to Abydos – and possibly Busiris in the delta – by the funeral processions of the kings of the Old Kingdom.

At the entrance to the tomb, the mummy was raised to an upright position in the sand and low-ranking priests purified it with water and incense, while the *sem* priest intoned the words of a ritual which dated back to the Archaic period. At that time a chisel was raised to the mouth of the god in the temple, to allow him to eat from the daily offerings. During the Old Kingdom, the same rite applied to royal mummies. By the time of the New Kingdom, it was part of the conventional burial of anyone wealthy enough to be accorded a full funeral. (The words the priest actually recited had their origin in the offering ritual of the Pyramid Texts of the Old Kingdom.) The priest twice raised an instrument that looked like an adze to the face of the mummy and to the *ka* statue. The priest also touched the mummy and the statue with a forked instrument called a *pesesh-kef* knife, or wand. By magic, the senses of the body – sight, hearing, speech, taste and touch – were now restored. An ox was slaughtered, and one of its forelegs cut off and presented to the face of the mummy. The purpose of this is not known, but it is thought that it may have had something to do with restoring full sexual powers.

While this ceremony was taking place, the lector priest recited 'glorifications', and other aspects of the ritual, such as the breaking of two red vases, were enacted. Members of the funeral party began preparing a funeral feast. The widow made a final farewell, clutching at the mummy in a final expression of her sense of loss.

EVOLUTION OF THE SARCOPHAGUS

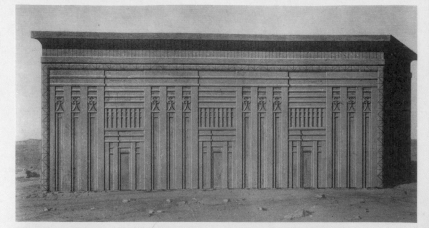

The word sarcophagus comes from the Greek for 'flesh eater', reflecting the Hellenic belief that the container 'devoured' the flesh of the body inside it. Egyptian sarcophagi were invariably made of stone, and held one or a whole nest of coffins. From the start of Egyptian history, with the king owning all land and all rights to its wealth, it was only the king who could order stone to be cut for a sarcophagus.

The earliest sarcophagi were rectangular, with immensely heavy lids that were cut square at each end, but barrel-vaulted between the end pieces. Jutting projections were left temporarily at each end to provide hand-holds while the sarcophagus was lowered into position in the tomb; the bosses were then cut off. During the Middle and New Kingdoms, commoners rarely had a sarcophagus at all. But those of royalty were elaborate indeed, often oval with a cavetto cornice edging like that of a pylon

Sarcophagi changed *through Egyptian history. Some of the earliest, like that of Mycerinus at Giza (right, above), were carved to resemble temples or shrines. The sarcophagus of Tutankhamun (right, below) has retained the curved cornice at the top, but its sides are inscribed with hieroglyphs and the figures of four protective goddesses are carved at the corners.*

or temple. In fact, the whole structure imitated the shape of a temple. The sarcophagi were made of quartzite or granite, and were finely cut, polished and carved with the names of the deceased and figures of protective deities.

From the end of the New Kingdom, sarcophagi grew even larger and took the shape of the mummy. The lid was frequently carved into the form of a recumbent mummy and the whole sarcophagus became much heavier. During the Greek and Roman periods mummies may have been kept in the houses of the living until a large number accumulated. These were then buried without sarcophagi in caches in long-empty tombs in the desert. During the Christian era, sarcophagi and coffins merged to become shouldered stone coffins into which the deceased were placed wearing their daily clothing.

The lid of the *sarcophagus of Ramesses III (below) is carved with the figure of the king as Osiris, and the goddesses Nephthys and Isis. Down both sides of the king are also images of the human-headed snake goddess Meretseger who guarded the Valley of the Kings.*

The offering ritual

After the ceremonies outside the tomb were finished, the lector priests recited the offering ritual at the false door of the tomb. At this point, in some depictions, a man is often shown kneeling before the offering table in front of the false door. The table itself was frequently in the shape of the hieroglyph *hetep*, formed by a loaf of bread on a table; it meant 'offering' or 'to offer'. The lector priests, usually three or four, then knelt with their left arms brought up to the chest and their right arms raised behind them. The inscriptions above them read *sakh*: 'causing to become an *akh*'. Thus the sustenance of the *ka* was assured and the deceased had become an *akh*. Throughout the whole procedure priests read from scrolls they held in front of them. Either before or during the offering ritual, the mummy in its coffin was placed inside the burial chamber, perhaps in a sarcophagus. All the grave goods that had been carried so lovingly in the procession were put in the tomb, as were the important *ushabti* figures and canopic equipment.

When all was completed, the priests withdrew from the tomb, one in place of the god Thoth (god of scribes whose duty it is to record all the souls as they enter the underworld) sweeping the floor as they went. Outside, the mourners shared in a feast, including meat from cattle ritually slaughtered for the funeral. Eventually, priests and mourners made their way back to the Nile to cross again to the area of the living. And, behind them, in the tomb all was silent. Cemetery workers filled the entrance passage with rubble, to make it virtually impassable; and masons closed the entrance, probably covering it with a final coat of plaster into which they pressed an official necropolis seal – the most well known shows a recumbent jackal over nine bound captives.

The estate or family of the deceased continued to make offerings outside the tomb for as long as they had means to finance it. The reiteration of the ritual was essential if a second death in the afterlife were to be avoided – for this death would be one from which there was no return. Sometimes the dead person left an indication of specified feast days on which the offering rituals were to be carried out. But the dead were never forgotten. For example, an annual festival called the Feast of the Valley took place in Luxor. The living crossed over to the necropolises on the west bank and, celebrating among the tombs with feasts and festivities, remembered their dead. To the ancients their ancestors were among them, even if not in a physical sense; and at least for this short time, the dead could partake of the joys of family and friends. To the ancient Egyptian, the idea of being remembered – by name – was inextricably linked with the idea of immortality.

Other funerals

This then was the ideal funeral. It was, in effect, a pale imitation of that which a king or queen might expect. But for the great mass of the people, such a burial was a dream beyond all expectation. For the peasant, the simple labourer, the beggar, there might have been a grieving family, and possibly even the simplest of mummifications, but the final resting place would not have been a grand tomb, cut from the rock and laboured over by artisans, but a shallow pit, to be shared with others of similar class or status.

In a late story, a character called Setne has his attention caught by sounds of lamentation and observes the funeral procession of a rich man. Noticing a funeral of a poor man at some distance, the body wrapped only in a mat and no mourners to grieve for him, Setne comments: 'How much happier is the rich man who is honoured with the sound of wailing than the poor man who is carried to the cemetery.' According to the story, Osiris rewarded the peasant, who had led a good life, with the riches of the wealthier, but morally inferior man. But the poor themselves left no records and it will probably never be known what sort of afterlife – if any – they expected.

The mortuary cult

Preparation for the afterlife was not a thing to be left to chance and often began long before death was anticipated. A rich Egyptian did not risk leaving the planning to others, but arranged for his tomb and the continuation of the offering ritual himself. To do this, he endowed a mortuary cult, which meant that he set aside, or was rewarded by the king or temple with, a piece of arable land (called the mortuary estate). The produce from this land would both provide daily offerings and support the family of the priest who had been appointed to continue the offering ritual. A Fifth Dynasty inscription recommends that one 'Choose for him [the mortuary priest] a plot among your fields. He profits you more than your own son. Prefer him even to your [heir].' In actual practice, this priest (known as the 'servant of the *ka*') was often the deceased tomb owner's son, who by virtue of his appointment could both fulfil his filial obligation and gain a secure living. One Old Kingdom tomb records the setting up of a system whereby the deceased's family took the duty in turns, on a rota basis. In return, they received shares of the land endowment. This would seem an ideal way of ensuring immortality and keeping land in the family.

To ensure that the name of the deceased would not be forgotten, and would continue to be spoken through the long centuries after death, one final measure was sometimes taken. Statues or stelae were erected in temples or places of pilgrimage, such as Abydos, where in the Middle Kingdom these memorials lay in an area set aside for them, and allowed the dead to take part in religious rituals and celebrations. By the Late period, commemorative statues were almost totally covered with an inscribed autobiography of the dead person extolling his many virtues and great deeds – no doubt the way he would choose both to meet the gods and to be remembered on earth.

The tomb: a house for eternity

The ancient Egyptian word for house and tomb was the same – *per*. So there was a house during life and a house after death, the one for the body, the other for the spiritual aspects that inhabited the shadowy world of the afterlife.

In earliest times, the dead were curled into a foetal position, no doubt associated with the idea of rebirth. The body was placed on its left side in a simple hollow in the sand, with its head generally to the south and the face towards the west. So it seems that the idea of the west being the place of entrance into another existence may well have been in the minds of Nile dwellers long before it was written down. Nor did it take long for the living to start to make this eternal desert bed more comfortable. First the body was laid upon a mat, with another rolled mat or a pad of linen to serve as a pillow; a final mat was laid over the body to shield it from the sand. Then it was only a short step from this to the use of simple wooden coffins – the panels and the barrel-vaulted lid copying, it is believed, the houses of the living.

Physical provision for the dead improved as the expectations of the living improved. At the cemeteries of Naqada and Hieraconpolis, in Upper Egypt, excavations have revealed areas where some tombs exceeded in size and quality those of adjacent burials. These larger tombs were undoubtedly the eternal homes of the chiefs of the regions. The burial pit was lined with either mud bricks or stone to create a neat vault. Over the top, large wooden timbers formed ceilings; and in some of them, small side chambers were provided around the burial chamber where jars of food and drink, garments and perfumes for the body could be stored. In a few of these tombs, the walls were plastered over. In the finest of six large tombs in Hieraconpolis so far examined (known as Painted Tomb 100), these

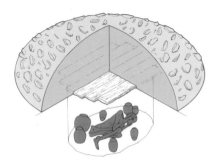

In Predynastic burials *the body was placed in a shallow oval pit in a flexed position, its head to the south, the face to the west. Grave goods, such as pottery, surround the body. The pits were often roofed with wood and a pile of stones placed over the top.*

Painted tomb 100 *at Hieraconpolis is of late Predynastic date and its walls (left) were covered with scenes of everyday life. Significantly, there are depictions of funerary boats and mourners as well as symbols of kingship. It is therefore likely that this tomb contained the burial of a chieftain.*

walls were painted with scenes similar to those on the jars of the living. Here for the first time scenes from life were portrayed, though crude in comparison with later pictures. In this instance, the funeral of a chief was shown, with mourners in attendance. Around the funerary boats, activities of the living – the taming of animals, the conquest of enemies – perhaps feats of the dead leader, were shown.

Examination of cemeteries from later periods shows that improvements in standards in tombs began with the higher ranks and then spread down to the lower classes. The idea of side chambers, of increasing quantities of grave goods, and of more substantial walls around the tomb spread from the chiefs to their families and officials within a few years.

Abydos: burial place of Osiris

Around this time, Abydos, a town that lies on the west bank of the Nile, some 60 miles (100 km) north of Luxor, emerged as a particularly sacred site. From the time of the Middle Kingdom, Egyptians placed cenotaphs (funeral monuments of people buried elsewhere) and stelae there. In later periods, the importance of Abydos was explained in terms of its role as the burial place of the god of the dead, Osiris.

A papyrus now in Turin records that the Egyptians believed that before human beings existed, the gods themselves ruled Egypt. And according to the Greek writer Plutarch, Osiris was once a great king of Egypt, the person who introduced agriculture into the Nile valley. During the Ramesside period, the tombs of the kings of Egypt's first two dynasties were discovered by priests on the desert plain behind the town of Abydos. They were perceived as being so old that some of the priests identified one of them as the tomb of Osiris himself. But there is no evidence that the first kings had been buried at Abydos for reasons of its holiness or even that these kings considered Osiris as being the local god of Abydos. The Pyramid Texts refer to Osiris only as a god among other gods.

Saqqara: early mastaba tombs

When, eventually, Upper Egypt conquered Lower Egypt, and formed a united country that extended right to the Mediterranean, Abydos must have been considered too remote from the delta for the king to exercise his authority effectively. So, around 3100 BC, or perhaps slightly later, Memphis was founded at the junction of the valley and the delta.

The wealth that must have flowed into the newly established capital would have made the royal officials men of enormous prestige and power, for it was they who controlled all the produce and imports of the new united country – and it might be expected that the size and equipping of their tombs at Saqqara would reflect this. Excavations at Saqqara, beginning in 1934, have uncovered the remains of massive mud-brick rectangular tombs, which proved to belong to the officials

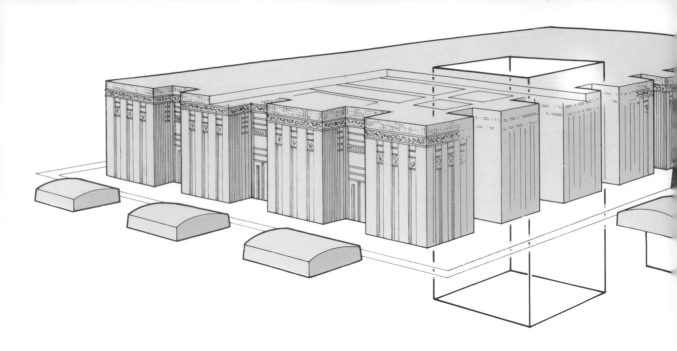

of the rulers of the first two dynasties. The elements of these so-called mastaba tombs, burial chamber, store rooms, false door and, sometimes, boat pits, were archetypes of later structures and present (in some way) in all of them.

The burial chambers of these tombs lay underground, cut out from the rock and mainly undecorated, although some were panelled in wood. The body of the deceased, in a wooden coffin, was lowered in place through the roof of the superstructure. Only one intact burial from this period has ever been found, but if that burial can be taken as an indication of standard, it would appear that at that time the body was probably simply wrapped in linen bandages. When the burial was complete, the underground chamber was roofed over, and the upper storechambers were then packed with goods that the *ka* was thought to need in its afterlife. But the roof proved an easy way of entry for robbers – and almost all the mastabas at Saqqara so far found have been violated.

The Step Pyramid

The Step Pyramid at Saqqara, built for the Third Dynasty king Netcherikhe, better known as Djoser, developed from a single mastaba. The plan was evidently the invention of Djoser's architect, Imhotep, who after enlarging the initial tomb, added a series of five superimposed mastabas in decreasing size on top, thus forming a pyramid of steps. Imhotep was also a priest of Heliopolis, a centre of sun worship, and there is a theory that the steps may have been seen as symbolizing the dead king's ascent to the sun. The burial chamber

Massive mastaba tombs (above), with mud-brick walls imitating palace façades, developed during the Archaic period – the First and Second Dynasties. The mastabas were surrounded by a low wall. The largest of these tombs belonged to officials of the earliest kings and queens and were surrounded by smaller tombs containing bodies of their followers; the mastabas of courtiers were surrounded by servant burials. The underground burial chamber was in the center, and filled with rubble after the body was in place beneath the superstructure. This building was subdivided into chambers for grave goods, which (like the body) were put in place from above. When preparations were completed, the whole complex was roofed over – there was no entrance. This elaborate style was gradually simplified into the more familiar mastabas of courtiers, such as those seen at Saqqara.

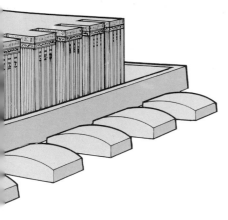

was designed to be underground as was customary, but instead of rooms in the superstructure for the provision of burial goods, storehouses and magazines were erected separately in the immediate vicinity of the pyramid. The *ka* of the king, inhabiting the burial chamber, needed a place through which it could emerge to gain the benefit of the funerary equipment. As a result, against the northern face of the pyramid, a mortuary chapel was built. And it was here every day that royally appointed priests would bring offerings of food and drink. On the common wall of the pyramid and chapel, a false door was carved in the stone through which the *ka* could gain access to the offerings.

Mastaba tombs of Djoser's courtiers

Djoser's Step Pyramid complex seems to have been designed as a copy in stone of the palace in Memphis that he had occupied during his life. And just as the palace would have been surrounded by the smaller houses of the king's family and courtiers, so his tomb was surrounded by the tombs of courtiers. These tombs were built in a similar manner to the mastabas of the courtiers of the first two dynasties, but they were now erected in stone and not mud brick.

The tombs of the nobility at Saqqara are some of the finest ever found in Egypt. The burial chamber, undecorated in any way, still lay underground. The walls of the chambers above ground were erected in fine-grained white limestone that had been quarried nearby. The upper rooms acted as a mortuary chapel to which offerings could be brought, and the walls of these rooms are delicately carved in raised relief, and show every stage of the provision of these offerings. Food is not only shown carried in the hands of offering bearers, but through the entire process of growth and preparation. Boats are depicted being made, from the cutting of the timbers to the rigging of the

Djoser's Step Pyramid *at Saqqara (right) was constructed in stages, as shown in this isometric view. It indicates the three building stages of the original mastaba (1, 2 and 3), the shafts leading to the subsidiary tombs (4) and the internal buttress walls (5) of the superimposed pyramid structure. The initial pyramid with four steps (6) was first extended to the north and west (7) and then further enlarged and raised to a height of six steps (8).*

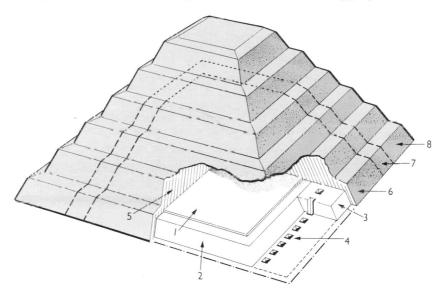

In Mereruka's *Sixth Dynasty mastaba tomb at Saqqara, his life-like* ka *statue (left) seemingly steps out from the wall to accept the offerings brought to the false door – and to greet the modern tourists who, by voicing his name once more, keep alive his immortality.*

The delicately carved *figures from the Old Kingdom tomb of Ptah-hotep at Saqqara (below), are part of a procession of people (each of whom personifies one of Ptah-hotep's estates) bearing offerings for the deceased. Long after actual food and drink have ceased to be brought by dutiful relatives and priests, the gifts brought by these silent figures magically sustain the* ka *in the afterlife.*

finished vessel. Some of these were obviously provided to carry the soul of the deceased south to Abydos to join in the festivities of regrowth. It is apparent that the burial site of the first kings at Abydos was already attracting an aura of mysticism that would be exaggerated in future periods.

The focal point of the upper chambers was a false door, located close to the entrance to the underground room, indicating that the *ka* of the deceased was expected to rise from the burial chamber into the upper chambers whenever food and drink offerings were provided. To focus the attention of the *ka*, an image of the deceased was often carved in the middle of the false door. In the tomb of Mereruka, the owner is shown as a three-dimensional statue which actually appears to be stepping out from the solid wall. In that of Neferseshemptah, he is depicted, unusually, as rising head and shoulders from the ground. In these tombs, in front of the false door was an offering table, cut in the shape of the hieroglyph *hetep* ('offering'). Sometimes images of food and drink were carved on the table, as if the images themselves could replace the actual food if the offering were forgotten.

Magic in the tomb

The details of what burial goods were actually provided within the chambers of the mastabas is still open to question. In many of the tomb inscriptions, the hieroglyphs were shown mutilated: snakes cut in half or pierced by knives, bulls without horns, lions, scorpions and bees beheaded, implying that the figures themselves were capable of taking on a life of their own, that they might actually harm the deceased. If this were true, then one could take it that the offering scenes on the walls could well have been seen as sufficient to provide the *ka* with everything needed after death.

There is no indication in the inscriptions or the pictures carved at this time that the soul of the deceased courtier was expected to live eternally in any other place. Depictions of the gods, the judgment of the dead and signs of any expectations of a land of the dead are missing. It would appear that only the *ka* and *ba* of the deceased were thought to survive, and they were expected to remain in the proximity of the tomb. If the pictures could supply their eternal needs, and the public areas of the tomb were entered, then there would be little need for the actual objects to be provided. In any event, no mastaba yet entered has contained anything significant in terms of intact funerary goods.

Pyramids: tombs of the god kings

As Egypt's wealth grew, her king became a living god, and efforts were made to create a tomb that fitted his status and, in death as in life, set him apart from other men. And so developed that most distinctive and famous of all funerary monuments – the pyramid. Over forty monumental pyramids – not all of them royal – have been discovered, dating from the Old Kingdom to the end of the Middle Kingdom, when they ceased to be built. Some are surrounded by one or more smaller, subsidiary pyramids (including these, the total number would probably be more than doubled). Some are unfinished, others are in a state of collapse. A few are similar to Djoser's Step Pyramid, and at least one is designated as 'bent' because of the change in its angle. But to the modern mind, the classic pyramid shape is smooth-sided and none fascinates more than the Great Pyramid at Giza, near Cairo. This massive structure was originally 481.4 feet (146 m) high, but the top 31 feet (9.6 m) are now missing; its sides are each 775 feet (238.5 m) long and its base covers approximately 13 acres. It was constructed of over two and a half million stone blocks, most of which weighed $2\frac{1}{2}$ tons (but some were many times this weight).

The form that the pyramids took, according to texts which appeared in the last of these monuments built in the Old Kingdom, was deliberately intended to recreate the mound that the Egyptians believed emerged from the waters of chaos at the time of creation. From the peak of this mound, the gods and then human beings were believed to have arisen. In a similar way, from the peak of the

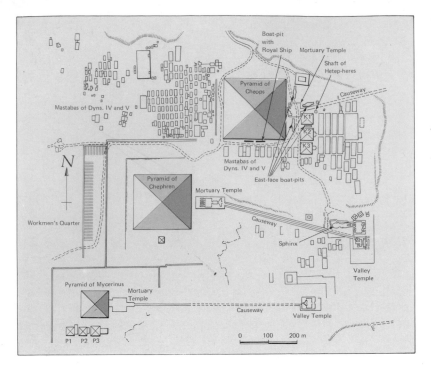

pyramid, the soul of the king – alone of all his people – was believed to be reborn in an afterlife. The Pyramid Texts suggest that in earliest times the soul was supposed to ascend to the stars. By the time the last pyramids were built, it was held that the soul of the king joined the sun in its passage across the heavens.

The pyramids built by the succesors of the Third Dynasty followed a set pattern. The structure itself was erected on a high and rocky part of the plateau. During construction, stone was dragged on sledges up a long causeway connecting the pyramid with a canal or the river itself. After completion, the causeway was roofed over, its walls delicately carved like those of the superstructure chambers of the adjacent mastabas. At the head of the causeway, a mortuary chapel contained a carved false door through which the soul of the king could emerge. At its foot, near the river, a valley temple was built, and this was probably the place where the body of the king was prepared for burial. During the Fourth Dynasty, purification, mummification and the Opening of the Mouth ceremony took place here. Eventually, these procedures were carried out in the mortuary temple. The causeway and attached buildings equated with the superstructures of the mastabas.

Royal grave goods

If the pyramid was seen solely as the means by which the soul of the king attained its afterlife, then there would have been little reason to include any treasure within its chambers. If funerary goods were

XVII The Step Pyramid *of Djoser and his architect Imhotep dominates the horizon at Saqqara today as it did when it was built some 4,600 years ago.*

XVIII An aerial view *of the Giza plateau reveals the scale of the enormous city of the dead that grew up around the three monumental Fourth Dynasty pyramids.*

included in the pyramid complex, it is reasonable to suppose that they would have been placed within the peripheral buildings (as they would have been placed in the mastaba superstructure). But no pyramid has been found unrobbed; and no royal burial chamber from the Old Kingdom has been found to contain anything other than an empty stone sarcophagus, minor remains and fragments of material.

An indication that funerary goods were sometimes placed within some of Old Kingdom burial structures can be seen in the contents of the tomb of Queen Hetepheres, mother of Cheops, builder of the Great Pyramid. This material, including some of the earliest furniture found anywhere in the world, was found in 1925 in a shaft, some 99 feet (30.4 m) deep, near her son's pyramid at Giza. Although badly damaged by dampness, careful excavation made possible a reconstruction of pieces of furniture including a bed with a silver headrest and an elaborately gilded canopy frame, two armchairs, and a palanquin, or carrying chair. In addition, there was a gold-covered box for the curtains of the canopy; silver bracelets, engraved with the queen's name and titles and inlaid with lapis lazuli, malachite and carnelian; eight alabaster vases filled with unguents, a manicure set of gold; and some gold and copper vases. On the whole, this seems a modest assemblage for the mother of the greatest pharaoh to have ruled during the Old Kingdom. But the tomb itself is still a mystery, for although the viscera of the queen were found in the canopic jars, her body was missing – all these grave goods surrounded an empty sarcophagus. (The theory of the discoverer, George Reisner, was that Hetepheres had been buried at Dahshur near her husband Snofru's pyramid; later her son found that her tomb had been robbed, and ordered a reburial at Giza. Recent research has, however, strongly called this into question and rejects the Giza site as a reburial.)

Changing expectations after the Old Kingdom

The collapse of royal power at the end of the Old Kingdom and the rise of an independent nobility brought about a change in beliefs. Now every Egyptian, not just the king, could expect to ascend to the land of the gods.

During the confused years at the start of the Middle Kingdom, the provincial tombs of the nobility had to be decorated and provisioned by local craftsmen untrained in the national traditions of funerary art. And so, a third type of Egyptian tomb was created – the rock-cut tomb. These burial monuments were cut in the cliff faces, far south of Saqqara, and often on the east bank of the Nile. Local artisans simply levelled the tomb walls so that they could be painted. Registers (horizontal bands) on the walls show consecutive figures of men engaged in military training and wrestling, and of women dancing and singing. Although some scenes, such as those of hunting and fishing, of bird catching and of boats sailing to Abydos, can be interpreted as references to ideas of a future existence, they could equally refer to events that took place during someone's lifetime. The

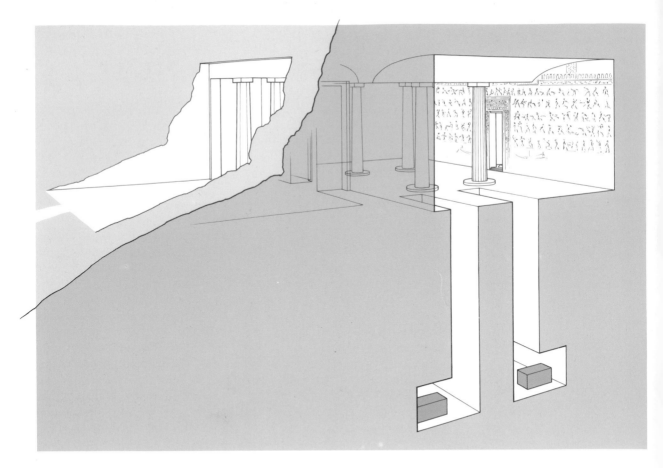

burial chambers, still underground and entered from a shaft sunk in one of the inner rooms, were plain and undecorated, with space only for a coffin or sarcophagus. On a nearby wall, a false door would be painted through which the *ka* could enter the upper chambers to receive offerings of food and drink.

Just as in earlier years the tombs of the nobility had formed 'cities' around the pyramids, so now the burial chambers of the families and nobles who served the local rulers, or mayors, were clustered into the hillsides in front of their rock-cut tombs. Often there were hundreds of subterranean burial chambers in the vicinity of each major tomb. These small chambers contained the owner's body in a painted coffin and, on top of each, a bewildering selection of painted wooden models were provided. As in Old Kingdom times, the needs of the *ka* of the deceased were met through depictions on the walls, but now they were also met by the activities of these models. Tiny jointed figures, often dressed in miniature linen kilts, represented workers of all varieties – butchers, bakers, brewers, carpenters.

At the end of the Old Kingdom, the nature of the god Osiris had begun to change. From the Pyramid Texts it was already evident that Osiris had begun to fuse with the characteristics of Khentiamentiu of

Rock-cut tombs *of the Middle Kingdom (above) cluster along the cliffs that line the Nile banks far south of the ancient capital of Memphis, at such places as Beni Hasan and Meir. They had porticoed entrances, and the walls of their large, bright, columned halls were covered not only with funerary scenes, but also those depicting everyday activities – wrestling, games, dancing, hunting. The coffins of the tomb owner and his wife were set in small chambers off shafts below the floor of the tomb.*

The characteristic coffins *found in many Middle Kingdom burials were accompanied by miniature models depicting the activities of everyday life. The photograph above shows a complete set of models as they were found in Tomb 366 in Beni Hasan. These models were meant to work for the deceased in the afterlife and included such things as butchers slaughtering cattle; women carrying water, rolling grain for flour and making dough; brewers soaking barley for beer; and fishermen and boats.*

Abydos, and that now he was associated with ideas of resurrection. And new ideas were starting to be represented on the coffins themselves. Texts on the outer surfaces referred to Osiris as 'Foremost of the Westerners' (or god of the dead), and Anubis as the guardian of the dead. On the inside of the coffins, new spells were painted. These Coffin Texts show the fear now felt by these people as their *akhs* proceeded through complex and twisting routes, filled with perils, that would lead them to another existence. On the interior floor of these coffins, the first maps were painted: diagrams of the rivers, fields, mountains and roads of the world of the dead, which had to be traversed.

The Valley of the Kings

By the time of the New Kingdom, around 1550 BC, the pharaohs no longer felt confident in the security that a pyramid could offer. The necessity for the provision of daily food and drink offerings for the *ka* remained unchanged. But the positioning of the mortuary chapel itself was now reviewed, and rulers chose to separate their tombs from their mortuary chapels in the hope of diverting potential robbers. Moreover, since the living entered only the mortuary chapel and

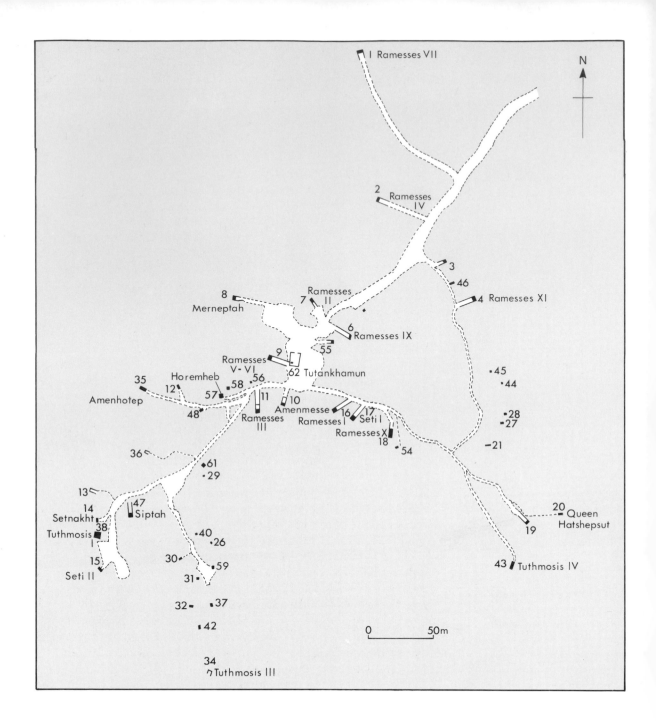

N

1 Ramesses VII

2 Ramesses IV

3

46

4 Ramesses XI

8

Merneptah

7 Ramesses II

6 Ramesses IX

55

9

62 Tutankhamun

Ramesses V-VI

35

Horemheb

45

44

12 58 56

Amenhotep

57

48

11

10

Amenmesse

28

27

36

16 17 Seti I

Ramesses I

21

Ramesses III

Ramesses X

18 54

61

29

13

20 Queen

14

47

Setnakht Siptah

19 Hatshepsut

Tuthmosis I

38

40

26

15

30

43 Tuthmosis IV

Seti II

59

31

32 37

42

34

Tuthmosis III

0   50m

never the burial place, the separation of the two funerary locations meant that richer offerings could be placed inside the tomb.

The kings of the New Kingdom also chose an unknown site for their burials in the area of Luxor from which the royal family came. A suitable area on the west bank, two quiet and hidden valleys behind the hills, were selected. The tombs were cut into the rock like the cliff tombs of the provincial nobility, but these royal burial places were revolutionary in style and truly grand in their execution, with large, high corridors and chambers, and painted in brilliant colours. The first tomb excavated here was that of Tuthmosis I, whose adviser and architect Ineni records that he built the tomb of his king in utmost secrecy, 'no one seeing, no one hearing'.

Records found at Deir el Medina, the village which housed the tomb builders and their families, clearly detail the process of excavation and decoration. The site was considered secure, and instead of a maze of labyrinthine passages and false entrances such as the pyramids contained, the tombs descended straight into the heart of the rock, sometimes as much as 600 yards (500 m) deep.

Inscriptions painted on the long walls of the passages in some of the tombs show that the *ka* of the king was believed to enter the world of the dead along with the setting sun. Here, like the sun god himself, the king had to overcome attackers to emerge safely the following dawn into the land of the living. The royal *ka* would then accompany the boat of the sun across the sky during the day, but must once more enter the tomb at dusk for another journey into the afterlife. The tomb was seen as this passage. And so the corridors follow a sequence, from the doorway inwards: the direction that the *ka* must follow daily.

The various halls, inscribed with spells to attract the soul ever downwards, culminate in two rooms, the first known as the 'Hall of Chariots'. On the evidence of the tombs of Tuthmosis IV and Tutankhamun, this could perhaps have been interpreted literally as the place in which the king's chariots were placed. Beyond this lay the 'Hall of Gold', in which stood a stone sarcophagus, holding the king's coffins. The innermost might well have been made of gold. And no doubt the royal sarcophagus would have been enclosed in a series of gilded shrines, whose walls contained additional spells. These gave the *akh* of the king access to a different afterlife, often identified with the god Osiris. Just as the living monarch had been seen as Horus (the son of Osiris), so at his death his *akh* assumed the persona of Osiris himself. There were frequently side rooms off the burial chamber, known as 'Treasuries', which might have been meant to hold precious objects, including the viscera of the king, stored in a canopic chest.

Interestingly, pits, or wells, were cut in these passages. Their purpose is a matter of modern debate, but they may have been intended either to cope with the torrential floods that occur sporadically in the valley, or to trap unwary robbers attempting to find their way to the burial chamber through the pitch black of the tomb.

A ROYAL TOMB IN THE VALLEY OF THE KINGS

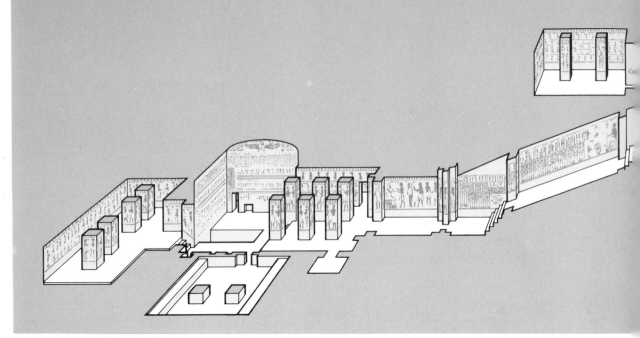

The tomb of Seti I *is grand in size and visually stunning as befits this great warrior king who was the father of Ramesses II. The tomb is one of the longest of all in the valley, descending hundreds of feet down into the rock (right to left); and finely painted examples of several of the major funerary texts fill its walls.*

After the first staircase, just inside the entrance, Seti makes an *offering to the sun god. This is followed by the text of the Litany of Re, a New Kingdom religious composition, showing the god Re in all his manifestations.*

Along the walls of the second staircase and the following corridor are scenes from the Book of What Is in the Underworld. The deep well room shows Seti making offerings to a number of gods. Two small columned rooms *continue on from the well room and were probably meant to confuse robbers. Scenes here are from the Book of What Is in the Underworld and the Book of Gates, but in the second room are unfinished.*

A staircase in the middle of the tomb takes us into a second set of chambers that actually end in the burial chamber. The first two corridors (the second just past a

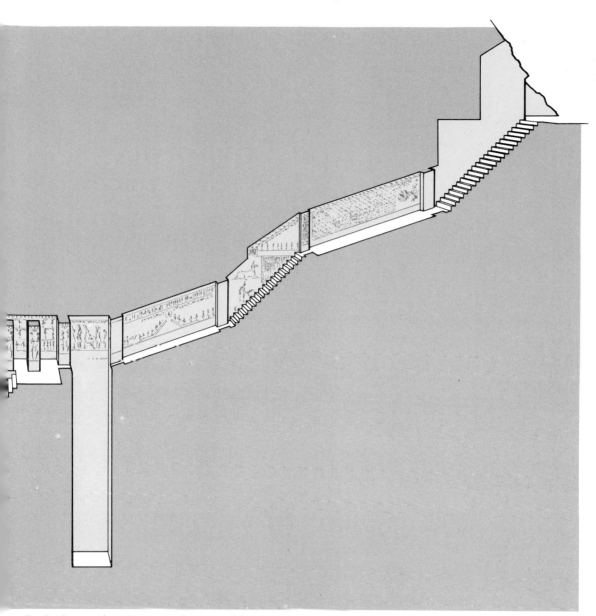

final, short series of stairs) shows
funerary rituals such as the
Opening of the Mouth and the
ritual offering list. Just before the
large columned hall (the burial
chamber) are more scenes of Seti
offering to the gods.

Finally, we reach the burial
chamber itself, with a recess that
once held the sarcophagus. The
walls are covered with vignettes
from the Book of What Is in the
Underworld; the ceiling is an
astronomical map of the heavens.
The large side chamber, which
contained the royal grave goods,
is decorated not only with
funerary texts, but also with
depictions of funerary equipment,
such as amulets and shrines.
Smaller side chambers contain
illustrations from the Book of
Gates and the Book of the
Heavenly Cow.

This relief from *the tomb of Ramose (Tomb 55 of the tombs of the nobles on the west bank at Luxor), shows Amenhotep and the Lady May, the brother and sister-in-law of Ramose – also Ramose's parents-in-law, since he appears to have married his niece. Theirs was obviously a powerful family, Ramose was a vizier under Amenhotep III and Akhenaten, his brother was a high official and chamberlain. Amenhotep holds a sceptre signifying his rank and around his neck is a double 'gold of honour' collar given to him by the king. In this delicately detailed scene, Amenhotep and May sit among their family at a banquet.*

Funerary cones *were set into the clay in rows over tomb entrances, and have been found dating from the Eleventh Dynasty. But during the New Kingdom they were stamped with the name and titles of the deceased. The cone face shown below reads: "The Osiris, the Hereditary Noble and Prince, the Fourth Prophet of Amun, the Scribe of the Temple of Amun, the Controller of the Prophets, the Governor of the South, Montemhet, justified.'*

The design changed somewhat through the 500-year history of the royal cemetery. The earliest of the valley tombs were simpler – that is, they had fewer chambers – and, in plan, also generally turned at an angle just before or after the burial chamber. By the end of the Eighteenth Dynasty, however, the plan was straight; the tombs of the Ramesside pharaohs were very long indeed and sometimes the number of chambers within the tomb were doubled – in which case the exact sequence repeated itself; the burial chamber was the final room of the repetition.

Mortuary temples of the New Kingdom

The royal mortuary complexes were located a few miles away from the Valley of the Kings, between the hills and the fertile strip on the west bank at Luxor. Each was designed on the same plan as an ordinary religious, or cult, temple (i.e. one for the worship of a god). It may have been at the mortuary temple that the king's body was prepared for its last journey; and where, later, daily offerings were made to sustain his *ka*. It seems, however, that the cult of a royal *ka* did not last long after the pharaoh's death. Examination of the mortuary temples on the west bank at Luxor reveals that successive kings used the mortuary temples of their predecessors as ready-made stone quarries. It appears that a king felt few qualms about demolishing an earlier temple – even if it had belonged to his own father.

Rock tombs of the nobles

The hills in front of the Valley of the Kings, facing the Nile, are honeycombed with the burial places of nobles and courtiers from the Middle Kingdom onwards. But those of the New Kingdom are some of the finest in all Egypt, and their wall paintings are beyond compare. The tombs were modest in size, and shaped like a letter T, with a transverse chamber inside the entrance doorway, and a long chamber beyond. In the floor of this long chamber, or sometimes just outside the entrance to the tomb, was cut the entrance to the underground burial chamber. The entrance to the tomb was marked with the owner's name and titles on a baked clay cone which was pushed into soft mud laid over the lintel. (These first appeared in the Eleventh Dynasty, but became common during the early New Kingdom.) The interior walls of the tombs were smoothed and then plastered over, the plaster layer becoming increasingly thicker the later in the New Kingdom the tomb was cut. Over this plaster layer, registers of painted pictures show not only aspects of daily life in Egypt, but also the expectations of the ordinary person of his or her afterlife: a life in a land of pleasure, cool verdant trees, unlimited food and drink, eternal youthfulness and constant happiness in the company of loved ones.

Several tombs of the period have been found intact, and contained the body of the owner, often with that of his wife and perhaps some of his children, all laid in painted anthropoid wooden coffins. An innovation that appeared at this time was the laying of a painted linen shroud over the top of the coffin. Tomb equipment was generally simple, from a few pieces of furniture to ordinary funerary statues or *ushabti* figures.

It is now known that, contemporaneously with the painted tombs at Luxor, even grander carved and painted tombs were being built at the Memphite cemetery of Saqqara for the high officials. Here the tombs resembled miniature pyramid complexes, with outer walls, subsidiary buildings, and deep underground shafts cut into the bedrock. Some of these even had small pyramids at one end of an open courtyard. The shafts were deep and led to burial chambers whose walls are painted, though not as brilliantly as those in Luxor. Scenes portrayed the gods and goddesses who presided over the afterlife rather than scenes of life in Memphis. It is becoming increasingly apparent that the carving of superb raised reliefs at Giza and Saqqara did not cease with the end of the Old Kingdom – on the contrary, the tombs of Luxor may, in time, prove to be provincial adaptations of the national style.

After the Valley of the Kings

In the second half of the Eighteenth Dynasty, Egyptian tombs began to reflect a new seriousness of purpose. Their owners seem to have been obsessed with appeasing the gods who may have been offended during the brief rule of Akhenaten and the sun god, the Aten, that he promoted. Tombs dating from the end of the New Kingdom became more sombre places, peopled by deities – a custom that may well have spread south from Saqqara. From around 1200 BC, the kings increasingly chose to abandon Luxor and to spend most of their time in their delta palace. The Valley of the Kings was finally abandoned during the reign of the last Ramesses, the eleventh of that name. The workmen deserted Deir el Medina and with their families moved into the precincts of the mortuary temple of Ramesses III, now called Medinet Habu. The valleys of the west bank of Luxor no longer rang with the sounds of artisans, no more royal tombs were cut there, and the only movement was that of drifting sand. From now on, the kings of Egypt were once again buried in the north.

The royal burials of the Third Intermediate period discovered at Tanis were mean affairs, in comparison with royal tombs of the New Kingdom. The chambers were small, barely large enough to contain the sarcophagus. The amount of burial equipment provided for each of the royal interments was meagre. Although the bodies of the pharaohs were encased in coffins of gold and silver, much of the material had been reused, borrowed from the burials of previous rulers. Osorkon III was found inside a coffin belonging to Takeloth II; the finest burial, that of Psusennes I, was laid within a coffin of Amenemope, while his viscera were in canopic jars bearing the inscriptions of four different kings who had died over a century earlier.

The tomb of Psusennes *at Tanis in the delta was entered in 1940 by Pierre Montet. The silver coffin, containing the body of the Twenty-first Dynasty pharaoh, lay within two sarcophagi, the inner of black granite, the outer of pink granite. On the top of the outer one, the sculptured body of Psusennes lies outstretched, his arms holding the royal regalia – the crook and flail – and crossed on his chest. Kneeling behind him, her arms outstretched and gently, protectively touching the sides of his head, is the carved figure of the goddess of the north wind.*

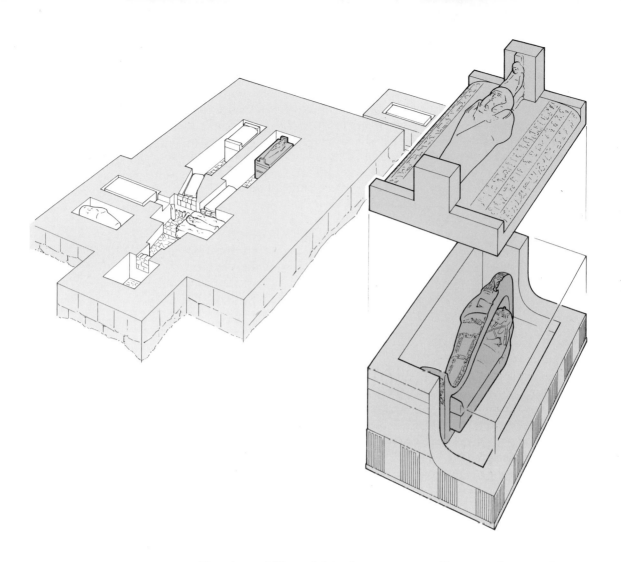

For the nobility of this chaotic time in Egyptian history, burial equipment focused on a superbly decorated coffin, frequently made of cartonnage. This consisted of layers of linen or papyrus wrapped around the bandages and then impregnated with plaster or resin until they hardened to form a solid impenetrable shell. In some cases, these coffins must have been made on a mould and later split, because a cut the length of the coffin was frequently stitched on the back. Within the cases, all the protection the deceased might need would be included in the form of amulets and papyri. Instead of a tomb for each individual, earlier tombs were reused and the mummies in their coffins placed together in large groups.

Foreign influences on Egyptian tombs
In the eighth century B C, under a series of Nubian rulers, there was a revival of the finest of Egyptian traditions. And the courtiers began

once more to build splendid tombs. At Saqqara and in Luxor, rock-cut chambers were again decorated with carved scenes – but they were copied directly from tombs often more than a thousand years old. The artists copied pictures exactly, their carvings and paintings often exceeding in fineness of detail the ancient originals. At Saqqara, a great underground catacomb was created with spaces cut out of the stone exactly in the form and size of a mummy; rows of mummies were then placed neatly within them.

The Persians, who took the throne in the Twenty-Seventh Dynasty, appointed deputies, or satraps, to rule for them. Princely burials from this time at Saqqara consist of underground chambers at the foot of very deep shafts. The whole shaft was filled with sand, and the sarcophagus placed over the top. A long, sloping tunnel to the bottom of the shaft was built with its entrance at some distance. As loose sand was removed through the tunnel, the sarcophagus slowly descended to rest on the bottom of the shaft itself, which was then filled with rubble and sand. Emphasis was still on the coffins and the provisioning of the mummy rather than in the supply of elaborate funeral equipment.

The arrival of the Greeks in the fifth century BC heralded a new era in funerary beliefs. A few tombs of the early Greek era can be seen at Tuna el Gebel, which was the necropolis of the Middle Egyptian city of Ashmunein. The superstructures of these tombs were temples in miniature. Their wall reliefs depicted the supply of food and drink offerings. It is as if the wheel of time had turned full circle, for the scenes shown here resemble in almost every way those of the Saqqara mastabas that were then over 2,000 years old – the only exception being the Greek dress worn.

During the Roman period, burial customs became confused. Roman citizens, often mummified according to old Egyptian customs, and dressed in everyday clothes, were laid to rest in low, barrel-vaulted brick vaults above the ground. Their stelae were carved in a mixture of Egyptian and Roman style. With the introduction of Christianity, another type of burial evolved, for the Coptic Christians, unmummified, were generally buried in simple graves with no special grave goods.

Over the full era of pharaonic history, beliefs in the afterlife underwent significant changes and with them, changes in the equipping of tombs and the expectations of an afterlife. But probably only some two per cent of the population at any time could have afforded a tomb at all. For the remainder, burial involved the digging of a hollow in the sand and the placing of the deceased in a shallow grave, equipped with the few possessions with which the bereaved could afford to part. Presumably the beliefs of the Egyptians placed in these simple graves would have reflected those of the better-off minorities. Through Osiris, every person had the hope of a joyous eternity dependent not on wealth, but on truth and honesty; and in their graves and tombs, these expectations would have been manifest.

Chapter Five
Gods, Spells and Amulets

TO THE EGYPTIANS magic was a real and potent force. What we might trivialize and dismiss as superstition was for the ancients a tangible method of communicating with the gods and seeking their favour. The very words used when reciting the sacred rites were considered to have power, for sound itself was an important and mystical element. In the embalming and funerary rituals the written word became reality as the priests spoke the spells, and spoke them in tones that imbued them with an other-worldliness.

Just as speaking had the ability to bring life to the dead, and allow humanity to gain the ear of the gods, so the wearing or keeping of images of gods or sacred symbols had another kind of power. These small images were known as amulets. Some took the form of the gods themselves, of animals connected with specific deities, or parts of the human body. Other amulets represented abstractions, the *ankh* symbolizing life, for instance. Wearing amulets during life was a way of seeking the gods' protection. But after death, a special protection indeed was required, for this had to last through all eternity.

Communicating with the gods

It is easy to conclude from tomb paintings that the Egyptians worshipped dozens of gods. But, in fact, the ordinary Egyptian would have recognized very few deities. Foremost of these would have been the god of the immediate area, statues of whom stood in the local temple beyond the sight of all but the priests. This deity was conceived of as an ancestral hero whose *ka*, if treated correctly, would bring benefit to every individual still living within his locality. The Egyptian would be unlikely to have worshipped this god, as we understand it, but would rather have negotiated with him.

Bargaining with the gods
As a first step in this procedure, gifts were offered to attract the attention of the god. If the offering was seen as acceptable, the god might consider the request favourably. Should the gifts be insufficient for the god to hear the plea, more gifts could be offered. As a last resort the supplicant could make one final strong demand. Should this too fail, the donor might actually curse the soul of the divine, for not responding in the expected manner.

Each local god had a 'wife', a goddess associated with him, and this female deity was the being to whom the women of the village or town made their pleas. The divine couples often had a son or daughter, the unit frequently represented as a triad, and thus taking on the familiar shape of a family and giving the goddess the enhanced status of the mother.

From the time of the Middle Kingdom, the Egyptians tried to attract the attention of demigods within their houses. Figures of Bes, a little dwarf god, would bring luck and good humour and might divert anger and sadness; those of Taweret, a standing, pregnant hippopotamus, would help women to conceive, or to survive childbirth. Strangest of all, perhaps, was Meskhent, the birth stool of each person which, because it was the first object encountered on earth, could be blamed when things went wrong. These were not gods in the true understanding of the word, but more like talismans.

A deity recognized by all Egyptians was Maat, a goddess shown as a woman with a standing feather on her head, and who represented all that was the opposite of chaos. If Maat were satisfied, she would bring equilibrium and balance to daily life. And when the heart of the deceased was judged by gods, it was weighed against the feather of truth, symbolizing the goddess Maat. The individual Egyptian could have done very little to influence Maat – this lay in the all-powerful hand of the pharaoh.

Gods of the dead

The only deities that the Egyptians undoubtedly feared were the gods of the dead, chief of whom was Osiris, who was killed by his jealous brother Seth and went on to become the ruler of the Duat, the

The gods of the dead *can be divided into two groups, those to do with the Judgment of the Dead and those who presided over and protected the inhabitants of the underworld.*

The first four gods shown below are part of the judgment (left to right): Thoth, the scribe who recorded the actions of life; Anubis, who supervised the balancing of the heart on the scales; Haroeris (Horus the Edler), who guided the deceased through the chambers of the underworld; and Maat, whose feather symbolizing truth was weighed against the heart of the dead person.

In the middle, seated on a throne, is Osiris, chief deity of the underworld. Behind him stand four goddesses who protected the dead (left to right): Isis, sister and wife of Osiris; Nephthys, sister of Osiris and wife of Seth; Neith, with crossed bows on her head; and Selket, with her scorpion headdress. These four goddesses are carved at the corners of the sarcophagus of Tutankhamun and gilded statues of them surround the canopic chest holding his internal organs.

Egyptian underworld. It was in the Middle Kingdom that Osiris came to be regarded as the chief god of the underworld. As such he is represented in the form of a mummy, wearing a royal crown and beard. Anubis was the jackal-headed god of cemeteries, who played a crucial role in the embalming process. One of his titles was 'Foremost of the Westerners', showing his prominence in the West, the land of the dead. (By association, Osiris came to take on this title as well.) Anubis was involved in the Opening of the Mouth ceremony at the time of burial and, when the heart of a dead person was weighed against the feather of Maat, it was Anubis who balanced the scales.

Osiris had two sisters, Isis (also his wife) and Nephthys. In Old Kingdom mythology, Nephthys leads the pharaoh into the land of the dead. The king's mummy wrappings were referred to as the 'tresses of Nephthys'. But her role, which appears to have lessened with time, is not clear. She and Isis are two of the protective goddesses who appear at each of the corners of the great gold shrine that enclosed the sarcophagus of Tutankhamun.

Hathor, 'Lady of the West', was the protectress of the cemetery at Luxor. She protected the dead as they made their way along dangerous paths to the underworld.

The god Thoth, who presided over writing and knowledge, was the scribe of the gods, and known for his wisdom, honesty and uprightness. He recorded all that was on the hearts of those who entered the underworld and, as the heart was weighed, it was Thoth who wrote the result.

The world of the temple

On temple walls, hieroglyphic inscriptions recounted stories connected with the local god or the founding of the temple. (Interestingly, hieroglyphs, or *medu-netjer*, are literally the 'language of the god'.) The gods themselves were considered remote from the ordinary person who could not approach them directly under any circumstances. If one wanted to make a plea to the local god, one had to make an offering to any of a series of statues placed around the open court of the temple in the hope that the *ka* of the figure would carry

the request; or make the offering of a creature who was sacred to the deity; or take the plea to one of the priests within the temple in the hope that as he entered the god's home (the sanctuary) with the daily offerings, he might speak on behalf of the supplicant.

The principal workers in the temples were not strictly priests, as we invariably call them, but literally the 'god's servants'. Once appointed to the highest rank in the temple, either by royal decree or by birthright, they alone could enter the dark sanctuary of the temple, touch the statue within the shrine designed to call up the *ka* of the god, and speak in the divine presence. If the cult of the temple was mysterious to the outsider, then the words used by the temple attendants were even stranger. The priest would use established ancient rituals, whose sound and rhythm were calculated to strike awe into the hearts of his listeners. In this way magic was truly born. Evidently it was neither necessary nor fitting that the words used when speaking to the gods should be understood by others.

Speaking to the gods

At times of illness especially, the physician priests from the temple, men trained all their lives in the study of medical papyri, would be called. The priest would consult the writings, and from the symptoms of the illness would declare whether or not he was able to treat the problem. If the disease was found to have been brought upon the person by the god as a lesson, an admonishment for some wrong, or to draw an end to life at the due time, then the texts would inform the physician that nothing could be done: 'A disease I cannot treat'. If on the other hand the disease was found to have been brought by a demon or demiurge using the body as a battleground against the god, then the texts would inform the physician that something could be done: 'A disease against which I can fight'. In the latter instance, the god had to be urged to enter the battle within the body of the sick person. The priest might administer a potion the purpose of which was not to relieve the symptoms, but to be so unpleasant that the evil force would leave. A few words would be spoken by the priest; and finally an amulet would be given to the patient to wear which would focus the power of the god against the invading demon.

If the uninitiated could not be expected to understand the words of everyday ceremonies, how could he or she be expected to converse with the gods when, after death, the *akh* was brought into the deities' presence? The temple libraries held rolls of leather or papyrus on which speeches to the gods were written – what we today would call spells. Before and directly after death, an ordinary person would need every assistance from the priests with their magic words to ensure safe transition from this world to the next. And just as the god more readily accepted the words written down by his servants, who understood his needs and desires, so the wearing of certain lucky charms or amulets would be sure to attract his attention even more quickly.

XX The jewellery *of Queen Mereret from Dahshur, now in the Cairo Museum, is a fine example of the use of amulets. The falcon pendant holds the* shen *sign, symbolizing eternity, in its talons. The necklace has as its clasp two so-called* sa *signs flanking a central* ankh; *together they read 'all protection and life'. The five inlaid 'motto' clasps in the middle include a large* shen *sign and a number of heart amulets.*

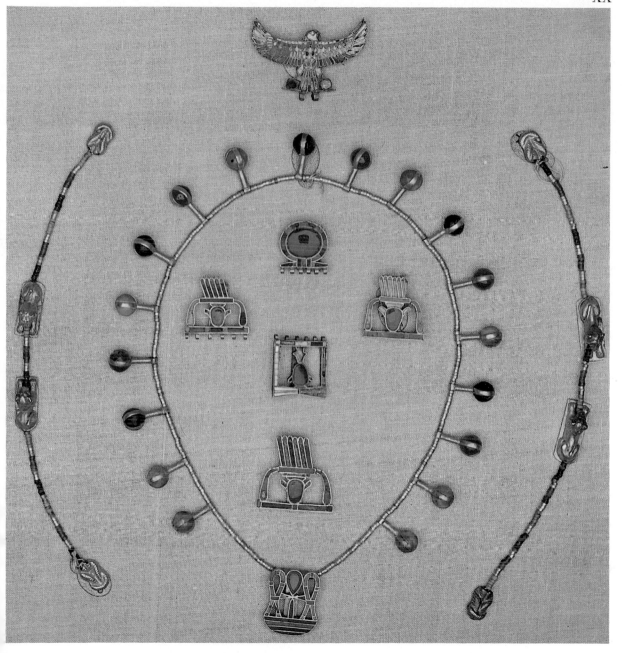

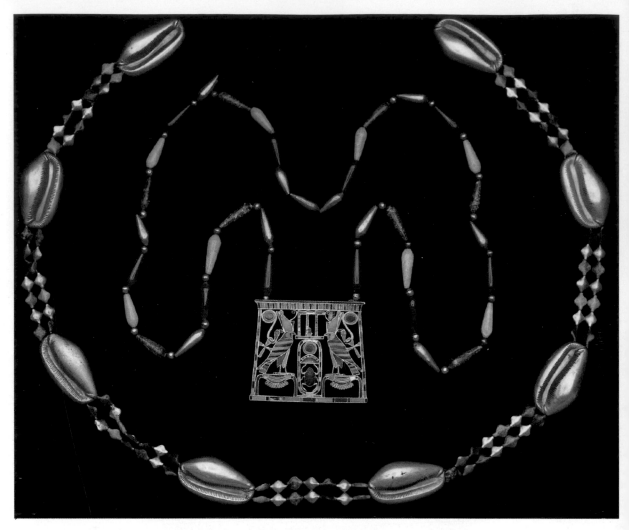

XXI

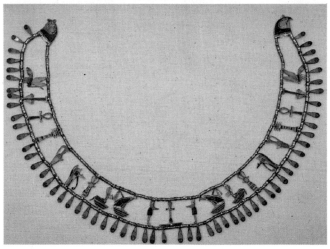

XXII

MAGIC FOR THE DEAD

We have no idea exactly when the idea of using magic to protect the dead came into being. Provision of food and drink within predynastic graves implies that some aspect, like the *ka* in later times, was deemed to continue living in and around the tomb for eternity. But the appearance of amulets in the grave in the form of shapes worn on thongs around the neck, on belts around the waist, or of small figures simply laid around the body, indicates the possibility that some magical protection was thought necessary.

The Pyramid Texts

There is no evidence to indicate the nature of the eternal expectations of the pharaohs for whom the early pyramids were built. The first pyramid, the Step Pyramid at Saqqara, appeared at the beginning of the Third Dynasty. But it and its immediate successors were bare of any inscription indicating the purpose of their construction. At the end of the Fifth Dynasty, the walls of the burial chambers of several pyramids were covered with lengthy hieroglyphic inscriptions. These are known as the Pyramid Texts and incorporate a total of over 750 individual spells. The characters are cut into the limestone covering of the walls, and filled with a blue paste which renders them clear and easy to distinguish. The words and sentiments in them are far more difficult to comprehend, however, for the spells contain the ideas and beliefs of over a thousand years or more of Egyptian development.

The Pyramid Texts comprise short statements or collections of statements aimed at urging the soul of the king to go to its eternal rest. It seems from the language in them that they were intended to be spoken or read aloud, and so may have formed a major part of the royal funerary ceremonies. Folk memory must have preserved some of these spells for many centuries, and the earliest ones refer to a time at least a millennium before they were committed to writing. In those long-gone days, when the body of the ruler like that of any Egyptian was placed in a simple grave in the sand, words spoken over the grave exhorted the monarch: 'Rouse yourself, O King. Go so that you may govern the mounds of Seth. Go so that you may govern the mounds of Osiris' (Spell 224). This appears to refer to the time when Egypt was still divided – i.e. into the delta area and the Nile valley – to the time when the first great princes from areas of Upper Egypt faced each other for control over the Nile valley.

Pharaoh as victor

The king's soul was still regarded as a conqueror, and it was as such that he was to enter the presence of the gods: 'Lift up your faces, you gods who are in netherworld, for the king has come so that you may see him, he having become the great god' (Spell 252). As a victorious god, all others must bow down before him with fear in their hearts: 'Fear and tremble, you violent ones who are in the storm clouds of the sky. He split open the earth by means of what he knew on the day when he wished to come there' (Spell 254).

Having been carried into the presence of the gods by the words of magic and the force of his strength, the king arrived as a victor, determined to conquer all the gods and become supreme among them. To this end, words urged him to kill his enemies, the weaker gods, and then to devour them so that he could absorb their strength. Whether this reflected a custom of the living king is hard to gauge: 'The planets are stilled, for they have seen the king appearing in power as a god who lives on his fathers and feeds on his mothers . . . It is the king who eats their magic, who gulps down their spirits. Their great ones are for his morning meal, their middle-sized ones for his evening meal, their little ones for his night-time meal, and their old men and old women are for his incense burning' (Spell 273).

Pharaoh among the gods

Other spells make it plain that the king was not only to reach the stars, or gods, but to become one of them: '. . . your bones are those of the divine falcons who are in the sky . . . But you shall bathe in the starry firmament . . . the sun folk shall call out for you, for the imperishable stars have raised you aloft' (Spell 214). 'Your limbs are the two children of Atum, O imperishable one. You shall not perish and your *ka* shall not perish, for you are a *ka*' (Spell 215). If the *ka* of the king became a star, then his *akh*, the transformed, brilliantly lit aspect his body took upon entering the tomb, was to enter the company of the greatest stars: 'O flesh of the king, do not decay, do not rot, do not smell unpleasant . . . You shall reach the sky as Orion, your *akh* shall be as effective as Sothis; be powerful, having power; be strong, having strength; may your *akh* stand among the gods as Horus who dwells in Iru' (Spell 412).

As Horus, the king was considered strong enough now to become a god after his death without recourse to violence. Just as all Egypt recognized his authority, he was regarded after death as being rightful heir to the position of the god Horus. It seems likely that at the time of the Great Pyramid, Cheops, its builder, expected to rise to the stars after his death in this way, for two narrow passages connect the burial chamber of his pyramid with the outside face. Modern observations have suggested that these passages would have been aimed directly at the two stars mentioned in these sections of text – Sothis being the ancient name for the star Sirius, whose rising heralded the annual Nile flood; and the constellation of Orion.

The Pyramid Texts and burial ritual

During these years, the bodies of the kings were being artificially prepared before being placed in the burial chamber. Whether the full

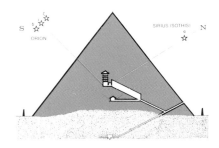

mummification process was then being used is doubtful, but we can be certain that the body was being bandaged, and it is likely that amulets would have been placed within the wrappings. Many of the spells of the Pyramid Texts are the words spoken by the funerary priests as the body was being prepared and placed in the burial chamber. The spells not only give the words to be spoken, but list the offerings to be made: 'Take the two eyes of Horus, the black and the white; taken them to your face so that they may light up your face – the lifting up a white jar and a black jar' (Spell 43). 'O Osiris, the king, take the foreleg of Seth which Horus has torn off – four-weave divine linen' (Spell 61). 'Recite four times, O Osiris, the King. I paint an uninjured eye of Horus on your face for you – green paint, one bag' (Spell 78).

After all the correct rituals had been followed, the body of the king would be made ready to be carried into the pyramid, but first, an adze was held up before the mummy by a high-ranking priest, who would apply it to the hardened wrappings over the eyes, mouth, nose, ears, hands and feet, as if actually lifting the fabric. By this means, he 'opened the mouth' of the king, or restored the senses to the body so that the *akh* could function readily in its next life: 'I split open your mouth for you, I split open your eyes for you. O king, I open your mouth for you with the adze of iron which split open the mouths of the gods' (Spell 21).

The Pyramid Texts and the influence of the sun cult

There is evidence for the possibility of sun worship as early as the Second Dynasty. But at the beginning of the Fifth Dynasty, the throne was taken by a family claiming to be descendants of the sun god Re himself, through the wife of a priest of Heliopolis, and the cult of Re assumed a new importance. The kings now called themselves the 'sons of Re', and there are spells of the Pyramid Texts which relate to the king joining the sun in the heavens: 'O Re-Atum, this king comes to you, an imperishable spirit . . . May you traverse the sky, being united in the darkness; may you rise on the horizon, in the place where it is well with you' (Spell 217). 'The king takes possession of the sky, he cleaves its iron. The king is conducted on the roads to Khepri [the rising sun]; the king rests in life in the West and the dwellers in the netherworld attend on him; the king shines anew in the East and he who settled disputes will come to him bowing' (Spell 257).

The king was to attain this position by sailing up to the sky: 'The reed floats of the sky are set in place for Re that he may cross in them to the horizon . . . the reed floats of the sky are set in place for me that I may cross on them to the horizon, to Re' (Spell 263). In 1954, a pit alongside the Great Pyramid at Giza, was opened. Inside, sealed for over 4,800 years, were all the components of a magnificent boat, complete with oars and rigging. There has been much discussion about whether this was a solar boat. But it is a controversial subject and one which scholars still debate.

The Great Pyramid *of Cheops at Giza shows evidence both of the solar and stellar cults. Its shape is thought to symbolize the rays of the sun, while two very narrow channels in the structure point towards Sothis (i.e. Sirius, the Dog Star) and the constellation of Orion.*

The coffin texts

In the Middle Kingdom cliff tombs of the local rulers, following the decline of the monarchy, painted coffins bear witness to the fact that changing beliefs allowed an afterlife to every man and woman. For the words painted on the inner and outer surfaces of these wooden coffins were spells to protect and speed the deceased on their perilous journey.

The afterlife for the ordinary Egyptian

The spells in these Coffin Texts reflect the dread and terror in the hearts of the deceased that they might not actually manage to speak the words that the demigods understood to allow them to pass into their paradise. The soul of the deceased had to pass into the company of the supreme god Osiris: 'The great god lives fixed in the middle of the sky which is his support; guide ropes are adjusted for that great hidden one, the dweller in the sky' (Spell 664). The earth, or Geb, the father of Osiris, was separated from the god's mother, Nut, by the air, Shu; and the spirit of the dead had to cross this enemy of the sky in order to reach Osiris. Shu would try everything he could to prevent the spirit from reaching its home: 'I am the strongest and most energetic of the company of the gods' (Spell 75).

To enable the rebirth of the soul of the deceased, grains of corn were often included within the tomb, and a spell encouraged it to grow, for as it grew, the deceased would gain the strength of Osiris himself: 'I am the plant of life which comes forth from Osiris; it grows from the ribs of Osiris and allows people to live. Whether I live or die, I am Osiris, I enter and reappear through you . . . the gods are living in me for I live and grow in the corn that sustains the spirits of the dead' (Spell 330).

The illustration (right) *from the papyrus of Nisti-ta-Nebet-Taui shows the Egyptian concept of their world. The sky goddess Nut is eternally separated from her brother the earth god Geb. Shu, their father and god of the air maintains this forced separation. Nut's hands and feet touch the four cardinal points, thus defining the extent of the universe. Nut and Geb are the parents of Osiris, Isis, Seth and Nephthys.*

Coffins such as *the one shown below are typical of the Middle Kingdom. They often had inscriptions painted on the inside and outside; some were almost completely covered in writing. These inscriptions consisted of spells whose purpose was to help the spirits of the dead on their journey to the afterlife.*

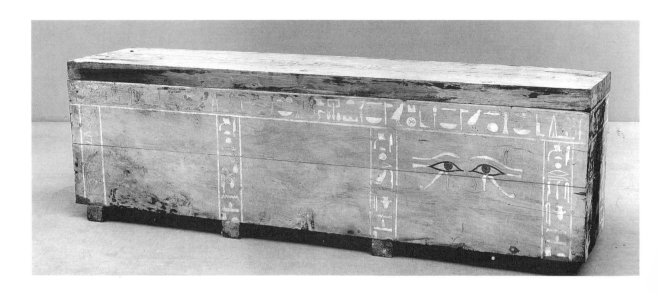

Ushabtis: workers of the next world

The location of their new eternal existence with Osiris was the Field of Reeds, and the soul dreaded that it would be required to work forever in the fields to serve the god. So, from the start of the Middle Kingdom, worker figures were placed in the tomb. The earliest of these were merely crudely cut wooden pegs, but they were succeeded by more elaborate faience ones bearing the words that would give them life. These figures were called *ushabtis*, from the Egyptian verb *usheb*, meaning to answer or respond. The sixth chapter of the Book of the Dead, the so-called 'ushabti' chapter, is often found inscribed on the figures, and reads: 'O *ushabti*, given to me, if I am summoned or if I am called upon to do any work which has to be done in the realm of the dead; if indeed any obstacles are placed for you as for a man with his tasks, you shall respond for me on every occasion – of fertilizing the fields, or irrigating the banks, or of carrying sand from the east bank to the west bank, "Here I am," you shall say.'

The figure above is an Eighteenth Dynasty faience ushabti *from the tomb of Ptah Mès. These small mummiform figures were placed in the tomb and were intended to carry out any tasks in the afterlife that the deceased might be called on to perform by the gods.*

The Book of the Dead

During the early New Kingdom, when strong pharaohs ruled a united Egypt with a far-flung empire, the Egyptians felt a renewed sense of pride and confidence. In contrast with the Middle Kingdom, these people saw little need to fear the afterlife.

Afterlife beliefs in the New Kingdom

During this time, the *ka* was still considered to be earthbound. Tombs continued to be filled with offerings of food, drink, linen and furniture; appointed *ka* priests carried on the mortuary cults. Just as in the Old Kingdom, the *akh* was thought to enter into the land of the dead. Here it would be judged by the gods before passing into a land where, forever young and in the company of family and loved ones, it would spend an eternity untroubled by material needs. But the passage into that other existence was by no means assured.

After the Opening of the Mouth ceremony, when the coffins were placed in the burial chamber, the body was deemed to take upon itself a new form of existence. The *ba* had already left the body at the point of death and now hovered in the tomb, and the *ka* was able to feast on the offerings which had been provided. But a night of trouble awaited the *akh*, and it would need all the protection the magical words of the priests and powerful amulets could supply to gain admittance to the paradise for which it hungered.

Amulets protect the akh

Preparations for the *akh's* perilous journey were made while the body was being bandaged. Among the linen wrappings, priests placed amulets – charms designed to strengthen every muscle, every limb. Spells were spoken over the amulets, each of which was made by the funerary priests from a selected material and anointed with special substances and, some, suspended from traditional cords. Copies of these spells (such as those found in the Ritual of Embalmment papyrus), together with words of protection for the *akh*, were presumably stored in the temple libraries. Anyone who could afford a mummification would be provided with an illustrated copy of these texts. To the Egyptians, they were known as The Book of Coming Forth by Day, since the ancients expected to emerge into a new, eternal day, but to us they are better known as the Book of the Dead.

When it came to protecting the vulnerable *akh*, the Egyptians took no chances. It is not unusual to find hundreds of amulets within the wrappings of just one mummy. And each had its appointed place over a particular part of the body – though placement was not always perfect, by any means. The most important was the heart amulet, or heart scarab, which was inscribed with a spell from the Book of the Dead, and was made of lapis lazuli, nephrite (green feldspar) or carnelian, and sometimes set in a gold frame, making it a prime target for tomb robbers. Very common was an amulet of the *djed* pillar. The mummy of Tutankhamun had two golden *djed* pillars hung around his neck, but it is more usual to find this amulet on the abdomen or chest. The meaning of this symbol is unclear, but it is widely thought to have represented the backbone of the god Osiris.

Some common amulets portrayed green plants, the parts of the body, or parts of animals. Those of animals were thought to transfer their characteristics, such as strength or fertility, to the dead person.

This mummy *of an elderly lady from the Graeco-Roman period is a fine example of a burial well provided with protective amulets.*

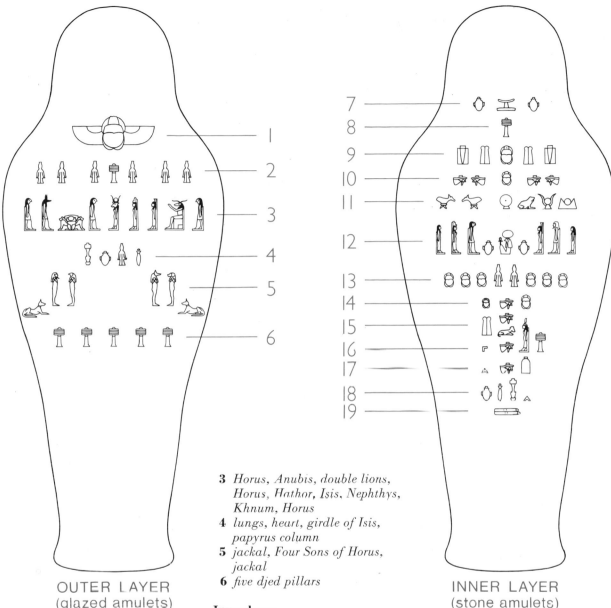

OUTER LAYER
(glazed amulets)

INNER LAYER
(stone amulets)

3 *Horus, Anubis, double lions,
Horus, Hathor, Isis, Nephthys,
Khnum, Horus*
4 *lungs, heart, girdle of Isis,
papyrus column*
5 *jackal, Four Sons of Horus,
jackal*
6 *five djed pillars*

Inner layer
7 *heart, headrest, heart*
8 *djed pillar*
9 *(unknown), two feathers,
heart scarab, two feathers,
(unknown)*
10 *two wadjet eyes, scarab, two
wadjet eyes*
11 *two bound gazelles, sun disc,
frog, sun disc between horns of
Hathor, horizon*
12 *goddess, Isis, Horus, heart, Re
seated, heart, Nephthys, god,
goddess*

Some mummies *contained dozens
of amulets. These two drawings
show amulets positioned row by
row as they were found in the
wrappings of the mummy of
Djedhor, dating from c. 380 BC,
found at Abydos by Flinders
Petrie in 1902.*

Outer layer
1 *winged scarab*
2 *three girdles of Isis, djed
pillar, three girdles of Isis*

13 *three scarabs, two girdles of
Isis, three scarabs*
14 *scarab, wadjet eye, scarab*
15 *two feathers, wadjet eye over
recumbent animal*
16 *carpenter's square, wadjet eye,
Maat, djed pillar*
17 *carpenter's or mason's level,
wadjet eye, necklace
counterpoise*
18 *heart, papyrus column, lungs,
carpenter's or mason's level*
19 *two fingers*

Other amulets alluded to mythical aspects. The *tyet*, or *tit*, amulet is thought to have symbolized the girdle of Isis and was always red. The colour may have represented the blood of the goddess and been linked with childbirth. One strange amulet was in the shape of a headrest and was placed at the neck, as if giving eternal support.

One amulet with a long history and found in burials as far back as the late Old Kingdom, was the *wadjet* eye, symbolizing the healed, replaced left eye of Horus, ripped out in his battles with Seth. This amulet was seen as having great protective powers, and capable of restoring health and giving new vitality. The *wadjet* eye is perhaps one of the most common symbols of Egyptian civilization.

Spells to be spoken over the amulets were included in the Books of the Dead, although no two texts are identical: 'Raise yourself, Osiris, place yourself upon your side so that I may pour water beneath you and that I may bring you a djed pillar of gold so that you may rejoice over it. To be said over a golden djed pillar, placed on a sycamore cord, to be placed on the throat of the deceased on the day of burial. As for him on whose throat this amulet has been placed, he will be a worthy *akh* who will be in the realm of the dead on New Year's Day, like those who are in the following of Osiris.' 'O my father, my brother, my mother Isis, release me, look at me, for I am one of those who should be released when Geb secs them. To be said over a broad collar of gold with this spell written upon it; it is to be put on the throat of the deceased on the day of burial.'

The *djed* pillar *was a very important amulet and symbolized strength and power. One theory is that it represented the backbone of Osiris. In these scenes from the Osiris hall at the Temple of Abydos, Seti I is shown (left) raising the* djed *pillar with the help of the goddess Isis. Next (right) we see Seti offering two rolls of cloth to another* djed *pillar which is adorned with a long kilt. The inscription reads: 'Giving cloth to his father, Osiris, that he may make a granted life.'*

THE HEART SCARAB

The heart scarab amulet came into use during the First Intermediate period and was traditionally made of a dark green stone such as serpentine; later examples were found in basalt or even obsidian. On some New Kingdom and Second Intermediate period heart scarabs, a human head replaced that of the beetle.

A finely carved *heart scarab, and (below) the inscription which appears on its underside and contains the words of Spell 30B from the Book of Coming Forth by Day.*

The most important amulet to be included in the mummy wrappings was a large stone scarab beetle. According to Egyptian beliefs, the scarab, or dung beetle, regenerated itself magically. The Egyptians saw the larvae emerge from the ball of dung pushed between the beetle's forelegs, but never realized that it contained eggs. So the scarab came to be associated with miraculous rebirth.

The stone scarab was wrapped within the bandages of the body in close proximity to the heart. The deceased was expected to produce his or her heart to place on the scales of Maat, goddess of truth, in the hall of judgment. The spell inscribed on the back of the scarab – Spell 30B in the Book of Coming Forth by Day

– not only enabled the dead person to produce the heart, but also begged that it should not betray its owner: 'Oh, my heart [which I had] from my mother! Oh, my heart [which I had] from my mother! Oh, my heart of my coming into being! Do not stand as a witness against me. Do not contradict me with the judges. Do not act against me with the gods. Do not be my enemy in the presence of the guardian of the balance [i.e. Anubis]. You are my *ka*, which was in my body, the protector who made my limbs healthy. Go forth to the happy place towards which we are hurrying. Do not make my name stink to the gods who made mankind. Do not tell lies about me in the presence of the great god. See, you will be selected to exist.'

The journey of the akh

After the *akh* entered the region over the western horizon with the setting sun, protection from a host of dangers in the form of demons was needed: 'O *rerek* snake, take yourself off, for Geb protects me; get up, for you have eaten a mouse, which Re detests' (Spell 33). The *akh* might even have to assume different forms to defeat these enemies: 'Spell for being changed into a lotus flower. I am this pure lotus which went out from the sun which is at the nose of Re. I have descended so that I may seek it for Horus, for I am the pure one who issued from the marshes' (Spell 81). The spirit needed to survive through many hours of trials before it entered into the judgment chamber. To do this, spells were included to allow it to breathe and to find food.

If these trials were successfully met, the *akh* came to a river which presented a new difficulty. The ferryman, Makhaf, woke the protesting owner of the boat, Aken, who took much persuasion to carry the *akh* across – and only after the soul correctly named all the parts of the boat. This accomplished, the *akh* was safely carried to the hall of Osiris.

The weighing of the heart

Once the soul arrived in the hall of judgment, Horus led it by the hand to the waiting Osiris, seated upon a throne. Here the *akh* had to declare every living action in the form of 42 negative confessions: 'Behold I have come to you. I have brought you truth. I have done no falsehood against men. I have never impoverished my associates. I have done no wrong in the Place of Truth. I have not learnt that which does not exist. I have done no evil.'

Sins, or transgressions, committed during life also caused the heart to be burdened. Every wrong action, every wrong word – all had their effect, making the heart heavier than an untroubled one could be. So the *akh* was then led into a second hall where the heart was laid on a set of scales to be weighed against the feather of the goddess Maat, she who represented justice and moral order in the universe. Anubis, guardian of the dead, checked the scales to see that the two elements balanced. If they did not, the Gobbler, a monster with the jaws of a crocodile, the forepart of a leopard, or lion, and the hindquarters of a

This famous scene *from the Book of the Dead of Hunefer, who lived about 1310 BC, shows the crucial moment when the heart is weighed against the feather of the goddess Maat. The god Anubis, kneeling at the midpoint of the scales, checks them for accuracy. As Hunefer's immortality hangs in the balance, the god Thoth solemnly stands on the right ready to record the verdict. The monster Ammit (the Gobbler) looks eagerly towards the recorder since, should the verdict be negative, Hunefer's heart will be the monster's prize.*

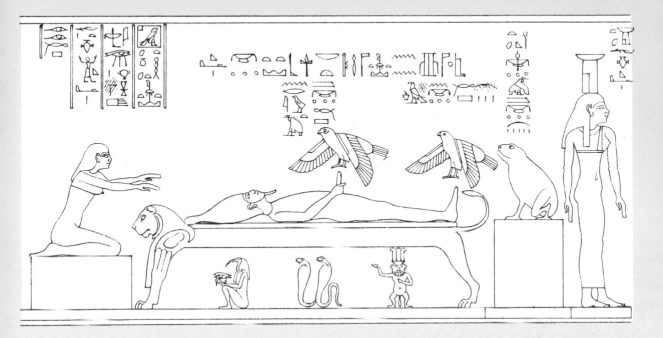

After the end of the Old Kingdom, all Egyptians came to believe that they might live again in the next world thanks to the god Osiris.

According to legend, Osiris was a prince of Egypt, born in Heliopolis to the goddess Nut. He had two sisters, Isis and Nephthys, and a brother Seth. Osiris grew to maturity, strong, handsome and popular and, in time, became King of Egypt and married his beautiful sister Isis, called 'Great of Magic'. Seth, married to Nephthys, became obsessed by his brother's good fortune.

When Osiris returned victorious from a campaign, Seth invited him and his companions to a great banquet. At the end of the celebrations, Seth produced a magnificent, inlaid coffin, and ordered it as a prize for the one whom it fitted best — the coffin had been made to Osiris' own measurements. As he stepped inside it, Seth slammed the lid shut, and threw the coffin into the Nile.

The waters carried the coffin as far as Byblos, where it became encased in a tree later used by the king there as a column. Seth took his brother's place as King of Egypt. Isis grieved for the loss of her husband, and searched with great tenacity for his remains. Eventually she found her way to Byblos and retrieved the coffin with the body of Osiris, which she brought back to Egypt and hid in the marshes. Unfortunately, Seth found the body and tore it to pieces, throwing them in the river.

Isis found all but one of the pieces — his genitals had been eaten by a fish. The other parts were collected together and bandaged to form the first mummy, and then transformed into an *akh*, which

In one of the *legends of Osiris, Isis as a kite hovers over the god's body to bring life to it. She succeeds and becomes pregnant with Osiris's son and heir, the god Horus. The goddess Nephthys stands at the foot of the lion-headed funerary bier.*

travelled down to the underworld, where Osiris became the King of the Dead.

Isis swore her son Horus to avenge his father's murder. When he grew to manhood, Horus fought his uncle Seth bitterly for many years until finally the gods declared him the rightful King of Egypt.

Eventually, every Egyptian believed they possessed the right, like Osiris, to be transformed and to live in the hereafter; and every king of Egypt was considered the successor of Horus.

hippopotamus, devoured the soul. And what was worse, if the soul were devoured it did not simply cease to exist, but was believed to become an evil spirit that would bring bad luck or illness to the living. The devoured soul was condemned to a continual existence of struggle with the gods and the priests. The torment of this existence was to be deprived eternally of comforts, and be removed forever from the company of loved ones.

Provided the heart and the feather of Maat balanced, the *akh* of the deceased passed into paradise, to be greeted by those who had died before. Here the *akh* would be served food and drink from a limitless store, while sweet music played. The sun shone, but never too hotly; the breeze brought the 'sweet breath of the north wind', but never too fiercely.

The akh of the pharaoh in the New Kingdom

The afterlife of the king was seen somewhat differently. His *akh* had, after all, been associated with the company of the gods for hundreds of years, and for him to become subject to the will of Osiris and one of millions of ordinary souls was inconceivable. The walls of the royal tombs are covered with texts that belong to a whole series of 'Books', referring to difficult aspects of the king's future existence. Pictures make it clear that he was first welcomed directly into the company of the great gods, whose images appear to emerge from the burial chamber with hands outstretched in greeting.

If the king's *akh* were to enter the underworld, then the demons he must face, as one of the gods, would be all the more horrific and many of the spells were aimed at protecting him from them. Other demiurges would come to fight on his side, and are shown fighting on his behalf armed with sharp knives and razors. The king's soul could also enter the sun ship in the heavens. Once at its helm, in the company of Re and other gods, the royal soul would need further protection. As the ship carrying the sun sank below the western horizon at sunset, it too would be beset by problems that had to be overcome. Powerful magic was needed if the king were safely to navigate the troubled waters of the night. The books describing the

The journey to the underworld is perilous and the help of the gods is neccessary to overcome the danger. In this scene from the papyrus of Her-Uben in the Cairo Museum, the god Seth spears the serpent of darkness from the prow of a solar barge on which rides the hawk-headed sun god, Horus and Thoth. Four jackals tow the barge which is supported by the sign for the heavens.

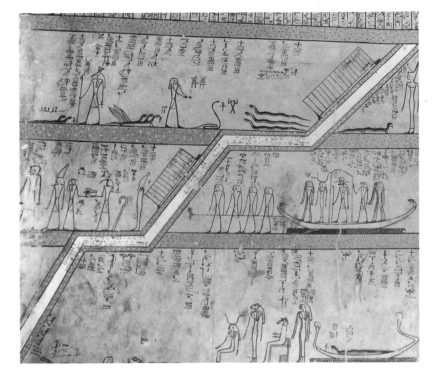

This painting *from the burial chamber of the tomb of Tuthmosis III illustrates the fourth hour, or division, from the Book of What Is in the Underworld. Each of the twelve hours is made up, as here, of three horizontal bands of figures (top to bottom). The solar barge is in the cental register of each hour. In this hour the barge is towed by four gods. On the other side of it stands the god Osiris and two other gods, one hawk-headed and one ibis-headed with a* wadjet *eye between them.*

denizens of the underworld and the journey of the sun were collectively known to the Egyptians as the *Amduat* (i.e. 'The Book of What Is in the Underworld'); others include The Book of Gates and the Book of Caverns.

Beliefs after the New Kingdom

Ideas that developed and became prevalent during the New Kingdom were to remain in force for the rest of Egyptian history, until superseded by those of Christianity. Confidence in Osiris continually gained in strength. The Books of the Dead, at one time placed within the wrappings of the mummy, were secreted inside the base of a wooden statue, called a Ptah-Sokar-Osiris figure. Although placed apart from the mummy within the tomb, this was considered sufficient protection.

The use of amulets seems to have declined as years went by. Mummies from the Late and Graeco-Roman periods have very little in the way of magical protections included around the body, with the exception of a magical plate placed over the abdominal incision through which the viscera were removed. Where things could leave the body, others could enter, and some form of protection was considered necessary.

The equipping of a mummy and the tomb was vital for future life, but none of it would have been sufficient without the added protection of magic.

Chapter Six
Animal Cults

THE BELIEFS AND STORIES attached to the Egyptian gods, and even the nature and appearance of the gods themselves, changed at various times during pharaonic history, becoming increasingly complex down the centuries. An unchanging element, however, was the importance of animals in religious practices.

Animals in Ancient Egyptian belief

Early depictions of animals

There are no written records for the period up to the unification of Egypt around 3100 BC, and images of deities are rare, but from what can be understood, Nile dwellers appear to have revered a universal mother figure, fat and fertile. Images of bulls, however, are very common. And from about 3100 BC, the bull, a strong and fearless fighter, came to be associated with the leader of men – the king himself.

On the Scorpion macehead (which is now in the Ashmolean Museum, Oxford), found in Hieraconpolis, and many of the carved slate palettes dating from the beginning of Egyptian history, animals and birds start to appear. These creatures are mounted on the tops of poles carried in ranks by servants of the king. Similar creatures on the Libyan palette fragment (in the Cairo Museum) are seen carrying mattocks and undermining the walls of enemy cities that the king is attacking. From this we must understand that each local area of Egypt, called by the Greeks 'nomes', or perhaps every town or major settlement, adopted an animal, bird or reptile as its figurehead. This symbol, mounted on a flagpole, would have served as a rallying point for soldiers in battle.

Many towns and villages adopted similar creatures. Hawks and falcons were especially favoured, given their swiftness and their habit of hiding from their prey by hovering between it and the sun, then apparently descending from the sun itself. Crocodiles, seen all along the banks of the Nile, were adopted by several towns as images

Animals are widely depicted *in Egyptian art. Below is a Twenty-sixth Dynasty representation of an ichneumon ('pharaoh's rat'), a type of Egyptian mongoose. The section of the schist palette (opposite), known as the Libyan palette, shows a number of creatures undermining enemy towns (the niched squares symbolize individual towns whose names are represented within by other creatures or flowers). Each figure – the hawk, scorpion or lion – could have been immediately identified by the ancients as the place or area with which it was associated.*

designed to instil terror into the hearts of enemies. Snakes were also regarded as frightening, and the adoption of the ichneumon (Egyptian mongoose) as a totem can only be seen as the hope that that town or village could 'devour' the serpent followers as the ichneumon devoured the snake itself. Dogs, cats and geese were popular because they were seen as being loyal and provided protection against strangers.

Gods and local heroes

From texts inscribed on later temple walls and in papyri, it is also evident that each town or village also revered a local deceased hero. This person was thought of as having existed after the creation of the world, but before the appearance of human beings. Local legend may have credited him with some special contribution to the area, agriculture or written records, for example. The people of each village or town would make funerary offerings of food and drink for the *ka* of this long-dead hero in the hope and expectation that they would receive material benefits in return. The identities of these heroes could be adopted by more than one village, though with slightly different attributes and legends. It was, then, but a short step for the deity to become identified with the town totem figure. So Amun, for instance, was identified with a goose in one town; in another, with a ram, and so on.

As history progressed, some of the gods became important nationally. Amun for instance, rose from being a demiurge in Ashmunein (Hermopolis) and a local deity in Luxor to becoming the king of the gods. He achieved this status solely because one of his followers became pharaoh. As a man changed from local dignitary to king, so the status of his god must change; as the man rose above men, so his god must rise above other gods. The adoption of Amun of Luxor as a national god resulted in the various towns who revered Amun adding their stories and images of him to those of Luxor. As a result, Amun became man, ram and goose. When Thoth, in the form of a baboon, rose from being a demiurge and supporter of the sun god to be the supporter of Osiris, king of the dead, he adopted another local image, that of the ibis.

Animals as the god's creatures

The Egyptians never worshipped animals. Indeed, it could be said that they seldom worshipped any god, but merely expected that, by offering service to the spirit of a deceased deity, they could effect an agreement that would be mutually beneficial. The Egyptians were never foolish enough to bow down in veneration in front of a crocodile, for instance, for they knew the crocodile would attack them. Similarly, seeing a scarab beetle crawling on the ground, they would be unlikely to have killed it, for it represented an image of the sun god as the bringer of life – but they would not have worshipped the beetle.

The depiction of gods and goddesses within tombs and temples with the heads of the creatures identified with them was intended to indicate clearly the god to whom the pictures or pleas were addressed. In a like manner, the image of the deity kept within the temple sanctuary would most probably have taken the form of the creature associated with the god because the spirit of the god was certain to recognize it. In this way there could be no confusion over the deities as there might have been if anonymous pictures or statues of men and women had been used.

Archaeology has helped to confirm this view of the role of animals in the Egyptian religious system. It appears that before unification, two towns along the Nile valley may have fought for supremacy over all of Upper Egypt. The god of the town on the west bank near modern El Kab (Nekheb) was Horus, and the local totem under which the town fought was that of the falcon. Its opponent was the town of Naqada, north of Luxor, which venerated Seth, shown on their totem as a curious cross between a dog, a pig and a creature resembling an ant-eater. The wars between the two towns were remembered as the 'Battles of Horus and Seth'; and they were later incorporated into the

This scene *(above) from the papyrus of the royal scribe Ani relates to spells 185 and 186 of the Book of the Dead. To the far right is Ani's pyramid-topped tomb entrance, typical of Nineteenth Dynasty burials. Three gods are shown (left to right): the hawk-headed Sokar-Osiris; the hippopotamus goddess Opet, who wears horns and a disc and stands by a sa amulet, a sign of protection; and Hathor as a cow-headed goddess.*

By using animals *associated with gods to represent them, the symbolism of a particular scene was immediately apparent to the Egyptians. Here (left) the hawk-headed god Horus stands as victor on his defeated uncle Seth, represented as a hippopotamus: a simple graphic device to illustrate a major Egyptian myth of the triumph of one god over another.*

legends of Osiris (Chapter 5). The king of Egypt was ever afterwards thought of as the living embodiment of the victorious Horus.

The growth of animal cults

During the late New Kingdom ordinary Egyptians were given more opportunity to come into contact with the gods, eventually consulting them as one would an oracle. And it was during this time that animal cults began to flourish on a massive scale. A person who wanted to attract the favour of a god was believed to be able to do it in several ways. He or she could consult the oracle of the god, but in that case could offer nothing and so might not be granted an answer. The supplicant might offer a figure made of faience or bronze, representing the animal associated with the god in the hope that the gift would attract attention. Or, probably most effective of all, an offering might be made to the god of one of the creatures – in mummy form – that he would recognize as his own.

The animal catacombs

The sands of Egypt are filled with many tombs, but few stranger than the labyrinthine and complex subterranean passages throughout Egypt that contain the mummies of animals. The walls of corridors and side-chambers are packed with pots or linen-bandaged packages that contain the bodies of the god's creatures. Some of these underground complexes contain millions of them. At Tuna-el-Gebel, the cemetery associated with the town of Ashmunein and dedicated to Thoth, for example, is crammed with mummified baboons and ibises. The ibis mummies alone are estimated to number in excess of 4,000,000, and some scholars believe it could well be twice this figure.

The remains of the nearby temple of Thoth contains a compound in which, it is believed, the birds and baboons were reared. It is highly unlikely, given the number of mummies, that the creatures died of natural causes. It seems probable, then, that a person who wanted something from Thoth would go along to the temple and pay over a certain amount of grain, linen, or whatever else might be suitable, choose either an ibis or a baboon, and have it killed. The creature would then be taken along to a workshop where the body was packed for a few days in natron to desiccate it. The body would then be wrapped, according to the amount paid.

At this late date, bandaging was at its most elaborate, and the creatures would be wrapped in tiny strips of coloured linen to form diamond-shaped patterns. The features of the animal might be painted on the head; it could even be set with inlaid eyes and gilded beaks. The mummy was then placed in some kind of container. From the ibis mummies examined at Tuna-el-Gebel, it appears that pots were favoured. The more elaborate the pot, the less well wrapped was the mummy within, while the plainer pots seem to contain the finest wrapped examples. A larger payment might secure a wooden or even a bronze container. The wooden variety would have been carved in two halves, fitted together with dowels, the outside carved to represent the animal; it may have been painted. A bronze container, clearly the most expensive kind, would have been rectangular and copied the shape of the walls of an Egyptian temple, with its curved cavetto cornice. A bronze figure of the creature was placed at its head. Very few of these have been found in the catacombs themselves. It is possible that they were considered too precious, and may have been stored within a chamber of the temple of the god himself.

Consequences of animal sacrifice

The raising and slaughter of millions of birds must have had some effects on the fauna of each area. Birds that were killed and mummified in honour of the god Horus, generally depicted in paintings as a lanner falcon, have been revealed by X-ray analysis to cover a whole variety of birds, including kites, vultures and even songbirds. It may be that it was the outer appearance of the animal mummy that was significant — or perhaps the embalmers merely allowed the supplicant to believe the shape indicated what was within the wrappings.

The offering of these animal mummies had other consequences. It resulted in animosity between areas. During the Greek era, two neighbouring towns in Middle Egypt came to blows over the matter.

The Egyptians mummified

animals of all kinds. Often they were given as a sacrificial offering to a temple. Here are shown (left) an ibis and (left below) a baboon, both identified with the god Thoth; (below) a hawk, the animal associated with Horus; and (below right) two crocodiles, one wrapped, one unwrapped, representing the god Sobek.

In Oxyrhynchus, a fish (called after the name of the town) was revered, and mummified in thousands for their local god. In Cynopolis, the locals mummified wild dogs – but ate the fish. The people of Oxyrhynchus asked the Cynopolitans to respect the fish, but to no avail. In the end, they staged a feast at which they roasted and served the dogs of Cynopolis, with the result that local civil war erupted.

Which animals were mummified?

The full range of ancient Egyptian wildlife has been found mummified and crammed in catacombs from the Graeco-Roman period. Burials of mice and rats have been found; snakes of all varieties; every imaginable type of bird; lizards, ichneumons and crocodiles; dogs, gazelles and rams. In a museum in Grenoble, there is even a mummified egg.

Many of the creatures mummified, though, were considered as far more important than mere spiritual messengers. The cost and time spent mummifying a mouse, snake or ibis was minimal; the time spent over a larger animal made it a different prospect. The mummification of a ram, for example, was rare, and could be afforded by very few ordinary people. On Elephantine Island, Aswan, a number of mummies of the ram of Khnum were found, and one of them is displayed in the museum on the island. It is ornately wrapped, gilded and painted, and was presumably prepared by the priests of the temple of Khnum on behalf of the entire population. There is no evidence, though, that the creature itself was especially revered as containing the spirit of Khnum himself. The same can be said of the gazelle or oryx mummy fragments in a museum in San Jose, California.

Cats and other pets

The Egyptians were great pet lovers. On the outside wall of the tomb of Sarenput, a prince of Aswan during the Twelfth Dynasty, his pet dogs are shown, one a saluki (still called the hound of the pharaohs), and the other resembling a corgi or dachshund, but clearly a bitch which had just given birth. Mahirpa, a soldier from the Eighteenth Dynasty, cared enough for his pet dogs for two of their leather collars to be included in his burial goods.

Many tomb paintings show the family pet lurking under the chair of the deceased, often eating food that they had mischievously taken from the offering table. These are usually dogs, cats or monkeys. Cats are most often shown and they are often depicted accompanying their owners on hunting trips into the marshes where they retrieve game knocked down by their master's throwsticks. They are shown as short-haired with marked coats of the kind we would call tabby. These pictures have been studied and the cats identified as most strongly resembling Abyssinians. Their names are also often found in the wall

*The **great cat** was hostile to snakes and sacred to the sun god. In this painting from the tomb of Inherkha the cat cuts off the head of the Apophis serpent which is threatening a sacred tree.*

164

This cat mummy (right) *was found at the great cult centre of Abydos. The intricate geometric pattern made by weaving bandages in and out, over and around each other is typical of the Roman period. It is one of thousands of cats that were mummified in Egypt and today it can be seen at the British Museum.*

inscriptions, and from this it is evident that the tomb owners wanted to have their pets with them in the afterlife.

The most popular of all Egyptian animal mummies without doubt are those of cats. The cats, representing the goddess Bast (sometimes called Bastet), was specially honoured in Graeco-Roman times in Bubastis in the delta region. X-rays, revealing deliberate separation of the neck from the body, demonstrate that many cats were sacrificed for mummification. Herodotus described the special regard for cats he observed when he visited Bubastis: 'What happens when a house catches fire is most extraordinary. Nobody takes the least trouble to put it out for it is only the cats that matter. Everyone stands in a row, a little distance from his neighbour, trying to protect the cats who nevertheless slip through the line, or jump over it, and hurl themselves into the flames. This causes the Egyptians deep distress. All the inmates where a cat has died a natural death shave their eyebrows . . . Cats who have died are taken to Bubastis where they are embalmed and buried in sacred receptacles.'

CULT OF THE APIS BULL

These small alabaster 'beds' at Memphis were probably used for the preservation of the internal organs, during the embalming of the Apis bulls, before they were transported for burial to the nearby Serapeum at Saqqara.

Considering the great antiquity of the cult of the bulls, it is not surprising that the bulls, and their mother cows, were revered above all other animals. And there is no doubt that the most sacred of all was the Apis bull. This was the incarnation of the god Osiris and, according to Herodotus, was identified by certain markings: 'This Apis – or Epaphus – is the calf of a cow which is never afterwards able to have another. The Egyptian belief is that a flash of lightning descends upon the cow from heaven, and this causes her to receive Apis. The Apis calf has distinctive marks: it is black, with a white diamond on its forehead, the image of an eagle on its back, the hairs on its tail double, and a scarab under its tongue.'

The mother of the Apis (the 'Isis cow') was equally revered, and at Saqqara a series of underground chambers cut in the time of King Nectanebo II contained their mummified bodies. As for the Apis, its identification as Osiris (or User in ancient Egyptian) resulted in its name being adapted to Serapis in the Roman period. The popularity of the cult of Serapis and his consort Isis spread throughout the Roman empire.

The appearance of an Apis was a time of great rejoicing. In 525 BC, Cambyses, King of the Persians, entered Egypt and took Memphis with great slaughter. According to Herodotus (although Egyptian records seem to indicate the contrary), the following morning Cambyses was perplexed to find the populace celebrating, and asked what kind of people would act like this after such a severe defeat. His men questioned the Egyptians and learned that they were overjoyed because a living god had been born among them. Cambyses requested that this god should be produced, and when the Apis calf was led before him, roared with laughter, calling the Egyptians pagans and fools. He stabbed the Apis in its hindquarters to prove its mortality, an event which led to the Apis' death. Cambyses had it cooked and served at a banquet. All the misfortunes that befell Egypt from this time were blamed on Cambyses' lack of respect.

The embalming of the Apis bulls took place in a temple in Memphis whose ruined foundations can still be seen. Here were great alabaster slabs, their sides carved to resemble the leonine beds so widely used by the Egyptians, with drainage channels through which body fluids could flow. Four smaller tables stood at one end of the hall, presumably for the preparation of the internal organs. After desiccation, the mummy of the bull, in a crouched position, was elaborately bandaged, its horns and facial features gilded. Then, with great ceremony, the mummy was carried to a catacomb (the Serapeum) a few miles away for burial. The only intact burial of an Apis bull was found by Auguste Mariette in 1851. The complex dates only to the time of Ramesses II, but we know of burials long before this time. Undoubtedly, several more Serapeums await discovery.

The bronze figure of an Apis bull is from the Twenty-sixth Dynasty, and shows all the specific natural markings by which the Apis is distinguished from all other bulls. In this votive figure, now in the British Museum, the bull wears the sun disc and uraeus on his head.

Bulls: animals as gods incarnate

Bulls were associated with the personality of the king from a time before records began. Many of the decorated slate palettes from around the time of the unification, 3100 BC, show him as a bull, and some of the tombs of the courtiers who served the first kings in Saqqara are decorated with bulls' horns. They represented his stout heart, great courage, determination to fight, strength beyond all reason, and virility. These animals were such fierce fighters and the king was frequently depicted slaying them, as a sign of his own might, although often after servants had taken the bulls into secure compounds. The cow, gentle-eyed and motherly, became the epitome of motherhood – fertile, meek, kind and generous.

The first references to the divine bulls of Egypt, bulls in whom the god had become flesh, appear early in the First Dynasty. The bull was identified by priests of his cult by physical signs. Once chosen, it would be taken to the temple precincts where it would be purified, given magnificent stabling, the finest foods, and a herd of the best cows. On state occasions, it was paraded publicly, adorned with gold and jewels. After its death, the body was mummified and placed in underground burial chambers. Only after the spirit of the bull had been freed by the funeral rites was a successor sought and identified. There appear to have been three divine bulls in particular: the Apis (see feature), the Buchis and the Mnevis.

The Buchis and Mnevis cults

Burials of mummies of the Buchis bull were found at Armant, south of Luxor. This animal was considered sacred to the god Mont, whose temple was at nearby Tod. The linking of Mont with the sun god Re

The idea of the sacredness *of the cow in ancient Egypt goes back to Predynastic times. This painting of seven celestial cows and a bull comes from a side chamber in the tomb of the chief wife of Ramesses II, Nefertari, in the Valley of the Queens. Inscribed on the walls are parts of spells from the Book of the Dead: Spell 94 (requesting a water pot and a palette) and 148 (spell for making provision for a spirit in the realm of the dead). In some versions of the Book of the Dead the cows are named – 'Mansion of Kas, Mistress of All', 'The Much Beloved, Red of Hair', 'Lady of the House of Exaltation', 'Ladies of the West', or 'Ladies of the Holy Land', for example. The bull is called in at least one instance 'The Holy Bull, Chief of the Beautiful Ones'.*

during the late Middle Kingdom resulted in the Buchis also being considered an aspect of the sun god. Like the Apis, the mummies of the Buchis bulls and their mothers were embalmed and buried in catacombs (the Bucheum). Unlike the Apis, however, whose bodies were placed in huge sarcophagi weighing in excess of 60 tons, the bodies of the Buchis bulls were placed on a wooden board and held in position by metal staples around the fore- and hind legs.

The third bull, about which very little is known, was the Mnevis. References link him closely with Re, the sun god of Heliopolis, and there are suggestions that he was sometimes identified with Min, the fertility god of Coptos (Qift). During the Eighteenth Dynasty, the cult of the sun reached new heights when Amenhotep IV, later Akhenaten, elevated the cult of Re-Horakhte, the form the sun took as it rose above the eastern horizon at dawn, into that of his new god, the Aten. This god was not, as is popularly believed, the disk of the sun, but rather the faceless form of the divine manifest in the sun. Akhenaten dedicated a new city to the worship of this god on the site now known as Tell el Amarna. When he established the city, the king swore to bury the Mnevis bulls there. As yet, however, no bull burials have been found on the site. Perhaps Akhenaten never carried out his vow; or perhaps no Mnevis died during his reign. The two Mnevis burials that have been found (in Heliopolis) so far, unlike those of the Apis and Buchis, are individual tombs, cut into the ground and sealed with a single granite slab.

The role of analysis

Many museums contain large numbers of animal mummies, very few of which have been examined. Often they are unprovenanced, bought and donated by travellers a century ago. Dating the remains is a great problem. Those animals whose wrappings are in the diamond-patterned style can only date from the Graeco-Roman period, but far more, in plain linen wrappings, could come from any era – including modern times. Since millions of these mummies survive, many in poor condition, radiocarbon dating could be performed on some with little loss, and might reveal much valuable information about the age of some of the cults.

The Curse and Other Myths

SOMEONE MAY SPEND MANY HOURS alone with a dying relative or spouse, but find it impossible to sit for even a few moments in their presence once they have passed away. In the same way, graveyards are seen as alien places where the living do not belong.

This unreasoning dread is exaggerated in the case of Egyptian mummies, for here the dead openly confront the living and inhabit their world. The remarkable preservation of the bodies only adds to the feeling of apprehension, because it leads to the ever-present thought that these people cannot truly be dead at all but are merely suspended in time. When added to this is the realization that the Egyptians used magic in their funeral ceremonies – much of which is still not fully understood – then the fear becomes palpably stronger.

The battle between the living and the dead

The so-called 'curse of the pharaohs' developed in a strange manner. When the Arabs arrived in Egypt in the seventh century, the old beliefs still flourished in some areas, and, though the ancient hieroglyphs could no longer be understood, enough of the language remained in common speech and Coptic to make it seem mysterious. These things they could not understand instilled a certain fearful respect among the Arabs.

The old word for Egypt was *keme*, the black land, referring to the fertile strip each side of the river. The Arabs picked up this term and referred to the ancient mysteries as 'the Egyptian matter' – or *al keme*. This became alchemy, the belief that the correct application of potions, mixtures and words could change the structure and appearance of matter. The Arabs believed implicitly that entering a tomb and uttering the correct magical formula would enable objects rendered invisible by the ancients to materialize: funerary equipment in solid gold and precious stones. They also believed that a people capable of such strong magic would not allow anyone simply to enter and rob a tomb. The result could only be a battle in which the living tried to appropriate the belongings of the dead which the dead would actively protect by any means in their power.

These concepts were expressed in many early Arabic texts, in which the writers sought to warn future generations of the things they knew. The belief that mummies could be restored to life grew from the paintings on the walls of ancient tombs, accessible to many, which showed the Opening of the Mouth ceremony. The idea that the dead could move, see, smell, hear, taste and touch made the mummy a powerful adversary – more threatening than a living enemy since this one was already dead and had nothing to fear.

'Death comes on wings . . .'

The curse of the pharaohs made headline news in 1923, six months after Howard Carter's discovery of the tomb of Tutankhamun, which he entered with his patron, Lord Carnarvon. The finding of this extraordinary and virtually intact tomb had two immediate results: the world's press besieged the Valley of the Kings, each reporter hoping for a scoop; and new, growing feelings of nationalism were directed against the English archaeologist Carter.

In an attempt to divert the constant pleas of the press for access to the tomb, Carnarvon appointed the correspondent from *The Times* in London as his sole agent. This meant that everyone – even the

George Herbert, Earl of Carnarvon *(1866–1923), limited by lifelong problems of ill health, was nevertheless an enthusiastic amateur Egyptologist and serious collector of artefacts. But he will be remembered first and foremost as the sponsor of Howard Carter. Without Carnarvon's enthusiasm and long financial support Carter would have had neither the time nor the resources to devote to his work in the Valley of the Kings that led eventually to the greatest archaeological find of this century: the tomb of Tutankhamun. It was Carnarvon's sudden death just weeks after entering the tomb that triggered the legend of 'the curse of the pharaohs'.*

Egyptians – had to contact London to find out what was happening. Carter and Carnarvon exacerbated the situation by their determination to regard the tomb as their own property. The Egyptian government retaliated by restricting access to the tomb. Carter raged that the choice of who entered the tomb was his alone and stalked out, locking the gates behind him. The authorities cut off Carter's locks and proceeded to stage a grand official opening of the tomb – to which only Egyptians were invited.

The press was left in an awkward situation, powerless in a hostile country with only copy on political arguments to send back rather than the stories of gold and treasure that the public demanded. Then, in March 1923, the American Gothic novelist Marie Corelli wrote a letter to the *New York Times*, stating that she had in her possession one of the early Arabic books concerned with the opening of Egyptian tombs in which it was stated that 'Death comes on wings to he who enters the tomb of a pharaoh'. Corelli foretold the deaths of all involved on working in the tomb. The story was taken up briefly by the press, and would have attracted no more than polite interest had not Lord Carnarvon died only days later.

Carnarvon, in ill health for many years, had originally gone to Egypt on doctor's orders to get away from the cold, wet English winters, but he was never strong. In early 1923, a mosquito bite had become infected and it was this that led to the pneumonia from which he died. The day that news of his demise reached England, a *Times* reporter was interviewing Sir Arthur Conan Doyle who, besides being known as the author of the Sherlock Holmes stories, was also famous as a medium and mystic. They discussed Carnarvon's death – and then the reporter mentioned Corelli's letter. Conan Doyle was much struck by it and said that he believed the death was indeed the vengeance of the dead pharaoh. On that day the idea of the curse became a fact, and the story made front-page news around the world. Details were added to embellish the tale. For example, at the time of Carnarvon's death, the lights had gone out in Cairo – a frequent occurrence even today – and this was taken as another sign that the ancient kings were punishing the violators of their peace. The words of the curse written by Marie Corelli now gained such an aura of authenticity that some newspapers declared the inscription had been found in the tomb itself.

The curse that would not die

As years went by, the legend gathered impetus. Every time someone associated with the original discovery died, the event was reported in the press. Hollywood produced numerous films, and books added yet stranger stories to the myth. One of the perpetrators of these stories was the otherwise highly regarded Egyptologist Arthur Weigall, who himself had discovered several tombs in the valley before Carter's sensational find. In 1924, in his book *Tutankhamen and Other Essays*, Weigall described more events that lent credence to the curse.

These included such stories as that of a cobra that swallowed Carter's pet canary.

Weigall told of two major incidents in detail. The first concerned an artefact he had acquired, the wooden figure of a cat that had been used as a container for an ancient cat mummy. He left it in his bedroom and, one night as he slept, the Egyptologist was awakened by a noise like the firing of a shot. As he opened his eyes, he found a large grey cat jumping onto his bed, while the coffin lay split in two on the floor. In the second story, Weigall told how he and an American artist friend, Joseph Lindon Smith, and their wives had decided to act out a play at the head of the Valley of the Queens. At a rehearsal, however, Mrs Smith was suddenly struck with a fierce pain in her eyes. Later the same day, Mrs Weigall developed severe abdominal pains. Both women were rushed to the hospital and, fearing the curse, the whole idea of the play was abandoned.

Looked at rationally, both stories have logical explanations. Wood from ancient sites frequently distorts as heat and humidity change, and as it breaks apart makes a loud cracking sound. Such a sound could easily have disturbed the cat which might have panicked and leapt onto Weigall's bed for protection. In the second instance, Mrs Smith suffered from ophthalmia, a common problem that afflicted westerners who spent hours in the brilliant Egyptian sunshine with no protection for their eyes. As for Mrs Weigall's pains, she was suffering a miscarriage. Neither medical condition needed the intervention of the supernatural. But Weigall's manner of telling the stories made them seem something more than ordinary events, and his final comment appeared to allow for the possibility of some otherworldly cause: 'I have heard the most absurd nonsense talked in Egypt by those who believe in the malevolence of the ancient dead; but at the same time, I try to keep an open mind on the subject.'

In 1972, the subject of the curse was revived. Selected treasures from Tutankhamun's tomb were permitted to be taken out of Egypt to certain museums in other countries to celebrate the fiftieth anniversary of the discovery of the tomb. The items were flown in crates to England in a Royal Air Force Britannia aircraft. Six years later, in September 1978, the 'awful truth' of the flight was revealed by the *News of the World* newspaper, in lurid tales told by the flight crew. One technical officer thought it amusing to kick the case containing the royal mask – and two years later broke the same leg. Another crew member was divorced several years after the flight and partly blamed the curse: 'I knew that during the flight we all talked about the curse,' he told the newspaper. 'Then it was just a big laugh. Now it's not so funny.' Two other members had had heart attacks and their families had little doubt that they were the fault of the offended pharaoh.

These people were not alone in their ideas. After the curse became news, many blamed bad fortune on Egyptian articles in their possession. Museum workers are sometimes confronted by members of the public who have dug up an Egyptian artefact in their garden, or back yard. Sometimes these articles are genuine, sometimes only copies, but in almost every case where the article can be traced, the explanation that eventually emerges for their having been buried is that the object was blamed for bringing bad luck and thrown out.

Even museums are not beyond these stories. The British Museum is reputed to have had a mummy with a curse upon it. Wanting to dispose of it, so the stories say, they sold it to an American institution and arranged for its transport – on the *Titanic*. This legend, like most others, is entirely fallacious. The mummy is in reality a coffin lid, still in the museum's collection and on display today in the mummy room (lid No. EA 22542).

The reality of the curse

It is evident from all tombs that have been found and the inscriptions on their walls that the dead positively welcomed the living. Their immortality depended on the survival of their name and the continuation of their funerary offerings – and these, in turn, depended on people entering the tomb with the proper intention.

There were, on rare occasions, inscriptions placed in tombs that were aimed not just at anyone entering the tomb, but specifically at those who had not been purified or those who had some grievance against the deceased. One typical inscription was found in the tomb of Meni, a courtier of the Fourth Dynasty: 'As for any man who did these things for me [i.e. prepared his tomb], he should not be dissatisfied, because, whether sculptor or stonemason, I paid him for it. Let the crocodile be against him in the water, the snake against him on land. I have never done anything against him and it is the god who will judge him for it.' In other words, Meni would do nothing against him and it was up to the god alone to judge him.

As is often the case with myths and legends, the truth can be somewhat disappointing. There was not and never has been a curse attached to any mummy or tomb. There was no threatening inscription found in the tomb of Tutankhamun. All the mysterious incidents connected with Egyptian sites or objects can be explained without reference to the supernatural. The curse simply does not exist.

The mummy of *Tuthmosis III (above), on which the film makers based the appearance of the mummy of Imhotep, as played by Karloff (opposite above).*

Imhotep, *having been released from his long death, adopts the guise of a modern Egyptian archaeologist (below). Assisted by his Nubian servant, Imhotep prepares to kill Helen Grosvenor so he can free the spirit of the ancient princess that inhabits her body.*

In 1932, *The Mummy* launched a new genre of films. In one of his earliest starring roles, Boris Karloff, surely the best known of all horror film actors, played the mummy of the priest Imhotep, who had been brought back to life by a hapless archaeologist reading aloud a spell from an ancient magical scroll.

The plot of the film concerns the efforts of Imhotep to revive the mummy of his lover, the Princess Ananka, whose spirit has unfortunately taken possession of another – who must be killed if the princess is to be restored to life. The film is truer to the lore of ancient Egypt in its props than in its plot – the Egyptians believed in an afterlife, but not in the physical resurrection of mummies so they could resume their amorous affairs in this one; nor did they believe in reincarnation or spirit possession. Nevertheless, the film was probably the first introduction for a popular mass audience to the myth and magic of mummies.

175

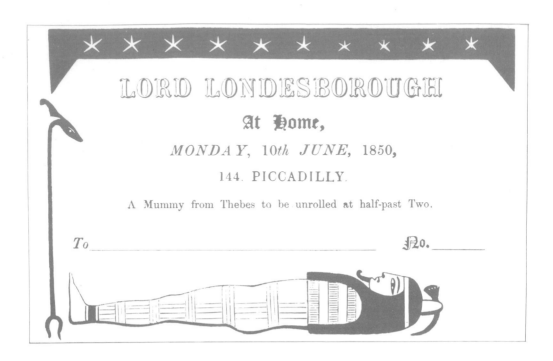

LORD LONDESBOROUGH

At Home,

MONDAY, 10th JUNE, 1850,

144. PICCADILLY.

A Mummy from Thebes to be unrolled at half-past Two.

To _____   No. _____

Mummy Factfile

A number of museums and universities have physical remains of ancient Egyptians, both human and animal. Many are on public display. Still others are part of study collections; not on view, but available to scholars from around the world. What follows is a selection of most of the major and some of the smaller international institutions holding Egyptian mummies.

AUSTRALIA

Sydney: Macquarie University
1 human mummy – sex unspecified; 5 animal mummies, all birds.

In addition, the collection contains fragments of mummies, including: 7 heads, 3 feet, 1 jawbone.

AUSTRIA

Vienna: Kunsthistorisches Museum
33 human mummies – sex unspecified; 67 unspecified animal mummies.

The human mummies are currently under detailed study for publication.

BELGIUM

Antwerp: Museum Vleeshuis
2 human mummies – 1 female, 1 sex unknown; 2 animal mummies, both ibises.

Brussels: Musées Royaux d'Art et d'Histoire
A number of fine human and animal mummies.

The collection holds a number of fine coffins and sarcophagi, and a selection of grave goods and amulets. One interesting mummy from Antinoë has ac- quired the name of 'the mummy of the embroideress', after the quantities of finely embroidered cloth which accompanied her burial and covered the body.

CANADA

Montreal: Redpath Museum, McGill University
3 human mummies – 1 male, 2 female; 16 animal mummies – 2 cats, 7 crocodiles, 4 hawks, 2 ibises.

Toronto: Royal Ontario Museum
7 human mummies – 3 male, 2 female, 2 sex unknown; 30 unspecified animal mummies.

EGYPT

Alexandria: Graeco-Roman Museum
20 human mummies – 6 male, 6 female, 8 sex unknown; 10 unspecified animal mummies.

Aswan: Aswan Museum (Elephantine Island)
4 human mummies – 2 male, 2 female; 1 animal mummy, a ram.

The male mummies are those of two priests who served the ram-headed god Khnum; the female mummies are their wives.

Cairo: Egyptian Museum
Numerous mummies, human and animal, spanning all periods of Egyptian history.

There is no up-to-date catalogue of Cairo's mummies, which constitute the finest collection in the world. It holds most of the royal mummies* which have been discovered, including the remains from the two caches (see pp. 36–7, 38–9); the remains from Tomb 55 (see p. 47); the bodies of Yuya and Thuya (see pp. 54–5), and Mahirpa (see p. 164); and many of the mummies from the cache of the high priests (see p. 38). The royal mummies rest in a room sealed off from even the most important visitors, but there are many which can be seen throughout the vast collection.

*Tutankhamun's mummy (see pp. 40–6, 48–9) is still in his tomb in the Valley of the Kings. The remains of the mummies from Tanis (see pp. 46, 136–7) are still in the Department of Anatomy in Cairo where they were initially examined.

FRANCE

Avignon: Musée Calvet
2 human mummies – 1 male, 1 sex unknown; 9 animal mummies – 2 cats, 3 crocodiles, 2 falcons, 2 ibises.

Grenoble: Musée des Beaux Arts
7 human mummies – 2 male, 3 female, 2 sex unknown; 21 animal mummies – 1 bird, 6 cats, 3 crocodiles, 3 falcons, 4 fish, 2 ibises, 1 monkey, 1 egg.

Limoges: Musée Municipal de l'Eveche
1 animal mummy – an ibis.

Paris: Bibliothèque Nationale
1 human mummy.

Paris: Louvre
2 human mummies – 1 male, 1 uncertain, possibly male; numerous unspecified animal mummies.

The collection also presently contains 1 human head.

Paris: Musée de l'Homme
4 human mummies – sex unknown.

Toulouse: Musée de Toulouse
1 human mummy – female.

GREECE

Athens: National Museum
15 human mummies – 8 male, 7 female; 6 animal mummies – 1 crocodile, 4 falcons, 1 ibis.

HUNGARY

Budapest: Szépmüvészeti Múzeum
5 human mummies – 3 male, 2 female; 13 unspecified animal mummies.

IRELAND

Dublin: National Museum of Ireland
5 human mummies – 1 male, 3 female, 1 sex unknown; 6 animal mummies – 2 cats, 1 crocodile, 1 hawk, 2 ibises, and the bones of a jackal.

ITALY

Bologna: Museo Civico
7 human mummies – 3 male, 3 female, 1 sex unknown; 5 animal mummies – 3 cats, 2 crocodiles.

Cortona: Museo dell'Accademia Etrusca
2 human mummies – possibly female.

Florence: Museo Archeologico
16 human mummies – 8 male, 5 female, 3 sex unknown; numerous animal mummies, including 4 cats, 7 crocodiles, 1 dog, 8 falcons, 6 fish, 2 ibises, 1 monkey, 3 snakes, miscellaneous parts, including 1 ram's head.

Milan: Castello Sforzesco
Numerous human mummies – male and female; numerous unspecified animal mummies.

Rovigo: Museo dell'Accademia dei Concordi
2 human mummies.

Trieste: Civico Museo di Storia ed Arte
1 human mummy – female; 1 animal mummy, a cat.

Turin: Museo di Antropologia e Etnografia
25 human mummies – sex unspecified; 3 animals, all dogs.

In addition, the collection holds 80 human heads and 100 other parts of human bodies.

Turin: Museo Egizio
70 human mummies – 30 male, 23 female, 17 sex unknown; 100 animal mummies, including birds (duck and ibis), bulls, cats, crocodiles, dogs, monkeys, snakes.

The mummies of Kha and his wife Meryt, found in their intact tomb, have been subjected to X-ray analysis (see pp. 76–7).

NETHERLANDS

Amsterdam: Allard Pierson Museum
1 human mummy – male; 7 animal mummies – 1 bird, 1 cat, 2 fish, 2 ichneumons, 1 scarab.

Leiden: Rijksmuseum van Oudheden
Approximately 30 human mummies.

POLAND

Warsaw: Muzeum Narodowe
2 human mummies – 1 male, 1 sex unknown; 8 unspecified animal mummies.

SWEDEN

Lund: Kulturhistoriska Museet
1 human mummy – sex unknown.

Lund: Universitets Historiska Museum
1 human mummy – male.

SWITZERLAND

Geneva: Musée d'Art et d'Histoire
2 human mummies – 1 male, 1 female; 21 animal mummies – 12 birds, 4 cats, 5 crocodiles.

Lausanne: Musée d'Yverdon les Bains
4 human mummies – 2 male, 1 female, 1 sex unknown.

Neuchâtel: Musée d'Ethnographie
1 human mummy – male; 6 animal mummies – 1 cat, 3 crocodiles, 1 ibis, 1 ichneumon.

UNITED KINGDOM

Blackburn: Blackburn City Museum
1 human mummy – female.

Bolton: Bolton Museum
2 human mummies, 1 male, 1 female; animal mummies are uncatalogued.

Bristol: City of Bristol Art Museum
9 human mummies – 6 male, 1 female, 2 sex unknown; 5 unspecified animal mummies.

Among the human mummies is that of Horemkenesi, a Twentieth Dynasty male whose remains formed the subject of a detailed analysis project (see pp. 98–9). The results are the focus of a permanent display.

Cambridge: Fitzwilliam Museum
1 human mummy – male; 2 animal mummies, both cats.

Dundee: Dundee Museum and Art Gallery
1 human mummy of unknown sex.

Durham: Durham University Oriental Art and Archaeology
2 human mummies – sex unspecified.

Edinburgh: Royal Museum of Scotland
10 human mummies – 6 male, 3 female, 1 sex unknown; 1 unspecified animal mummy.

Glasgow: City of Glasgow Art Gallery and Museum
2 human mummies – 1 male, 1 female; at least 8 unspecified animal mummies.

Glasgow: Hunterian Museum
1 human mummy – female; 2 unspecified animal mummies.

Liverpool: National Museums and Galleries on Merseyside, Liverpool Museum
18 human mummies – 9 male, 6 female,

3 sex unknown; 72 unspecified animal mummies.

See pp. 92–3.

Liverpool: University of Liverpool
1 'human' mummy; 17 animal mummies – 12 fish, 2 hawks, 1 snake, 2 unspecified.

On examination, the 'human' mummy was found to be that of a cat inside a human coffin.

London: British Museum
78 human mummies – 37 male, 20 female, 19 sex unknown; 70–80 animals, unspecified and uncatalogued.

In at least two cases contents of coffins or mummies contained other remains. That of an adult male also contained the mummies of two infants and a ten-year-old child. Another 'mummy' proved to be two 'miniature mummies', one died after birth; the other was a five-month-old foetus.

Manchester: Manchester University Museum
18 human mummies – 2 male, 2 female, 14 sex unspecified; numerous unspecified animal mummies.

The museum's mummy analysis project has been one of the foremost researches in the field (see pp. 101, 102–3, 103–4). It has led to the setting up of the International Mummy Data Bank at Manchester, as a resource for scholars.

Norwich: Castle Museum
2 human mummies – 1 male, 1 female; 3 animals – 1 cat, 1 crocodile, 1 hawk.

Oxford: Ashmolean Museum
9 human mummies – 1 male, 4 female, 4 sex unknown; 28 animal mummies – 5 cats, 1 crocodile, 4 falcons, 8 fish, 6 ibises, 1 scarab, 1 package of shrews, 2 snakes.

Oxford: Pitt-Rivers Museum
2 human mummies – 1 female, 1 sex unknown; 20 animals – 1 cat, 2 crocodiles, 1 dog, 1 kite, 15 unspecified.

Plymouth: Plymouth City Museum and Art Gallery
Approximately 12 animal mummies, including 1 cat, 1 crocodile, 1 ibis, 1 package containing about 20 shrews.

When displayed, the collection is shown with X-rays of the contents of the wrapped mummies.

UNITED STATES

Ann Arbor: Kelsey Museum
1 mummy – sex unknown.

Atlanta: Emory University Museum
4 human mummies – male

Baltimore: Walters Art Gallery
1 human mummy – female.

Berkeley: Robert H. Lowie Museum of Anthropology
5 human mummies – sex unspecified; unspecified number of animal mummies.

Boston: Museum of Fine Arts
15 human mummies – 8 male, 7 female; 120 unspecified animal mummies

The museum also holds partial remains of a further dozen human mummies. Many of the mummies and associated funerary material in Boston's collection were featured in an exhibition in 1988, including Tabes (see illustrations pp. 78–9).

Cambridge: Harvard Semitic Museum
1 animal mummy – a falcon.

Chicago: Field Museum of Natural History
30 human mummies – sex unspecified; numerous unspecified animal mummies.

The Egyptian collection was reinstalled in 1988 and planned to recreate life in ancient Egypt. A focus of the new exhibition is mummification, including a complete, large-scale diorama of an embalmer's workshop. Fifteen of the museum's animal mummies and all but five of their human mummies are now part of the permanent exhibition.

Chicago: Oriental Institute Museum
6 human mummies – 1 male, 4 female, 1 sex unknown; 57 animal mummies – 20 birds, 3 cats, 1 chicken, 34 crocodiles.

The institute also holds 1 complete Predynastic contracted burial; the sex is unknown, but considered to be female. In addition, there are numerous partial remains, including 1 head, 1 foot and 1 hand.

Cincinnati: Cincinnati Art Museum
2 human mummies – both male; 7 animal mummies, unspecified.

Cleveland: Western Reserve Historical Society
1 human mummy – male.

The mummy, identified from his wrappings as that of a minor priest, has been X-rayed twice, most recently in 1985 when it was also the subject of a CAT-scan analysis.

Columbus: Ohio State Historical Society
1 human mummy – possibly female.

Denver: Denver Art Museum
1 animal mummy – an ibis, complete with coffin.

Detroit: Detroit Institute of Arts
4 human mummies – 1 female, 3 sex unknown; 1 animal mummy, an ibis.

The female, from the Roman period, is on permanent display.

Kalamazoo: Kalamazoo Public Museum
2 human mummies – 1 male, 1 female; 5 animal mummies – 1 bird, 1 cat, 1 crocodile, 1 ibis, 1 lizard.

The female mummy, that of an unknown woman aged about 40, has been the subject of a detailed analysis. This includes not only X-ray and CAT-scanning, but also a complete reconstruction of the head and facial details. The mummy, the analysis results and the reconstruction are the focus of a permanent exhibition.

Los Angeles: Los Angeles County Museum of Art
1 animal mummy – falcon (presumed)

Memphis: Institute of Egyptian Art and Archaeology
1 human mummy – male; 2 animal mummies – 1 cat, 1 duck.

Minneapolis: Institute of Arts Museum
3 human mummies – 2 male, 1 female.

The female mummy is that of Lady Teshat, of whom several studies, X-ray and CAT-scan, have been done (see pp. 80–1).

New Haven: Peabody Museum of Natural History (Yale)
2 human mummies – 1 male, 1 female; 2 animal mummies – 1 bird, 1 'wolf'.

The male mummy, Rha, found at Deir el Bahri, was a cook for the pharaoh Ramesses II.

New York: The Brooklyn Museum
6 human mummies – 3 male, 3 female; 48 animal mummies – 8 cats, 5 crocodiles, 1 fish, 28 ibises, 1 snake, 5 unspecified.

New York: Metropolitan Museum of Art
10 human mummies – 6 male, 3 female, 1 unknown; approximately 25 animal mummies.

Philadelphia: The University Museum
9 human mummies – 3 male, 6 sex unknown; 75 unspecified animal mummies

The analysis of the Pennsylvania mummies, PUM I, II, III and IV, by a team

from Detroit (see pp. 95–6), has been the most significant such research in North America. Members of the team also analyzed mummies in the Toronto collection.

Pittsburgh: Museum of Art, Carnegie Institute
4 human mummies – 3 male, 1 female; 46 animal mummies – 7 cats, 2 crocodiles, 4 falcons, 23 fish, 1 lizard.

Richmond: Museum of Fine Arts
1 human mummy – male.

St. Louis: Mr and Mrs Barney A. Ebsworth Foundation
1 human mummy – male.

San Diego: Museum of Man
1 animal mummy – an ibis.

San Francisco: Museum of Fine Arts
4 human mummies – 1 male, 2 female, 1 sex unknown

San José: Rosicrucian Museum
8 human mummies – 3 male, 3 female, 2 sex unknown; 17 animal mummies – 1 'animal', 1 baboon, 7 birds, 5 cats, 2 crocodiles, 1 fish.

Toledo: Stanford University Museum
1 human mummy – female; 2 unspecified animal mummies.

Washington DC: Smithsonian Institution
6 human mummies – 3 sex unknown, 3

unspecified; 17 unspecified animal mummies.

WEST GERMANY

West Berlin: Staatliche Museen, Ägyptisches Museum
1 human mummy – female; 2 animal mummies, both falcons.

Frankfurt-am-Main: Natürmuseum Senckenberg
4 human mummies – 1 male, 1 female, 2 sex unknown; 18 animal mummies – 2 cats, 6 crocodiles, 5 falcons, 5 ibises.

Heidelberg: Ägyptologisches Institut der Universität
3 human mummies – 1 male, 2 sex unknown.

Tübingen: Ägyptologisches Institut der Universität
3 human mummies – 2 male, 1 female.

Würzburg: Institut für Ägyptologie der Universität Würzburg
5 animal mummies, all cats.

A child's mummy was destroyed in the bombing of World War II.

YUGOSLAVIA

Zagreb: Archeološki Muzej
4 human mummies – all female; 6 unspecified animal mummies.

Glossary

adze Carpenter's tool, with a curved blade at right angles to a handle. This came to have a ritual use in the ceremony of the Opening of the Mouth at the time of burial. Touching it to the mouth of the mummy or statue of the deceased was believed to restore the senses.

akh State in which the deceased exists in the afterlife, both immortal and unchangeable.

Ammit Goddess called 'Devouress of the Dead', who sits at the weighing of the heart and will eat the heart of anyone who is judged unworthy to be admitted to the underworld.

amulets Good-luck charms, often in the form of hieroglyphs, gods or sacred animals; made of precious stones or faience. They were worn in life and were also included in large numbers within mummy wrappings.

Amun God of Luxor (Thebes) who came to favour during the Middle Kingdom. His name means 'hidden', 'secret'. During the New Kingdom, regarded as the king of the gods.

ankh Hieroglyph, resembling a looped cross, that means 'to live' and 'life'. It may represent a sandal strap or the handle of a mirror. Adapted by Coptic Christians as their cross. Widely used as an amulet.

anthropoid Greek: man-shaped. The term is used to refer to wooden coffins of human shape.

Anubis Wild-dog- or jackal-headed god, believed to preside over mummification and bandaging of the dead, and to control the balance at the weighing of the heart.

Apis Bull sacred to Osiris, revered from the earliest times, though it came to prominence during the Graeco-Roman period.

ba Aspect often incorrectly translated as soul. It is freed from the body at death, and often represented as a human-headed bird.

barrel-vault Term referring to a roof of semi-cylindrical shape. Used for lids of Old Kingdom sarcophagi, and also believed to have been used for mastaba superstructures.

Bastet Cat goddess, whose centre of worship was at Bubastis in the delta.

Bes Squat, grotesque god held to be protective and to ward off evil spirits.

Book of the Dead Modern name given to magical texts that protected the dead on their way to the afterlife. An assortment of different texts are often called by this generic term. The Egyptians called the principal text The Book of Coming Forth by Day.

canopic jar Four jars, often made of stone, used to store preserved internal organs. The term appears to refer to a Greek demigod, Canopus, venerated in the form of a jar with a human head. *See also Four Sons of Horus.*

cartonnage Papyrus or linen soaked in gesso plaster, shaped around a body, rather like papier mâché, and then painted when dry. Used for mummy masks and coffins.

causeway Pathway running from a pyramid to a canal cut from the Nile to meet the desert plateau. When the pyramid was finished this was generally decorated inside and roofed over to form a corridor.

cenotaph Greek: empty tomb. A tomb built for ceremonial purposes and never intended for the interment of a body.

Coffin Texts Spells written inside Middle Kingdom wooden coffins to direct the souls of the dead past the dangers and perils of the afterlife.

cult temple Temple for worship of a god. *See also mortuary temple.*

djed pillar Widely found amulet, whose exact nature and meaning are unclear, although it was believed to have been a fetish from prehistoric times. It is thought that it eventually came to symbolize the backbone of Osiris, and was sometimes painted inside the base of the coffin (i.e. under the back of the deceased).

duat Egyptian name for the land of the dead. Similar to Egypt itself, lying under this earth, and entered through the western horizon.

encaustic Wax-based paint used on boards for portraits during the Graeco-Roman period.

faience Glazed material comprising a base of either carved steatite (soapstone) or moulded clay with crushed quartz, with an overlay of coloured glass, usually blue/green.

false door Focal point of a tomb; a door carved or painted on a wall through which the *ka* could enter and leave at will to partake of funerary offerings.

Four Sons of Horus Gods who protected the internal organs of the deceased.

From the Nineteenth Dynasty, canopic jars had the heads of these gods as their lids. Wax figures of these deities were often contained within the mummy wrappings, sometimes the appropriate figure was placed with the wrapped, prepared internal organ which was specifically under its protection.

funerary cones Tapering cones of clay inserted above the entrances to tombs, often with the name and titles of the deceased on the flat, circular end.

funerary offerings Bread, beer, wine and other items provided initially by mourners and later, magically, through inscriptions and pictures in the tomb; essential for the well-being of the *ka*.

Geb God of the earth. With his sister the sky goddess Nut, he produced Osiris, Isis, Seth and Nephthys.

grave goods Equipment placed in the tomb to provide all that was needed in the afterlife.

Haroeris The mature Horus, with the capacity for ruling.

Harpocrates The immature Horus, often depicted on the lap of his mother Isis, with a sidelock of youth and sucking his fingers.

Hathor Egyptian goddess portrayed with cow's horns, often confused with depictions of Isis. Consort of Horus, her major temple is at Dendera.

Horus One of the oldest gods of Egypt and recognized in Hieraconpolis and Edfu as contemporary with and opponent of Seth. Later absorbed into the Osiris legend as the posthumous son of Osiris and Isis. *See also Haroeris, Harpocrates.*

Isis Greatest of goddesses. Wife of Osiris and mother of Horus. She was a powerful magician and also venerated as the ideal mother; especially revered during the Graeco-Roman period.

ka The spiritual (and physical) double of a human being, created at the time of

birth by the god Khnum, who fashioned beings on his potter's wheel, before placing them inside their mother. The *ka* could be released during life in dreams, but was finally released at death. It was symbolized by a pair of upraised arms. *See also akh, ba, false door, funerary offerings, mortuary cult.*

lector priest Recited the ritual at cult ceremonies and funerals; wore a broad white sash across his chest.

Lower Egypt Land around the Nile delta, from modern Cairo to the Mediterranean coast. *See also Middle Egypt, Upper Egypt.*

Maat Goddess depicted with a feather on her head; also the feather by itself. Both represented order, balance, correct attitudes and thinking, morality and justice. It was the feather of Maat against which the heart of the deceased was weighed.

mastaba Arabic: bench. Refers to large mud-brick, rectangular superstructures built over tomb shafts during the Early Dynastic period and the Old Kingdom.

Meretseger Cobra goddess who lives on the mountain that dominates the Valley of the Kings.

Middle Egypt Geographical term loosely applied to the area south of Luxor, especially to sites around Beni Hasan and Tell el Amarna.

mortuary cult The provision of regular funerary offerings for the eternal wellbeing of the deceased. *See also false door, funerary offerings, ka.*

mortuary priest Person appointed to bring funerary offerings daily to a tomb; known as the 'servant of the ka'. An endowment of land during the life or after the death of the deceased provided the offerings, which then reverted to the priest to maintain him and his family.

mortuary temple Place where the mortuary cult of a king was carried out. Originally part of the funerary complex; in the New Kingdom came to be separated from the tomb, often by some miles. *See also cult temple.*

mummy A preserved corpse. This might be by 'natural' or artificial means. The latter involved removing all sources of moisture (i.e. as cause of decay) and thoroughly drying the body. Name derives from *moumiya*, or bitumen, with which the Persians mistakenly thought the bodies were coated.

mummy mask *See cartonnage.*

natron Naturally occurring salt from the area of the western delta, used as a cleansing agent for washing clothes, bodies and teeth. It was also used as a preservative during mummification.

necropolis Greek: city of the dead. Refers to Egyptian cemeteries from all periods, and includes the Valley of the Kings, Giza, Saqqara.

Nephthys Goddess, sister of Isis, Osiris and Seth, whose wife she was in the Osiris legend. With Isis, referred to one of the 'two kites', screeching birds that sounded like mourning women. She was a protectress of the dead.

Nut *See Geb.*

Opening of the Mouth Ceremony performed at the funeral to restore the senses of the deceased. *See also adze, Ptah, sem priest.*

Osiris God and king of the dead. Linked with both resurrection of the dead and regrowth of vegetation. Eventually, any dead person came to be referred to as 'an Osiris', i.e. a dweller in the land of the dead.

per nefer 'House of beauty' or 'good house'. Place where part of purification and mummificaton procedures or rituals took place.

pharaoh Literally the 'great house' or house of the king. From the time of the New Kingdom, the term came to be used for kings of Egypt.

Ptah Creator god of Memphis. It was Ptah whom the sem priest emulated at the Opening of the Mouth, for Ptah was believed to have carried out a similar action on the gods at the time of their creation.

pyramid Monumental burial places for kings between the Third and Twelfth Dynasties.

Pyramid Texts Spells carved on the walls of burial chambers of pyramids of the Fifth and Sixth Dynasties.

Re The sun god of Heliopolis, often shown as a falcon wearing a sun disk on its head; in the underworld, he is ram-headed. Came to prominence in the fifth Dynasty.

reserve heads Old Kingdom sculptures, found mainly in tombs at Giza, and considered by some to be true portraits of the deceased.

rock-cut tomb Method begun during Middle Kingdom of excavating tombs from solid rock. Examples are found in cliffs along the Nile, the burials in the Valley of the Kings and the tombs of the nobles at Luxor.

sarcophagus Greek: flesh eater. Name given to the rectangular or oval stone container within which the coffins and mummy were placed. Often used incorrectly for 'coffin'. *See also barrel vault.*

scarab Egyptian dung beetle, associated with spontaneous creation of life. Also

the god Khepri – kheper meant 'to come into existence'.

sekh **tent** A temporary structure at the tomb where the final funerary rites are thought to have taken place.

sem **priest** Associated with funerary ritual, especially the Opening of the Mouth ceremony; characteristically wears a leopard-skin garment.

serdab Arabic: cellar. Walled-up chamber provided in a mortuary chapel or burial shaft to contain an image or statue of the deceased.

Seth Brother of Osiris, Isis and Nephthys, whose husband he was. Personified evil; always represented with a strange black head of an unidentified animal. According to legend, his murder of Osiris was avenged by Horus.

shawabti See *ushabti.*

solar (or sun) boat Mythical, high-prowed boat in which the sun god was believed to navigate the heavens. Some Pyramid Texts refer to the king's going to join the gods in such a boat.

stela Slab of stone with an inscription, or a similar inscription carved on the face of a wall or cliff. Can be a memorial to a dead person (i.e. a gravestone), a com-

memoration of a victory or a major event, or a formal decree.

Thoth Ibis-headed god associated with scribes and learning. It was he who recorded the outcome of the weighing of the heart.

Upper Egypt Southern Egypt, generally referring to places between Luxor and Aswan; sometimes includes Middle Egypt.

ushabti Small wooden or glazed-stone mummiform figures placed in tombs to undertake work on behalf of the deceased, who might be called upon to perform tasks in the afterlife.

valley temple Place at the Nile edge where the king's body was received for final rites before being transported via the connecting causeway to the pyramid.

vizier Head of the bureaucratic administration, chief ambassador, supreme civil and criminal judge and the king's chief minister.

wabet Place where part of purification or mummification rites took place.

wadjet **eye** The left eye of Horus, restored by the god Thoth. It symbolized the power of healing and was a powerful protective amulet.

Suggested Reading

Abbreviations:

BMP *British Museum Publications, London*

CUP *Cambridge University Press, Cambridge and New York*

EES *Egypt Exploration Society, London*

IFAO *Institut Français d'Archéologie Orientale de Caire*

MFA *Museum of Fine Arts, Boston*

MMA *Metropolitan Museum of Art, New York*

MUP *Manchester University Press*

UCP *University of Chicago Press*

Selected General Books on Mummification

Adams, B., *Egyptian Mummies*, Shire, Aylesbury 1984.

Andrews, C. *Egyptian Mummies*, BMP and Cambridge, Mass. 1984.

D'Auria, S., Lacovara, P. and Roehrig, C., *Mummies & Magic, The Funerary Arts of Ancient Egypt*, MFA 1988.

David, A.R., *Mysteries of the Mummies*, MUP 1978.

Faulkner, R.O., *The Ancient Egyptian Book of the Dead*, BMP 1985.

Fleming, S., Fishman, B., O'Connor, D. and Silverman, D., *The Egyptian Mummy, Secrets and Science*, University Museum, Philadelphia 1980.

Hamilton-Paterson, J. and Andrews, C., *Mummies*, BMP and Collins, 1978.

Harris, J. and Weeks, K., *X-raying the Pharaohs*, Macdonald, London, and Scribner's, New York 1973.

Spencer, A.J., *Death in Ancient Egypt*, Penguin, London and New York 1982.

Taylor, J., *Egyptian Coffins*, Shire, Aylesbury 1989.

Selected General Books on Egypt

Aldred, C. *The Egyptians*, Thames and Hudson, London and New York 1984.

Baines, J. and Málek, J., *Atlas of Ancient Egypt*, Phaidon, Oxford 1983, repr. 1986.

David, A.R., *Ancient Egypt*, Phaidon, Oxford 1975, rev. 1988.

Hobson (El Mahdy), C., *Exploring the World of the Pharaohs*, Thames and Hudson, London and New York 1987, repr. 1989.

James, T.G.H., *Ancient Egypt, the Land and Its Legacy*, BMP 1988.

Kemp, B.J., *Ancient Egypt, Anatomy of a Civilization*, Routledge, London and New York 1989.

Romer, J., *Romer's Egypt*, Michael Joseph, London 1982.

Further Reading

Aldred, C., *Akhenaten, King of Egypt*, Thames and Hudson, London and New York 1988.

—'More Light on the Ramesside Tomb Robberies', in Ruffle, J. et al (eds.), *Glimpses of Ancient Egypt, Studies in Honour of H.W. Fairman*, pp. 92–9, Aris and Phillips, Warminster 1979.

Allen, T.G., *The Book of the Dead*, UCP 1974.

Balout, L., Robert, C. and Desroches-Noblecourt, C., *La Momie de Ramses II*, Paris 1985.

Bakry, H.S., *A Brief Study of Mummies and Mummification*, Cairo 1965.

Belzoni, G., *Narrative of the operations and recent discoveries within the pyramids, temples, tombs, and excavations in Egypt and Nubia*, London 1820.

Bierbrier, M.L., *The Tomb-Builders of the Pharaohs*, BMP 1984.

Breasted, J.H. *The Edwin Smith Surgical Papyrus*, UCP 1930.

Brothwell, D. and Sandison, A. (eds.), *Diseases in Antiquity*, C.C. Thomas, Springfield, Illinois, 1967.

Budge, E.A.W., *The Mummy*, 1925, repr. Kegan Paul International, London and New York 1987.

Carter, H., *The Tomb of Tut-ankh-amen*, (3 vols.) Cassell, London 1925; repr. (1 vol.) Sphere Books, London, and E.P. Dutton & Co., New York 1972.

Černý, J., *The Valley of the Kings*, Cairo 1973.

—*A Community of Workmen at Thebes in the Ramesside Period*, IFAO 1973.

—*Ancient Egyptian Religion*, Hutchinson's University Library, London 1957.

Cockburn, A. and E., *Mummies, Disease and Ancient Cultures*, CUP 1980.

Cottrell, L., *The Mountains of Pharaoh*, Evans, London 1956.

—*The Lost Pharaohs*, Evans, London 1960; Grosset & Dunlap, New York 1963.

David, A.R., *The Ancient Egyptians, Religious Beliefs and Practices*, Routledge and Kegan Paul, London and New York 1982, repr. 1986.

—*The Manchester Mummy Project*, MUP 1979.

David, A.R. (ed.), *Science in Egyptology*, MUP 1988.

David, A.R. and Tapp, E. (eds.), *Evidence Embalmed*, MUP 1984.

Dawson, W.R., *A Bibliography of Works Relating to Mummification in Egypt*, IFAO 1929.

Dawson, W.R. and Gray, P.M.K., *Catalogue of Egyptian Antiquities in the British Museum I: Mummies and Human Remains*, London 1968.

Desroches-Noblecourt, C., *Tutankhamen*, Michael Joseph, London, and New York Graphic Society, 1963; repr. Boston 1986.

Diodorus Siculus, *History*, (tr. C. Oldfield), Harvard University Press, Cambridge 1935; Loeb Classical Library, London 1968.

Drioton, E. and Lauer, J.-P., *Sakkara, the Monuments of Zoser*, IFAO 1939.

Ebell, E. *The Papyrus Ebers, the Greatest Egyptian Medical Document*, Levin and Munksgaard, Copenhagen 1937.

Edwards, I.E.S., *The Pyramids of Egypt* (rev.), Viking, London and New York 1986.

Edwards, I.E.S. and Shorter, A., *A Handbook to the Egyptian Mummies and Coffins Exhibited in the British Museum*, London 1938.

Emery, W.B., *Archaic Egypt*, Penguin, 1961 London and New York, repr. 1987.

Faulkner, R.O., *The Egyptian Coffin Texts*, Aris and Phillips, Warminster 1973.

—*The Egyptian Pyramid Texts*, Oxford University Press, 1969.

Gardiner, A.H., *The Attitude of Ancient Egyptians to Death and the Dead*, CUP 1935.

Garstang, J., *Burial Customs of Ancient Egypt*, Constable, London 1907.

Ghaliounghi, P., *Magic and Medical Science in Ancient Egypt*, (2nd ed.), Amsterdam 1973.

Ghaliounghi, P. and el Dawakhly, Z., *Health and Healing in Ancient Egypt*, Cairo 1965.

Goneim, Z., *The Buried Pyramid*, Longmans, London 1956.

Goyon, J.-C., *Rituels Funéraires De L'Ancienne Égypte*, Editions de Cerf, Paris 1972.

Goyon, J.-C. and Josset, P., *Un Corps Pour L'Éternité*, Le Leopard D'Or, Paris 1988. Note: this is the record of the Lyons mummy analysis project.

Grapow, H., *Grunriss der Medizin der alten Ägypter*, Berlin 1954 through present.

Gray, D. and Slow, E., *Egyptian Mummies in the City of Liverpool Museums*, 1968.

Harris, J. and Wente, E., *X-ray Atlas of the Royal Mummies*, UCP 1980.

Hayes, W.C., *The Scepter of Egypt*, (2 vols.), MMA, (vol. 1) 1953; (vol. 2) 1959.

Hornung, E., (tr. J. Baines), *Conceptions of God in Ancient Egypt*, Routledge and Kegan Paul, London 1983.

Lauer, J.-P., *Saqqara, Royal Cemetery of Memphis*, Thames and Hudson, London and McGraw-Hill, New York 1976.

Leca, A.P., *Cult of the Immortal*, Paladin, London 1980.

—*La Médicine Egyptienne au Temps des Pharaons*, Dacosta, Paris 1971.

Lortet, L. and Gaillard, C., *La fauna momifiée de L'ancienne Égypte*, Archives du Museum d'Histoire Naturel de Lyons, IX–X, 1903–9.

Lucas, A., *Ancient Egyptian Materials and Industries*, (4th ed., revised and enlarged by J.R. Harris), Edward Arnold, London 1962.

Manchester, K., *The Archaeology of Disease*, University of Bradford, 1983.

Manniche, L., *City of the Dead, Thebes in Egypt*, BMP 1987.

Mariette, A., *Le Sérapéum de Memphis*, Paris 1882.

Maspero, G., *Les Momies Royales de Deir-el-Bahari*, Cairo 1889.

Mendelssohn, K., *Riddle of the Pyramids*, re-issued Thames and Hudson, London and New York 1986.

Mohammed, M.A.Q., *The Development of the Funerary Beliefs and Practices Displayed in the Private Tombs of the New Kingdom at Thebes*, Cairo 1966.

Mokhtar, G., Riad, H. and Iskander, Z., *Mummification in Ancient Egypt*, Cairo 1973.

Mond, R. and Myers, O., *The Bucheum*, EES 1934.

Moodie, R.L., *Roentgenologic Studies of Egyptian and Peruvian Mummies*, Field Museum of Natural History, Chicago 1931.

Murray, M.A., *Tomb of the Two Brothers*, MUP 1910.

Peet, T.E., *The Great Tomb Robberies of the Twentieth Egyptian Dynasty*, Oxford University Press 1943.

Petrie, W.M.F., *Amulets*, Aris and Phillips, Warminster, 1972.

—*Royal Tombs of the Earliest Dynasties*, EES 1900.

—*Shabtis*, Aris and Phillips, Warminster 1972.

Pettigrew, T.J., *A History of Egyptian Mummies*, London 1834; repr. Los Angeles 1983.

Piankoff, A., *The Litany of Re*, Pantheon Books, New York 1964.

—*Mythological Papyri*, Pantheon Books, New York 1957.

—*The Pyramid of Unas*, Princeton 1968.

—*The Shrines of Tutankhamun*, Pantheon Books, New York 1955.

—*The Tomb of Ramesses VI*, Pantheon Books, New York 1954.

Porter, B. and Moss, R., *Topographical Bibliography*, (8 vols.), Oxford, 1927 through present.

Reisner, G.A., *Amulets*, Service des Antiquités, Cairo 1907.

—*The Development of the Egyptian Tomb down to the Accession of Cheops*, Harvard, Cambridge, Mass. 1936.

—*History of the Giza Necropolis I*, Harvard, Cambridge, Mass. 1942.

Romer, J., *Ancient Lives*, Weidenfeld and Nicolson, London 1984.

—*Valley of the Kings*, Michael Joseph, London 1981; William Morrow and Company, New York 1981; repr. 1988.

Ruffer, M.A., *Studies in the Palaeopathology of Egypt*, UCP 1921.

Sauneron, S., *The Priests of Ancient Egypt*, Paris 1957; London and New York 1960.

—*Le Rituel de L'Embaumement*, National Printing House, Cairo 1952.

Schiaparelli, E., *La Tomba Intatta dell'architetto Cha*, Turin 1927.

Schneider, H., *Shabtis*, (3 vols.), Leiden 1977.

Simpson, W.K., *The Mastabas of Qar and Idu*, MFA 1976.

Smith, G.E., *The Royal Mummies*, Cairo 1912.

Smith, G.E. and Dawson, W.R., *Egyptian Mummies*, London 1924; New York 1925.

Thomas, E., *The Royal Necropolis at Thebes*, Princeton 1966.

Thompson, D., *Mummy Portraits in the J. Paul Getty Museum*, Malibu 1982.

Vanlatham, Marie-Paule, *Cercueils et Momies de l'Égypte Ancienne*, Musées Royaux d'Art et d'Histoire, Brussels 1983.

Wilkinson, J.G., *Manners and Customs of the Ancient Egyptians* (2nd ed) London 1878.

Winlock, H.E., *Excavations at Deir-el-Bahari*, 1911, MMA 1942.

—*The Slain Soldiers of Nebhepetre Mentuhotep*, MMA 1945.

—*Materials Used at the Embalming of King Tut-Ankh-Amen*, MMA 1941; repr. Arno Press, 1973.

Acknowledgments

The author and publishers would like to thank the many scholars and institutions who have generously given their time and expertise to the preparation of this book. Special thanks are due to the Boston Museum of Fine Arts, the City of Bristol Museum and Art Gallery, the British Museum, the Committee of the Egypt Exploration Society, and Kodansha Publishers Limited of Tokyo, for their cooperation and invaluable assistance.

The publishers also wish to acknowledge the sources of the following photographs:

After *Art and Architecture of Ancient Egypt* 118. Ashmolean Museum 153. After *Barrow, Pyramid and Tomb* 130. Bildarchiv Foto, Marburg 19, 71. Boston Museum of Fine Arts 78, 79 (© Myron Marx). City of Bristol Museum and Art Gallery 98, 99. Trustees of the British Museum 12, 53, 67, 150, 158–9, 161, 162 (top), 163 (both); Pls. VII, XI. Emil Brugsch 10 (right, both), 36 (left, both centre), 37. Peter Clayton 10 (left, right top), 31, 47, 55, 56, 114; Pls. V, XV. Costa 111 (right), 159. After Davis, *A Corpus of Inscribed Funerary Cones* 135. *Description de l'Égypte* 25. Detroit Institute of Arts (© Nemo Warr) 95 (both), 96. Egypt Exploration Society 50, 140, 152. After *Egyptian Mysteries* 146. Fitzwilliam Museum 115; Pls. IV, VI. Griffith Institute 49, 171. J.E. Harris 76. André Held 164–5. Max Hirmer title page, 15, 134. Kodansha Pls. I, II, III (from *The Gold of Tutankhamen*, published by Kodansha Ltd, Tokyo 1978). Peter Lindman 80 (left). Liverpool Museum 92–3 (all). Louvre Pl. XIV. C.M. El Mahdy 166. Manchester Museum 20–1, 102. After A. Mariette, *Temple of Denderah* 155. Metropolitan Museum of Art 16, 17, 39 (bottom), 97 (both), 111 (left), 114–15, 148. Minneapolis Institute of Arts 80 (right), 81 (both). After *Mummies & Magic, the Funerary Arts of Ancient Egypt* 153 (bottom). Museum National d'Histoire Naturelle 89 (both). After Naville, *Das Ägyptischer Totenbuch der XVIII. bis XX. Dynastie* 13, 113. *Petri della Valle, Eines vornehmen Romischen Patritii Reissbeschreibung* 29. Photo Rosso 77. After A. Piankoff, *Mythological Papyri* 149 (top), 156; *The Tomb of Ramesses VI* 27. After *The Riddle of the Pyramids* 121. John Ross Pls. XII, XVI, XVII, XVIII, XIX. Service des Antiquités 122 (right). Albert Shoucair 122 (left); Pls. XX, XXI, XXII. G. Elliott Smith, *The Royal Mummies* 10 (right, top), 22, 36 (right), 38, 39 (top), 66, 67 (left), 85, 87, 88 (all), 91, 174. Frank Spooner Pls. IX, X. After *The Story of Decipherment* 160. Universal Pictures 175 (both). University of Liverpool 129. Roger Viollet 168. J.G. Wilkinson, *Manners and Customs of the Ancient Egyptians* 32.

In addition, the publishers wish to acknowledge the contribution of the following illustrators:

Christine Barratt 8
Ian Bott 48, 49, 57, 69, 118 (top), 128, 132–3, 137
Garth Denning half-title, 12 (both), 124
Tracy Wellman 8, 47, 112, 140–1, 151

Index

Page numbers in *italic* refer to one- and two-colour illustrations and captions; Roman numerals (*III*) indicate colour plate numbers

ABD EL RASSULS 34, 35, 36, 38, 40
Abu Simbel 46, 89
Abydos 113, 117, 119, *165*
   burials at 14, 122
   journey to 127
   Khentiamentiu of 128–9
   Osiris and 11
   Temple of *140*, *152*
adze 56, 57, 113, 147
afterlife 136, 138, 148, 149, 150, 175
   expectations of 135
   journey into 131
   of a king 156
Ahmose 35, 37, 85
Ahmose Hentempet 37
Ahmose Henttimehu 37
Ahmose Inhapi 37
Ahmose Meryetamun 37, 86, 87
Ahmose Nofretiri 37
Ahmose Sipair 37
Ahmose Sitkamose 37
Ahotep 35, 85
Aken 154
akh 11, 142, 150
   becoming 13, 116
   Book of the Dead 146, 152
   Coffin Texts 129
   journey of 154
   of Osiris 155
   royal 131, 156
Akhenaten 18, 46, 47, 54, *134*, 136, 169
alabaster *48*, 67, 127, 166
Alexander the Great 18
Alexandria 29, 94
   University of 76
aloes 28
Amarna 18, 46, *88*, 169
Amasis 52
Amduat *17*, 157
Amenemopet 22, 136
Amenhotep I 26, 35, 37, 75, *76*, 86, 87
Amenhotep II 38, 39, 40, 84, 87, *88*

Amenhotep III *39*, 54, 87, *88*, 90, *135*
Amenhotep IV *see* Akhenaten
Amosis *86*, 87
amulets 24, 58, 139, *151*, 152, *XX*, *XXII*; *see also* heart amulet
   against disease 142
   Amenhotep II 40
   cotton 97
   decline of 157
   Kha *76*
   mummies 26, 68, 94, 137, 145, 147, *151*
   protecting *akh* 150
Amun 54, *135*, 160, *XII*
   Chantress of 103, 104
Ani *12*, *160*
animal mummy 161, 162, 163, 165, 169
ankh 139, *II*, *XX*, *XXI*, *XXII*
Antiquities Organization 34, 35, 36, 38, 40, 75
   formation of 33
Anubis 72, *113*, 129, *XIV*, *XV*
   balancing scales 141, 153, 154
   mask of *56*
   tomb of Tutankhamun *48*
Apis bulls 59, 166, *167*, 169
Apophis *164*
Arabs 28, 35, 170, 172
Armant 169
arms, position of 68, *137*
Arsinoë *71*
arthritis *11*, 83, *86*, 87, 90, *92*, 99, 100
Ashmolean Museum 74, 158
Ashmunein 162
Aten 18, 54, 136, 169
Atum 146
Avaris 17
Ayrton, Edward 46

*B*A 11, *11*, 12, *12*, 13, *13*, 110, 123, 150
baboon 160, 162
balsam 28, 29
basalt 153
Bast 165
Bat *XXII* beads (*see also* jewellery) 52

bed 127
Belzoni, Giovanni Battista 30, *31*, 32, *115*
Beni Hasan *128*, *129*, *IV*
Bes 140
bier 9, 56
bitumen 10, *11*, 28
blood group 46, 49
boat 121, 127, *129*, 147
   Amenhotep II 38, 40
   ferry of soul 154
   funeral procession 112, *118*
   pits 120
Book of Caverns 157
Book of Gates *132–3*, 157
Book of Coming Forth by Day (*see also* Book of the Dead) 150, 153
Book of the Dead *12*, 58, 149, 150, 152, 137, *160*, *168*, *II*, *XI*
Book of the Heavenly Cow *132–3*
Book of What Is in the Underworld *132–3*
Boston Museum of Fine Arts 57, *78*, *79*
bracelets (*see also* jewellery) 127
brain 96
   removal of 49, 57, *86*, 94, 97, *IX*
Bristol City Art Museum 93, 99
   project 98–9, *98–9*
Britain 30, 76
British Museum 25, 30, *31*, 53, 74, 75, *165*, *167*, 174
bronze 46, 161, 162, *167*
Browne, Sir Thomas 29
Brugsch, Emil 35, 36
Bubastis 165
Buchis bulls 168, 169
bull worship 158, 166, 168–9; (*see also* Apis bulls, Buchis bulls and Mnevis bulls)
Burkhardt, Jean-Louis 31
Busiris 113
Byblos 155
Byzantine 155

CAIRO 14, *15*, 28, 29, 35, 89
   Antiquities Organization 33

examination of mummies 66, 76
removal of mummies to 46, 66
Cairo Museum 24, 36, 38, *111*, 158, *XX*
  catalogue of 76
  Faiyum portrait *19*, *71*
  papyrus *156*
  Ramesses II 89
  removal of mummies to 40, 75
  royal caches 84
  Tutankhamun *I*
California, University of 46
Cambyses 166
canopic jars 45, *56*, 60, 67, 112, 116, 131
  of Hetepheres 127
  re-use of 136
  of Tiye *47*
Canopus 67
canopy 112
carbon dating 94, 97, 169
cardinal points *148*
Carnarvon, Lord 40, 45, 171, 172
carnelian 127, 150, *I*
Carter, Howard 40, 45, 46, 49, 171, 172
cartonnage *19*, 67, 69, *71*, 72, *78*, *79*, 137, *V*
cartouche *17*
cassia 54
cat 93, 159, 164, 165, 173
CAT scanner 76, 78, *78*, *79*, 80, 94, *X*
catacombs 138, 162, 163, 169
cenotaphs 119
chair (*see also* furniture) 54, 127
Champollion brothers 75
chariot 111, 131
Cheops (*see also* Great Pyramid) 14, *15*, *124*, 127, 146
Chephren 14, *15*, *124*
children, mummies of 50, 74, 93
Chinese 10
chisel 113
Christianity 18, 28, 115, 138, 157
chromatography *79*
Clemens, Samuel *see* Twain, Mark
cliff tombs *128*
Cockburn, Aidan 94
coffin 34, 50, 56, 66, 70, 112, 114, 116, 120, 131
  cartonnage 137
  Christian 115
  first use of 53, 118
  inscription 84
  Middle Kingdom *129*, *148*
  Nakht 100
  Nesikhonsu 35

Nes-shou 94
  painted 69, 80, 128, 129, 135, 148
  Ramesses II *11*
  re-use 136
  Tiye 46, *47*
  tomb of Iurudef *51*
  Tutankhamun 45, *48*, 49
  Userhet *IV*
Coffin Texts 129, 148
Cook, Thomas 30
copper 127
Coptic 16, 18, 72, 138, 170
Coptos 54, 169
Corelli, Maria 172
cosmetics 111
cotton 97
cows *168*
crocodile 156, 158, 163
crook *48*, *137*
Crusades 29
curse 139, 170, 171, 172, 173, 174
Cynopolis 163

Dahshur *29*, 127, *XX*, *XXI*, *XXII*
dance (*see also* muu dancers) *111*
David, Dr Rosalie 101, *102*
Davis, Theodore 40, 45, 46
Deir el Bahri *11*, *16*, 22, 28, 34, 36, 38, 60, 66, 72, 84, 85, 89, 98, 100, *XII*
Deir el Medina 27, *56*, 76, 131, 136
Demos *71*
Diodorus Siculus 57, 58, 60, 70, 102
Djed-hast-inef-ankh *56*, *57*
djed pillar 150, 152, *152*
Djoser 120, 121, 123, *XVII*
DNA structure 78
dog 163, 164
Dog Star *see* Sothis
Doyle, Sir Arthur Conan 172
Dresden Museum *29*
dress 100, 111, 115, 118
Drovetti, Bernadino 30, 31, 32
Duamutef 67
Duat 140; (*see also* underworld)
dung beetle 153
dye 68, 69

Ebers, Georg 75
ebony *111*
Edwards, Amelia 33, 34
egg, mummified 163
Egypt Exploration Fund 98–9
Egypt Exploration Society 46, 50
Elephantine Island 163
embalming 18, 22, 80, 103
  Anubis 141

development of 54
fluids 95
incision 57, *57*
Nes-shou 94
Old Kingdom 15, *86*
priest 110, *XV*
process of 56–7, 58, 59, 65, 68, 104
Roman 72
styles of 92
texts 104
tools 65
endoscopes 78
Europe 28, *29*, 30
evisceration *see* internal organs, removal of
Exodus 91

Faience *48*, 69, 149, 161
Faiyum 15, *19*, *71*, 102, *VII*
falcon 158, 160, 162, *XX*, *XXI*, *XXIII*
false door 116, 120, 121, 122, 124, 128
Feast of the Valley 116
feather 140, 141, *151*, 154, *XIV*
Field of Reeds 149
fish 163
Fitzwilliam Museum 115, *IV*
flail *48*, *137*
flint knife 57
floral garlands 40, 70, 75, 111
Fontaine, Guy de la 29
food offerings 52, 111, 118, 121, 122, 128, 129, 150
Fouquet, Nicolas 29
France 29, 76
Francis I 29
frog *151*
funeral procession 9, *111*, 112, 117, *122*
funerary banquet 45, 113, 116
funerary cone 135, *135*
funerary ritual 70, 110, 111, 112, 113, 116, 139
furniture 84, 111, 127, 136, 150

Geb 148, 152, 154
Genesis 59
ghost 12, 34
Giza *115*, *124*, *XVIII*
  Hetepheres' tomb 127
  pit 147
  pyramids (*see also* Cheops, Chephren, Great Pyramid, Mycerinus) 14, *15*, 25, 123
  reliefs 136
  tombs 38
Glasgow, University of 39

glass *48, I*
Gobbler, the 154
gods 139, 140, *140–1*, 142, 146
gold 17, 26, 65, 75, *76, 111*, 127, 150
    coffin 131, 136
    mask 22, 70
    mummy case 9
    Tutankhamun 45, *48*, 49, 67, *I*
Goyon, Professor Jean-Claude 104
granite *27*, 115, 137
Gray, P.H.K. 76
Great Pyramid *25*, 123, 127, 146, *146*,
        147; (*see also* Cheops, Giza)
Greeks 18, 115, 138, 163
Grenoble 72, 75, 163

HALL OF CHARIOTS 131
Hall of Gold 131
Hapi *67*
Haroeris *141*
Hathor 141, *151, 160*
Hatshepsut 12, 87
Hawara *19, 71*, 102, *VII*
hawks 112
Hay, Robert 94
headrest amulet *151*, 152
heart 58
    amulet *151*
    balancing of 141, 153, *153*, 154,
        156, *XIV*
    disease *11*, 101
    scarab 58, 94, 150, 153, *XX*
height 87
Heliopolis 120, 147, 155, 169
henna 65
Henttawy *22*, 37, 65
herbs 28, 60
Herihor 28, 38, 75
Herodotus 52, 54, 56, 57, 58, 59, 60,
        70, 102, 165, 166
hetep 116
Hetepherakhet 25
Hetepheres 59, 127
Hieraconpolis 118, 145, 158
hieroglyphs *115*, 116, 123, 141, *XXII*
Hildesheim Museum *56*, 57
hippopotamus 156, *160*
Hittites 18
Hopkinson, Edmund 93
Horemheb 46, 51
Horemakenesi 98–9
horizon *151*, 154
Horus *140*, 146, *151*, 155, *160*, 162,
        XIII, XXI
    battles with Seth 160–1
    eye of 147, 152
    identification of king with 131,

155, 161
judgment of dead 154, *XIV*
    Sons of 67, 151
Hyksos 17, 85, 87

IBIS 160, 162
ibu 56, 57
ichneumon 159, 163
Imhotep 120, 175, *XVII*
Imseti *67*
Incas 10
incense 113
incision *see* embalming incision
indigo 68
Ineni 26, 131
Inhapi 28, 36
inscriptions 112, 116, 117, 141
    on bandages 68
    on coffins 84
    tomb 123, 131, 145, 165, 174
internal organs 46, 54, 60
    removal of 11, 53, 57, 58, 67
    see also Horus, Sons of
Ishtar 90
Isiemkheb 37
Isis *56*, 72, 76, 112, *115, 140*, 141,
        151, 152, 155
Islam 18
Itj-Tawy 15
Iurudef 50, 51

JACKAL *151*, 156
jewellery 24, 40, 49, 65, 68, *76*, 85, *97*,
        111, *XX, XXI*
Jonckheere, Frans 76
Judgment of the Dead *141*, 153, 154,
        XIV
juniper oil 58, 65

KA 11, 12, *12*, 25, 153
    of god 142
    of hero 139, 159
    of king 121, 131, 135, 146, *I*
    provision for 111, 116, 120, 129
    release of 110
    rising of 122, 123, 128, 150
    servant of 117
    statue of 113, 141
Kamose 85
Karloff, Boris 175, *175*
Karnak 26, 28, 38, 54, 89
Kha 76
Khayat, Dr 76
Khentiamentiu 128
Khepri 147
Khnum 12, *12, 151*, 163
Kingston Lacey *31*

kites 112, *155*, 162
Kiya 47

LADY MAY 135
Lady Teshat 80
lamp *48*
lapis lazuli 9, 127, 150, *I*
leather 69
Leiden Museum 46
leopard 156
Lepsius, Karl 46
Libyan palette 158, *159*
limestone 24, 67, 121, 145
Lindow Man 9
linen 30, 40, 75, 92, 118, 137, 169
    coloured 72, 136
    first use 53
    for mummification 45, 68, 69, 97,
        99, 120
    household 100
    offering of 111, 150, 162
    packing 60, 65, 69
    reuse for paper 33
    supply of 82
    Tutankhamun 49
Litany of Re *132–3*
Liverpool City Museum 76, *92–3*, 93,
        94, 100, 103
Loret, Victor 38, 40
lotus *48*, 154
Louis XIV, King of France 29
Lucas, Alfred 58
lung, illnesses of 101, 104
Luxor 15, 27, 40, 80, 116, 141, 160,
        XVI
    Amelia Edwards 33, 34
    Belzoni 31
    necropolis 46
    royal cache 74
    tomb of Wah 97
    tombs 131, 135, 136, 138
Lyons mummy 60, 68, 104, *X*

MAAT 140, 141, 151, 153, 154, 156,
        XIV
Maatkare Mutemhet 37
madder 68
magic 28, 123, 139, 142, 145
Makhaf 154
malachite 127
Manchester Museum 101, 102
    mummy analysis 102–3, *102*
Manchester University *21*, 78
maps 129, *132–3*
Mariette, Auguste 166
Martin, Professor Geoffrey 46, 50
Masaharta 37

mask *56*, 69, 70, *97*, *I*
Maspero, Gaston 34, 35, 75, 76
mastabas 14, 26, 110, 120, 121, *120–1*, 123, 124
Maya 46, 51
Medinet Habu 136
Memphis 14, 27, 59, 119, 121, *128*, 136, 166
Mentuhotep *see* Nebhepetre Mentuhotep
Merenptah 84, *88*, 90, 91
Mereruka 122, *122*
Meresankh 67
Meryetamun 11
Meryt 51
Meshkent 140
Metropolitan Museum of Art 40, 57, 68, *97*, *111*
Min 54, 169
Minneapolis Institute of Arts mummy analysis 80–1
mirror 111
Mnevis bulls 168, 169
Mohammed Ali 31
monkey 165
Mont 169
Montet, Pierre 46, *137*, *VIII*
mortuary chapel 121, 124, 129
mortuary cult 117
mortuary estate 117
mortuary temple 26, 98, 124, 135, 136
mourners, professional 111
mouse 154
mummy, animal *see* cat crocodile, falcon, ibis, monkey
mummy, derivation of term 10, *11*
movie of 174–5
in Tomb 55, *47*
mummy, unknown 66–7
mummy, unwrapping of 29, 30, *36*, 38, 75, 93, 94, 97, 99, 102
mummy, use of in industry 33
mummy, use of in medicine 28, 29
mummy, wrapping of 69
Murray, Dr Margaret *21*, 101
musical instruments 111
Mutnodjmet 51
muu dancers 9, 112
Mycerinus 14, *15*, 25, 67, *115*, 124
myrrh *28*, *54*, *60*

Nakht 100, 103
name, importance of 13, 110, 117, *122*, *174*
Napoleon 29, 74
Naqada 118, 145, 160
natron 11, 54, 56, 58, 59, 60, 65, 66,

91, *98*, 99, 162
Nebhepetre Mentuhotep 16
Nectanebo II 166
Neferseshemptah 122
Nefertari *168*
Nefertiti 51, 54
Neith *141*
Nekheb 160
Nekhtamun *56*
nephrite 150
Nephthys *56*, 112, *115*, *141*, *148*, *151*, 155
Nesikhonsu 35
Neskhons 37
Nes-shou 94
Nestanebtishru 37
Nile 14, 27, 28, 29, 30, 31, 35, 36, 112, 116, 118, 127
Nodjmet *36*, 37
north wind, goddess of *137*
Nubia 12, 17, 27, 28, 137
Nut *148*, 155, *II*

Oars *48*, 147
obelisk *31*
obsidian *111*, *153*, *I*
ochre 65
offering table 116, 122
Opening of the Mouth ceremony 13, 56, 110, 113, *113*, 124, *132–3*, 141, 147, 150, 171, *II*
Orion 146
Opet *160*
Osiris 11, 117, 128, *135*, 138, 145, 148, 149, 152, 156, 157
Apis bull 166
backbone of 150
god of the dead 72, 112, 129, 140, 141, 154, 160, *XIV*
king identified with 131
story of 155
Tutankhamun as *48*, *115*, *II*
Osorkon III 136
ox, sacrifice of 113
Oxyrhynchus 163

Paddles *48*
Painted Tomb 100 118–19, *118*
painting 13, 17, 29, 51, 112, 119, 127, *131*, *132–3*, 135, *157*, 164, *168*, *II*
palanquin 127
palette 158, *159*
panther skin 112
papyrus 27, 32, 34, 69, 94, 101, 119, 137, 142, *148*, *151*, 156, 159, *160*

parasites 101, 103, 104
Paré, Ambroise 29
Pennsylvania, University of 94–7
mummy analysis 94–6
perfume 11, 12, 28, 70, 111, 118
per nefer 65
Persians 58, 138, 166
pesesh-kef knife 113
Petrie, Flinders 35, 38, *71*, 75
Pettigrew, Thomas 30
pit graves 13, *53*, 110, 117, *118*
plaster 54, 69, 72, 116, 118, 135, 137
Plutarch 119
polio 90, *91*
portraits *19*, *71*
position of body 118
pottery 52, *53*, 67, *118*, 162
priests 70, 116, 117, 121, 139, 142, 147, 150, *XV*
burial of 54, *95*
embalming *56*, 57
mortuary 24
sem 110, 112, 113
tombs of 38
Psusennes 21, 46, 70, 136, *137*, *VIII*
Ptah-hotep *122*
Ptah-Sokar-Osiris 157
PUM I 94
PUM II 97
PUM III 94, 95, *95*
PUM IV 95, 96, *96*
purification 112, 113, 125
pyramids 14, 15, *15*, 25, *31*, 51, 110, 127, 136; *see also* Giza, Great Pyramid, Saqqara
construction of 124
development of 123
end of 129
Pyramid Texts 52, 113, 119, 124, 128, 145, 147

Qebhsenuef 67
quartzite *17*, *48*, 115
Qurna 34, 35

Radiocarbon Dating *see* carbon dating ram, mummified 163
Ramesses I 35, 90
Ramesses II *11*, 27, *31*, 37, 50, 51, 72, 75, 82, 84, 87, *88*, 89, 90, *132–3*, 166
Ramesses III 37, 86, 98, *115*, 136
Ramesses IV 39, 86
Ramesses V *38*, 39
Ramesses VI 27, *27*, 39, 45, 84
Ramesses IX 26, *27*, 37
Ramesses XI 98, 136

Ramose *135*, *XVI*
razor *111*
Re 147, 151, 154, 156, 169, *XIII*
rehydration 78
Reisner, George 127
reliefs 13, *115*, 121, *122*, *135*, 136, 138
resin 11, 28, 30, 35, 49, 53, 54, 57, 59,
    60, 65, 69, 75, 79, *88*, 91, 94,
    97, 137
ROM I 100
resurrection 129
rock-cut tombs 110, 125, 127, 128
Romans *19*, 71, 102, 115, 138, *165*,
    166, *VII*
Royal Ontario Museum 100

SAFFRON 68
Salt, Henry 30, 31
saluki 164
sandals 49, 72, 111
Saqqara 25, 54, 138, 166, 168, *XVII*;
    see also Step Pyramid
    mastaba tombs 119–20, 121
    necropolis 14, 46, 50, 74, 136
    tomb of Maya 51
sarcophagus *17*, 26, *27*, 114–5, 116,
    128, 131
    Amenhotep II 38, *38*
    Apis bull 169
    Hetepheres 127
    Mycerinus *114*
    Psusennes *115*, *137*
    Seti I *31*, *132–3*
    Tutankhamun 46, *48*, 114–5, *II*
Sarenput 164
scarab *76*, *151*, 153; (*see also* heart
    scarab)
sceptre *135*
scorpion *141*
Scorpion macehead 158
seals 45, 46, 116
sekh 70
Selket *141*
Sennedjem *XV*
Seqenenre Tao 35, 84, 85, *85*, 86
Sequence Dating 38
Serapeum *111*, 166
Serapis 166
serpentine 153
Sesostris I 9
Seth 140, *141*, 145, 147, *148*, 152, 155,
    156, 160, *XXI*
Seti I *31*, 35, *37*, 87, *88*, 90, *132–3*,
    140, *152*

Seti II 39, 90
shadow 13
shawabti see ushabti
shen 12, *XX*
shrine 47, *48*, 131, *132–3*
Shu 148
Siamun 35
Sicard, Père Claude
silver 26, *111*, 127, 136, *137*
Sinuhe 9
Sirius *see* Sothis
Siptah 90, *91*
Sitamun 54
Sit Hathor Yunet *111*, *XXI*
Sloane, Sir Hans 74
smallpox 79
Smenkhkare 47
Smith, Grafton Elliot 46, 76
snake 159, 163, *164*
Snofru 127
Soane, Sir John *31*
sobek 163
Sothis 59, 146
soul 11, 12, 15, 123, 124, 145, 148,
    156; (*see also* akh, ba, ka)
spectroscopy 79
Stanwood, Augustus 33
statue 117, 122, 136, 139, 141
stela 9, 117, 138
Step Pyramid 120, 121, *121*, 123, 145,
    XVII
sun god *132–3*, 160, *164*, 169; (*see
    also* Aten, Re)
sun ship 156
sun worship 120, 124, 131, 147

TAIT 9
Takeloth II 136
Tanis 22, 46, 70, 136, *137*, *VIII*
Taweret 140
teeth *11*, 49, 54, *76*, 82, 83, 87, *88*, 90,
    94, 95, 100, 104
temple 139, 142
Teshat, Lady 80–1
Thebes 14, *32*; (*see also* Luxor)
Thoth 116, 141, *156*, 160, 162, *XIV*
Thuya 54
Tia 46, 50
Tiye *39*, 46, 47, 54
Tod 169
Tomb 55 45, 46–7, *47*
Treasuries 131
Tuna el Gebel 138, 162
Turkey 18, 29, 31, 87

Tutankhamun 22, 40, 45, 46, 47, 60,
    67, 84, 131, 150, 171, 173, 174
    mask of 49, 70, *I*
    sarcophagus 115, 141
    tomb of 48–9 *II*, *III*
    unwrapping of 49
Tuthmosis I 26, *36*, 37, *88*, 131
Tuthmosis II 35, 37, 87, *88*
Tuthmosis III *17*, *36*, 37, 57, 87, *174*
Tuthmosis IV 39, 76, 87, *88*, 131, *157*
Twain, Mark 33
'Two Brothers' *21*, 101

UNDERWORLD 140, 141, 156, *II*, *XI*
uraeus 34, *167*
Userhet *IV*
ushabti 112, 116, 149

VALLE, PIETRO DELLA *29*
Valley of the Kings 17, 26, 27, 29, 84,
    98, 131, *132–3*, 135, 136, 171
    Belzoni 32
    Carter 40
    Horemheb's tomb 46
    Loret 38
    map *130–1*
    Seti I's tomb *132–3*
    Tutankhamun 49
    Yuya 54
Valley of the Queens *168*, 173
Van Dijk, Dr Jacobus 46
vulture 162, *XXII*
Vyse, Howard 25

WABET 57, 65, 70, 112
wadjet eye 151, 152, *157*, *XIII*
Wah 68, *97*
warning 25
Waty 54
wax 18, *19*, 65, 71
weapons 111
Weigall, Arthur 20, 46, 172, 173
weighing of the heart *see* heart,
    balancing of
whetstones *111*
wine 54, 60, 65, 72
Winlock, H.E. 11, 16, 40

X-RAY 20, 46, 49, 74, 75, *76*, 78, 80,
    87, *88*, 90, 92, 93, 94, 97, *98*,
    99, 100, 102, 162, 165

YOUNG MEMNON *31*
Yuya 54, *55*
Yverdon 94, 101